D0555067

THE GOD OF THE GOSPEL OF JOHN

The God of the Gospel of John

MARIANNE MEYE THOMPSON

WILLIAM B. EERDMANS PUBLISHING COMPANY
GRAND RAPIDS, MICHIGAN / CAMBRIDGE, U.K.

© 2001 Wm. B. Eerdmans Publishing Co.
All rights reserved

Wm. B. Eerdmans Publishing Co.
2140 Oak Industrial Drive N.E., Grand Rapids, Michigan 49505 /
P.O. Box 163, Cambridge CB3 9PU U.K.

Printed in the United States of America

15 14 13 12   7 6 5 4

Library of Congress Cataloging-in-Publication Data

Thompson, Marianne Meye.
    The God of the Gospel of John / Marianne Meye Thompson.
        p.   cm.
    Includes bibliographical references and index.
    ISBN 978-0-8028-4734-8 (pbk.: alk. paper)
        1. God.   2. Bible. N.T. John — Criticism, interpretation, etc.   I. Title.

BT102.T525   2001
226.5′06 — dc21

                                                    2001040379

www.eerdmans.com

To John

Contents

Acknowledgments

> Most people think mistakenly that writers are people who have something to tell them. Nothing I think could be wronger. If I knew what I wanted to say, I wouldn't write at all. What for? Why do it, if you already know the answers? Writing is the search for the answers, and the answer is in the form, the method of telling, the exploration of self, which is our only clew to reality.[1]

I have written this book in search of answers and, in the process, have discovered, as many writers do, that the questions themselves have changed. This was not the book that I set out to write a number of years ago. The table of contents has changed entirely; indeed, none of the chapters of the present book is as I initially projected them. Most are new, and those that I had thought would serve as the heart and soul of the present book have either disappeared or been absorbed into other chapters. Much of what I thought I would write about, including the topics I would cover and the arguments I would make, has changed.

The differences are only partially captured in my lament to my friend, Professor Andrew Lincoln, "Every time I try to write about God I end up writing about Jesus," and his response, "And what does that tell you,

1. Ralph C. Wood, "Review of *The Correspondence of Shelby Foote and Walker Percy*, ed. Jay Tolson," *The Christian Century*, November 12, 1997, p. 1048.

Marianne?" Yet I have not abandoned my original thesis, that the Gospel of John is theocentric, that it directs our attention to God, and that this is a better characterization than the more typical "Christocentric." If anything I am perhaps more persuaded of it than ever. Yet the ways that I have approached the topic and the subjects that I have written about, as well as the conclusions that I have reached, or at least the formulations that I have found most faithful to John, have indeed changed. Sometimes I have been surprised by these changes. I would like to think that they have been occasioned by careful and continued attention to the Gospel itself, and that the face at the bottom of the well is less mine and more the Gospel's. If I were to start the project today, or if I were to keep writing and tinkering, I think I might conceive of the project along different lines still. In the words of the Gospel, if everything were to be written down, "the world itself could not contain the books that would be written." Hence, it is time to say that "what I have written, I have written."

However, I do not say this with the defiance of Pilate; I say it rather all too aware of the books and articles left unread, the questions and texts left unexplored. It has been said that the Gospel of John is a pool in which a child can wade and an elephant can swim. I am lazily tempted to add, "and in which a scholar can drown." I am happy to acknowledge here, therefore, the invaluable counsel, encouragement, and wisdom of friends and colleagues.

Many people have contributed to this book in one way or another. I still keep on file the lengthy, detailed, and informative letters and e-mails from Larry Hurtado, offering invaluable bibliographical references and comments on first-century Jewish monotheism and worship. Conversations and e-mail exchanges with Andrew Lincoln encouraged me along the way, gave me freedom to pursue certain hunches and, with various probing and insightful questions, challenged me to be more precise and modest in my claims. Jack Levison carefully read and commented on the chapter on the Spirit and contributed much to its improvement. The "Johanneum," including Dale Brunner, Tom Elson, Darrell Johnson, and Donn Moomaw, also read the chapter on the Spirit and gave me good feedback. I am particularly grateful to Richard Bauckham, who read several of the chapters and whose comments and observations led me to abandon some unfruitful lines of thought. Although his own work, *God Crucified: Monotheism and Christology in the New Testament*, came to my attention only after my manuscript was nearly completed, readers will note significant points of contact in our arguments. Ellen Charry helped me to understand some current issues in thinking about God. My heartfelt thanks goes to all of them, and my apologies for ignoring advice I probably should have taken.

This project could not have been completed without the support of other friends and institutions. A grant from the Pew Evangelical Scholars Program in 1992-93 and another from the Henry R. Luce Foundation in 1995-96 gave me the time to research and write. I also appreciate the conversations with and feedback gained from other fellows during the gatherings of the recipients of these two fellowships. I am grateful also to the Trustees of Fuller Seminary for their generous sabbatical policy that afforded additional time to research and write. I want also to thank Diane G. Chen, my research assistant, who copied articles, chased down references, helped with matters of footnote and bibliography style, and prepared the indexes for the present volume. Her diligence, reliability, and perseverance are very much appreciated. Chris Spinks also helped with proofreading and checking references, and I am grateful for his help in the midst of a busy schedule.

Portions of chapter 2, "The Living Father," have appeared in *The Promise of the Father: Jesus and God in the New Testament* (Louisville: Westminster/John Knox, 2000) and "The Living Father," in *Semeia* (vol. 85; "*God the Father*" in the Gospel of John*). An earlier form of chapter 5, "The Worship of God," was delivered as the annual Thompson Lecture at Princeton Theological Seminary and subsequently published as "Reflections on Worship in the Gospel of John," *The Princeton Seminary Bulletin* 19 (1998): 259-78. Permission to reprint these materials is gratefully acknowledged.

Finally, a word of appreciation to my family. My daughters, Allison and Annelise, have cheered me on and celebrated with me milestones in the completion of this manuscript. Their love and joy for life enrich mine beyond measure. Above all, I want to say a heartfelt word of appreciation to my husband, John, for his friendship, collegial support, and love. The decade or so in which I have thought about and worked on this book has been marked by ups and downs, joys and sorrows, but through it all I have always been undergirded by his steady companionship, encouragement, and committed love. I dedicate this book to him.

The Neglected Factor in New Testament Theology

About twenty-five years ago, Nils A. Dahl, a professor at Yale Divinity School, wrote a now oft-cited essay entitled "The Neglected Factor in New Testament Theology."[1] That neglected factor, according to Dahl, was God. A decade later Leander Keck asserted that Dahl was indeed correct: "The understanding of God has been the neglected factor in the study of New Testament theology as a whole. This is particularly true of the study of New Testament christology, even though every statement about Christ implicates God, beginning with the designation of Jesus as the Anointed."[2] While there are numerous studies about God in the OT, focused variously on names for God or conceptions of God, "God" has largely been ignored as the proper subject of inquiry and reflection with respect to the substance of NT theology. Furthermore, the contrast with OT studies is only highlighted, not relieved, by the plethora of Christological studies in the NT.[3] Apparently scholars have concluded that the OT is about God and the NT is about Jesus, or else that God has but secondary importance in en-

1. Nils A. Dahl, "The Neglected Factor in New Testament Theology," in *Jesus the Christ: The Historical Origins of Christological Doctrine*, ed. Donald H. Juel (Minneapolis: Fortress, 1991), pp. 153-63. Originally published in *Reflections* 75 (1975): 5-8.

2. Leander Keck, "Toward the Renewal of New Testament Christology," *NTS* 32 (1986): 363.

3. See here Halvor Moxnes, *Theology in Conflict: Studies in Paul's Understanding of God in Romans*, NovTSup 53 (Leiden: Brill, 1980), pp. 1-2.

gaging the witness of the NT Scriptures. Needless to say, every page of the NT belies this conclusion.

Dahl suggested several reasons for such neglect in NT studies, including the general lack within the NT itself of thematic formulations about God, and the fact that most of the references to God occur in contexts that deal with some other theme. In those contexts, references to God function implicitly as warrants for promises, appeals, or threats; as statements about Jesus, the Jews, the Church, salvation, conduct, and so on. Hence, Dahl suggested that the indirection of NT language about God might have been one of the factors contributing to this neglect in NT scholarship.

To be sure, there have been exceptions, particularly in a number of older theologies of the NT, in which NT theology was structured according to the categories of dogmatic studies. Alan Richardson organized his theology of the NT along just such lines, discussing the various attributes of God, such as power, glory, and wrath.[4] When this approach was abandoned in favor of an approach that ordered the witnesses of the NT either chronologically or canonically, typically the various loci of dogmatics came up only as they were deemed to be relevant or important to understanding a particular writer or theological development. Thus, for example, Rudolf Bultmann's *Theology of the New Testament* includes, under the preliminary discussion of "The Message of Jesus," chapters on "Jesus' Interpretation of the Demand of God" and "Jesus' Idea of God." The latter heading may seem somewhat surprising, given Bultmann's aversion to "objectifying" God, but predictably Bultmann's interest lies not so much in the content of an idea as in the kerygmatic and existential elements of Jesus' preaching.[5] Moreover, Bultmann argues that since Jesus' expectation of the irruption of the kingdom did not materialize, it is necessary to ask whether the idea of God that comes to expression in his preaching is likewise illusory. Similarly, in his discussions of Paul and John, Bultmann includes, respectively, sections on "The Righteousness of God" and "Revelation," inasmuch as these are crucial to understanding the reality of God within that particular author's framework. In other words, "God" comes up as a topic to be discussed not in terms of traditional dogmatic catego-

4. Alan Richardson, *An Introduction to the Theology of the New Testament* (London: SCM, 1958).

5. Rudolf Bultmann, *Theology of the New Testament*, 2 vols. (New York: Scribner's, 1951, 1955). See the discussion in John K. Riches, *Jesus and the Transformation of Judaism* (New York: Seabury, 1980), in his chapter entitled "Jesus' Theism," pp. 145-67.

ries but as contextually situated in the different writings of the various authors of the NT.

While there is unquestionably value in an approach that treats the documents of the NT on their own terms, it nevertheless can leave the impression that understanding God is quite important for some parts of the NT but not for others. With respect to Bultmann's theology, one might conclude that "God" is important in grasping the teaching of Jesus since Jesus had an "idea of God," but that Paul's convictions about God are somehow less important for understanding his theology. Yet an assumption that God is unimportant in Pauline theology could scarcely be further from the truth. To be sure, Paul does not consider "God" in isolation or abstraction from such themes as the role of the law, the destiny of Israel, and the significance of the cross. On these he reflected a good deal. Did his reflections on these topics change or alter his convictions about God? In *Paul and Palestinian Judaism*, E. P. Sanders writes, "From [Paul] we learn nothing new or remarkable about God. . . . One could, to be sure, list further statements made by Paul about God, but it is clear that Paul did not spend his time reflecting on the nature of the deity."[6] Similarly, Joseph A. Fitzmyer comments that Paul's Damascus road experience changed his Christology, but not his theology.[7] In other words, Sanders and Fitzmyer contend that Paul's basic beliefs about God and God's character remained unchanged even after his convictions about Jesus of Nazareth had changed decisively. As Sanders put it, Paul did not spend his time "reflecting on the nature of deity." Paul, in other words, was not a speculative theologian. Yet we may well ask, When traditional statements or assertions are placed into new historical, literary, or theological contexts, does such reorientation not affect and alter the fundamental content of those statements? Thus, while Paul may not have drawn up a new list of beliefs about God or concepts of divinity when he began to confess Jesus as Messiah, he did reformulate his convictions about the manifestation of God's wrath and righteousness, the role of the law, and the character and scope of God's people. In that way, his convictions about God are reshaped.

6. E. P. Sanders, *Paul and Palestinian Judaism: A Comparison of Patterns of Religion* (Philadelphia: Fortress, 1977), p. 509.

7. Joseph A. Fitzmyer, *Paul and His Theology: A Brief Sketch* (Englewood, N.J.: Prentice-Hall, 1989), p. 30. See also Brevard S. Childs, *Biblical Theology of the Old and New Testaments* (Minneapolis: Fortress, 1992), p. 358: "Jesus brought no new concept of God, but he demonstrated in action the full extent of God's redemptive will for the world which was from the beginning."

The disjuncture between "Christology" and "theology" has recently and rightly been called into question. When the early Christians confessed Jesus of Nazareth as Messiah and Lord, how did such confession shape their convictions regarding the God of Israel? There is arguably today a rising tide of interest in just this question. Over the course of the last twenty years — and often cognizant of and responding to Dahl's alarm — an increasing number of works have focused specifically on Paul's thought about God.[8] What distinguishes these works is the contextual approaches they take. Various studies focus on Paul's thought in a particular letter, allowing the author to pay attention to historical context and rhetorical situation; others more narrowly on Paul's "language about God"; and others on Paul's thought in relationship to specific topics (divine impartiality, eschatology) in their historical setting. They thus avoid the trap of turning the NT into a collection of untethered theological statements, seeking instead to ground Paul's thinking about God in his historical contexts or to focus on the language and formulations that he called upon in speaking of God.[9]

Recently several works have addressed the need to articulate the theological question within the historical and literary framework of the NT documents. G. B. Caird's *New Testament Theology*, edited and published posthumously, contends in its opening chapter, suggestively entitled "The Divine Plan," that "the New Testament is from beginning to end a book about God."[10] In its manifold witnesses it testifies repeatedly to the salvific

8. See Jouette M. Bassler, *Divine Impartiality: Paul and a Theological Axiom*, SBLDS 59 (Chico, Calif.: Scholars Press, 1982); Moxnes, *Theology in Conflict*; L. Joseph Kreitzer, *Jesus and God in Paul's Eschatology*, JSNTSup 19 (Sheffield: JSOT Press, 1987); and Neil Richardson, *Paul's Language about God*, JSNTSup 99 (Sheffield: Sheffield Academic Press, 1994). See also Antoinette C. Wire, "Pauline Theology as an Understanding of God: The Explicit and the Implicit," Ph.D. diss., Claremont Graduate University, 1974. Studies such as J. Christiaan Beker's *Paul the Apostle: The Triumph of God in Life and Thought* (Philadelphia: Fortress, 1980; rev. ed., 1989) make explicit the theological underpinnings of Pauline thought.

9. Other works focusing on God in the NT do exist; see A. W. Argyle, *God in the New Testament* (Philadelphia: J. B. Lippincott, 1966) and the collection of essays in *La Notion biblique de Dieu*, BETL 41 (Leuven: Leuven University Press, 1976). There is also bibliography and discussion in Moxnes, *Theology in Conflict*, pp. 1-4; and Richardson, *Paul's Language about God*, pp. 1-25.

10. G. B. Caird, *New Testament Theology*, completed and edited by L. D. Hurst (Oxford: Clarendon, 1994), p. 31. See also G. B. Caird, "The Glory of God in the Fourth Gospel: An Exercise in Biblical Semantics," *NTS* 15 (1969): 265-77: "Much has been written on the glory and the glorification of Christ in the Fourth Gospel, but grammars, dictionaries, commentaries, and monographs are strangely inadequate, or even silent, on the kindred theme of the glory of God."

work and presence of God through Jesus Christ. That assertion might strike some as virtually a truism that needs no further unpacking. Yet it is precisely the failure to articulate the way in which the NT is "from beginning to end a book about God" that Dahl had already decried. Moreover, to say that the Christian NT is a book about God presumably means that it has something distinctively Christian to say about that God. N. T. Wright makes just this point:

> It seems to me that the early Christians, including the writers of the New Testament, wrestled with [the meaning of the word "God"] more than is usually imagined. The word *theos* for Greek-speakers (and its equivalents in other languages spoken in the first century) was not univocal, and the early Christians made out a fairly thorough case for understanding it in a particular sense.[11]

These and other works have profited from the explosion of interest in and study of first-century Judaism and early Christianity in relationship to it. Such study has sparked renewed interest in "Christian origins" and consequently has necessitated reexamination of the assumptions of either a radical discontinuity or a simplistic continuity between Christian and Jewish convictions about God.

The issue of early Christian views of God cannot simply be reduced to the question whether NT views of God are the same as or different from those of the OT or Judaism. To speak of 'beliefs about God," as though the project were simply to abstract, codify, and compare different beliefs, leads to the mistaken impression that early Christian understanding of God was achieved through dogmatic reflection on the being of God. Yet reflection on the character and actions of God was shaped out of the community's experiences with Jesus of Nazareth, their reading of Scripture, and the rapid growth of the Church among Gentiles.[12] Thus to reduce NT theology to "be-

11. N. T. Wright, *The New Testament and the People of God*, vol. 1: *Christian Origins and the Question of God* (Minneapolis: Fortress, 1992), p. xiv.

12. So also Paul W. Meyer warns against the attempt to abstract various assertions about God and then to place them in an artificial systematic pattern. Rather, attention must be paid to the creative reinterpretation of various beliefs about God as they are applied in new settings ("'The Father': The Presentation of God in the Fourth Gospel," in *Exploring the Gospel of John: In Honor of D. Moody Smith*, ed. R. Alan Culpepper and C. Clifton Black [Louisville: Westminster/John Knox, 1996], p. 257); see Dahl, "Neglected Factor," pp. 158-60. On the role of experience in the formulation of convictions about God, see David

liefs about God" without taking into account such crucial issues as the means through which God's activity in the world is manifested and may be discerned dismisses vital dimensions of any understanding of God. To say that Christian faith shares with Judaism basic beliefs about God, including an understanding of God as just, merciful, compassionate, holy, and righteous, is undoubtedly true; but to leave it at that is to discount the fact that early Christians argued that the fullness of God's mercy and righteousness had now been manifested through and in Jesus, the Messiah, of Israel. Such an argument does not and cannot leave "basic beliefs" about God unaltered.

The Fourth Gospel and the Question of God

Study of the Gospel of John has surely profited from renewed interest in early Judaism but, strangely enough, has not investigated very closely the question of God within the Gospel. This is strange because almost every survey of first-century Judaism emphasizes belief in the one God as one of its core convictions. Yet, in many ways, the Fourth Gospel has been a prime exemplar in recent scholarship of the neglect of the theological question, having been routinely read as a narrowly Christological and, even more acutely, "Christocentric" Gospel. In a lengthy "Report on Recent Research" on John, Robert Kysar summarized the situation when he noted, "No one seriously doubts that the heartbeat of the theology of the [Fourth Gospel] is found in its christology."[13] Kysar's assertion employs "theology" in its broadest sense — theology as the thought or conceptual world of the Gospel — and thus his assertion is symptomatic of the problem. However, it is also fair to take theology in its narrow sense, namely, as thought about *God*

Rensberger, *Johannine Faith and Liberating Community* (Philadelphia: Westminster, 1988), pp. 45-46. For a discussion of the importance of doctrine in early Judaism and Christianity, see the exchange between Neil J. McEleney ("Orthodoxy and Heterodoxy in the New Testament," *Proceedings of the Catholic Theological Society of America* 25 [1971]: 54-77; "Orthodoxy in Judaism of the First Century Christian Church," *JSJ* 4 [1973]: 19-42) and D. E. Aune ("Orthodoxy in First Century Judaism? A Response to N. J. McEleney," *JSJ* 7 [1976]: 1-10), as well as the comments of Moxnes (*Theology in Conflict*, p. 65).

13. Robert Kysar, "The Fourth Gospel: A Report on Recent Research," *ANRW* II.25.3 (1985): 2443. Kysar's assessment can be easily documented in many recent published writings on John. Thus Adele Reinhartz writes, "Christology is the central theme of this gospel," and adds, "this is virtually axiomatic in Johannine studies" (*The Word in the World: The Cosmological Tale in the Fourth Gospel*, SBLMS 45 [Atlanta: Scholars Press, 1992], p. 30 and n. 1).

— and then Kysar's statement might also suggest the solution. The heartbeat of the *theology* of the Gospel, of its convictions about God, is to be found in its *Christology*. As J. D. G. Dunn puts it, "New Testament Christology functions within theology."[14] Only if Christology remains the servant of theology — not vice versa — does it provide a hook sufficient to bear the weight of the Gospel.[15]

Other voices have been raised in defense of the *theo*logical center of John. Perhaps the clearest statement to date espousing a theocentric reading of the Gospel of John has been offered by the noted Johannine scholar C. K. Barrett.[16] As Barrett comments, "There could hardly be a more Christocentric writer than John, yet his very Christocentricity is theocentric."[17] Elsewhere he comments that "John is writing about, and directing our attention to, God."[18] Similarly, D. Moody Smith comments:

> The fundamental question of the Fourth Gospel is the question of God, not whether a god exists but who is God and how God reveals himself. Thus the fundamental question or issue of the Gospel can be stated as the nature of revelation. What God is revealed, and how is God revealed?[19]

14. James D. G. Dunn, "Christology as an Aspect of Theology," in *The Future of Christology: Essays in Honor of Leander E. Keck,* ed. Abraham J. Malherbe and Wayne A. Meeks (Minneapolis: Fortress, 1993), pp. 202-3.

15. Paul Meyer writes that Bultmann's emphasis on Jesus as the revealer of God who reveals nothing except that fact "seems to cut off even more conclusively any significant talk about God in distinction from the Christ and to signal a collapse of theology into Christology" ("'The Father,'" p. 255. See also Dermot A. Lane, *The Reality of Jesus: An Essay in Christology* (Dublin: Veritas, 1975), p. 142: "The ultimate purpose of christology is to illuminate our experience and understanding of the mystery of God. Christology if it is to achieve this goal must be theocentric."

16. C. K. Barrett, "Christocentric or Theocentric? Observations on the Theological Method of the Fourth Gospel" in *La Notion biblique de Dieu,* BETL 41 (Leuven: Leuven University Press, 1976), pp. 361-76.

17. C. K. Barrett, "'The Father is Greater than I' (John 14.28): Subordinationist Christology in the New Testament," in his *Essays on John* (Philadelphia: Westminster, 1982), p. 246. Similarly Rudolf Schnackenburg comments, "Attention is always directed toward the figure of Jesus, the revealer and bringer of life from God. To this extent everything is Christocentric and at the same time theocentric" (*Jesus in the Gospels: A Biblical Christology,* ET [Louisville: Westminster/John Knox, 1995], p. 247).

18. Barrett, "Christocentric or Theocentric?" p. 363.

19. D. Moody Smith, *The Theology of John* (Cambridge: Cambridge University Press, 1995), p. 75.

Exegetically considered, the Gospel provides abundant evidence to support contentions that its "fundamental question" is the question of *God,* and how God is known and revealed. The many Christological assertions make this very point. Jesus is the Word, Son, Messiah, and revealer *of God.* Jesus is the way *to God,* and Jesus is the life *from God.* Still, the case for a theocentric reading of the Gospel has been somewhat muted, so that one wonders whether William Loader's claim that "the theocentricity of the gospel is widely recognised" optimistically overstates the case.[20]

Various articles and books have addressed the question, "Does the New Testament Call Jesus God?" Here the Fourth Gospel in particular (John 1:1, 18; 20:28), which contains the NT's most explicit designation of Jesus as "God," receives pride of place.[21] However, this is not equivalent to the question of God in the NT, although in such a broader study it is impossible to ignore those passages in which *theos* (θεός) is used of Jesus. Indeed, in the essay cited above, as well as in another essay entitled "Sources of Christological Language," Dahl raised the question of the significance of the application to Jesus of terms and scriptural passages that refer in the OT to God.[22] If the early Christians used "theological" language to speak of Jesus, what accounts for such use? What does this language imply about Jesus? We can also turn the question around somewhat: What does this language imply about the content of the term "god"? Or, put differently, what is the significance of the theological language for Jesus adopted by early Christians for understanding their convictions about God?

Again, the Gospel of John has often been featured in discussions of revelation in the NT. Rudolf Bultmann's treatment of the Fourth Gospel, for instance, deals extensively with the question of the Revealer and the

---

20. William Loader, *The Christology of the Fourth Gospel: Structure and Issues,* BET 23 (Frankfurt am Main: Peter Lang, 1989), p. 140. In addition to the work by Barrett, Loader cites articles and works by Dodd, Haenchen, Hahn, and Schnackenburg.

21. Two passages in the Johannine literature, John 1:18 and 1 John 5:20, are debated. The textual variant at John 1:18 that reads θεός (God) in place of υἱός (son) is usually adopted today as the original reading. Yet John 1:1 and 20:28 still provide the clearest designations of Jesus as God in the NT. Similarly, in 1 John 5:20, the referent of the phrase "the true God" is disputed. Some commentators think that it designates Jesus, others that it refers to God (the Father). If it were taken to refer to Jesus, however, it would not add new content to the Gospel's affirmation of Jesus. Similarly, if it were taken to refer to God, then the Gospel's affirmations at 1:1 and 20:28 are not impugned. The question remains, however, what such predications actually intend.

22. Reprinted in Juel, *Jesus the Christ,* pp. 113-36.

problem of revelation.[23] It would be a short step from a study focusing on the theme of revelation to one that concentrated on God. Perhaps the most pertinent question in this regard arises from the assertion of the Fourth Gospel that the Son has made the Father known (e.g., John 1:18) If indeed Jesus makes God known, then what is it about God that Jesus reveals? It was to this question that Bultmann answered, "Nothing: but that Jesus is the revealer of God." It is not a "what" that Jesus reveals, but a "that" — he is the Revealer. Such a conclusion has scarcely gone unchallenged, and others have asserted that there is indeed a content and substance to the revelation of God in Jesus in the Fourth Gospel.[24] However, as is often admitted, such studies run up against the puzzling fact that although Jesus in the Fourth Gospel repeatedly states that he makes the Father known in word and deed, nowhere is it made plain what it is *about* God that is revealed.

Surely there are certain assumptions about God that underlie the Gospel, that provide the framework in which the Gospel is placed and read, and that make sense of the ministry of Jesus and of the statements that Jesus makes God known. As William Loader writes:

> The evangelist builds thus upon the presupposition that God is in some sense known. For all his claims, Jesus does not impart detailed information about God, but speaks on the assumption that God is a word that makes good sense to his hearers. Since this is so, it is equally important to examine the unexpressed assumptions about God present in the gospel, for Jesus' claim and significance is inseparably connected with them.[25]

There are implicit assumptions about God that provide the lens through which we read the Gospel and that illumine it and all the statements about the unity of the work of the Father and Son. The explicit statements in the

23. As John Ashton wrote, "[Bultmann's] fundamental insight, from which he never wavered, was that the central theme of the gospel is revelation" (*Understanding the Fourth Gospel* [Oxford: Clarendon, 1991], p. 63).

24. Most notably, Ernst Käsemann (*The Testament of Jesus: A Study of the Gospel of John in the Light of Chapter 17*, ET Philadelphia: Fortress, 1968], who argued that the dogma of the unity of the Father and Son is the content of the revelation of the Gospel.

25. Loader, *Christology*, p. 140; cf. Meyer, "'The Father,'" p. 257: "Not only individual verses in the Gospel of John but often logical and literary transitions as well are intelligible only if one is aware of some of [the] beliefs and teaching about God that are nowhere spelled out but are simply taken for granted by the writer."

Gospel about God articulate some, but not all, of these implicit assumptions. It is the explicit statements and implicit assumptions about God, and the ways in which they together provide the framework of the Gospel, leading directly and indirectly to new formulations about the very reality of God, that form the subject matter of the present inquiry.[26]

As noted above, it is surely the case that Johannine scholars have neglected to write of John's *theology* proper due to the common description of the Gospel as a thoroughly Christocentric document.[27] Yet the problem with — as well as promise of — the designation "Christocentric" is that the term already points beyond itself. If the Christ, the Messiah, is the one anointed and sent by God to carry out God's work, it follows that Christology makes sense particularly as it gives expression to theology. In his article "Toward the Renewal of New Testament Christology," Leander Keck makes the following suggestion in speaking of the "signification of Jesus for Christian theology":

> "Significance" is intelligible only in relation to something or someone. Accordingly, the subject-matter of christology is really the syntax of relationships or correlations. In developed christology this structure of signification is expressed in relation to God (the *theological* correlation proper), the created order (the *cosmological* correlation), and humanity (the *anthropological* correlation); each of these impinges on the others whether or not this impingement is made explicit. Consequently, from statements about God or world or humanity one can infer the appropriate christological correlates, and vice versa. Of these correlations, two have not got their due — the cosmological and the theological. Nils A. Dahl has rightly observed that the understanding of God has been the

---

26. Jerome Neyrey has pursued a similar question in several works. By investigating first-century conceptions of deity, he endeavors to illumine various affirmations about Jesus in the Fourth Gospel, particularly those that point to the deity of Christ. See "'My Lord and My God': The Divinity of Jesus in John's Gospel," *SBLSP* (1986): 152-71; and *An Ideology of Revolt: John's Christology in Social-Science Perspective* (Philadelphia: Fortress, 1988).

27. "John" here stands for the Gospel itself, rather than for the author of the Gospel (or, for that matter, other documents within the NT). When I speak of John's Christology or theology I refer primarily to that which is expressed in the Gospel itself. Here one must of course take into account historical context, which includes implicit theological assumptions. To explain the text is also to explain that which is implicit. I do not suppose that everything that the author of the Gospel or his community believed about Christ or God has come to expression either in the Gospel or the epistles.

neglected factor in the study of NT theology as a whole. This is particularly true of the study of NT christology, even though every statement about Christ implicates God, beginning with the designation of Jesus as the Anointed.[28]

Thus every Christological affirmation has a theological correlate. As Paul Meyer has put it:

> In its profoundest dimension — not just in this Gospel but in all its variations throughout the diverse traditions of the New Testament — [Christology] concerns not the person of Jesus or his identity ("who he is") and the consequences of his life so much as — first, foremost, and always — his open or hidden relationship to God, and of God to him. Without that, there may be a religious hero in the Gospels, but there is no Christology.[29]

Yet the theological correlates of Christological statements have often been neglected in Johannine studies because the widely shared understanding of the Gospel as "Christocentric" has often shaped and predetermined exegetical conclusions. The necessary correlation of Christology and theology implies that to label the Gospel of John "Christocentric" is inadequate and imprecise: *inadequate* because the label diverts our attention from the theocentric framework of the Fourth Gospel; *imprecise* because it ignores the prior question of the function and referent of John's Christology and because it obscures important observations about the text that might lead us to rethink and reformulate our understanding of Johannine theology.

Certain aspects of the historical and religious milieu of the first century are particularly illuminating for the Fourth Gospel. Attention has often been focused on the historical background of messianic or Christological designations. Of particular importance in delineating John's Christology are the concepts of Wisdom and Word, and considerable research has been done with respect to these "intermediary" or "agency" figures.[30] However, often the focus of such studies has been narrowly

28. Keck, "Renewal of New Testament Christology," p. 363.
29. Meyer, "'The Father,'" p. 259.
30. For example, James D. G. Dunn, *Christology in the Making: A New Testament Inquiry into the Origins of the Doctrine of the Incarnation*, 2d ed. (London: SCM, 1989 [1980]);

INTRODUCTION

Christological: With which of these figures, if any, was Jesus identified? What light does the use of such categories shed on early Christian understanding of the person of Jesus? Less often has the gaze of scholarship been trained on the question how the identification of Jesus with one of these figures impinges upon the understanding of *God*. In fact, as several authors have pointed out, those categories that are particularly useful to John, such as Wisdom and Word, posit a different sort of relationship between Jesus and God than the broader designation of "agency" or "intermediary" figures might imply, and hence those categories necessarily implicate early Christian convictions about God.[31]

There are also a number of recurring characteristics or traits of God that shed light on the God of the Fourth Gospel, including justice and mercy as God's "proper" attributes; "life-giving" as a prerogative unique to God; and God as Father, a term that describes God as the source of life and salvation. These characteristics figure centrally in Johannine depictions of the work of God in the world. The problem of discerning the work and presence of God arises for the Fourth Gospel as well as its contemporary Jewish sources.[32] How is God to be known? Ancient texts that treat God's dealings with the world speak extensively of God's revelation or manifestation through intermediaries — angels and prophets, Wisdom and Word, temple and Torah — and so deal as well with the questions of the manifestation and knowledge of God. These themes are central to John. Similarly, it can scarcely be disputed that worship of the one true God forms the basis of practice and belief in first-century Judaism and that issues surrounding proper worship, use of the temple, and carrying out of certain rituals surface in its literature. No less can be said of the Gospel of John. John repeatedly manifests contacts with the first-century social and religious

---

Larry Hurtado, *One God, One Lord: Early Christian Devotion and Ancient Jewish Monotheism* (Philadelphia: Fortress, 1988).

31. See especially Richard J. Bauckham, *God Crucified: Monotheism and Christology in the New Testament* (Grand Rapids: Eerdmans, 1998); James D. G. Dunn, "Let John Be John: A Gospel for Its Time," in *Das Evangelium und die Evangelien,* ed. Peter Stuhlmacher, WUNT 28 (Tübingen: Mohr, 1983), pp. 309-39; and Peder Borgen, "God's Agent in the Fourth Gospel," in *Religions in Antiquity: Essays in Memory of E. R. Goodenough,* ed. Jacob Neusner (Leiden: Brill, 1968), pp. 137-48.

32. Philo's speculations about the powers of God and knowing God through (or even as) the Word (Logos) certainly suggest the kinds of questions that fueled at least some ancient Jewish speculation about the character, activity, and manifestation of God.

12

world regarding questions of the activity, presence, revelation, knowledge, and worship of God.

This work, then, is a theological investigation of the Gospel of John, in that it takes as its central question the convictions and presentation of God, and does so in the hope of coming to theological conclusions. This investigation is carried on primarily through historical and exegetical means. What will be noticeably lacking from the present study, especially when it is compared with important works on the Gospel of John in recent decades, are attempts to reconstruct the history of the text or the community that lies behind it. Such reconstructions have been highly influential in shaping study of the Gospel. They have also contributed greatly to the predominant views of the Gospel's "Christocentricity." The seminal works by Raymond Brown and J. Louis Martyn have in common the view that so-called "high Christology" stands at the heart of the dispute between Church and synagogue and accounts for much of the hostility not only between "Christians' and "Jews," but also between various groups of messianists, some of whom were not willing to share the high Christology of the Johannine Christians. Brown in particular has argued that the history of the community can be traced in various stages of the text's composition, which reveals multiple layers even in its present form.

My interests lie elsewhere, in part because I believe that the Gospel itself invites — even compels — us to look first in other directions for proper interpretation, both by virtue of its genre and its explicitly stated purposes.[33] In terms of genre, the Gospel is a narrative of some aspects of Jesus' life, written to persuade its readers to take up its perspective of the significance of that life as their own. This is the intention embodied in the Gospel — and embodied by its primary author. To the extent that the Gospel can properly be classified an ancient biography, the audience of the Gospel remains unspecified, except of course that it consists of readers for whom the Gospel exerts normative force in their understanding of who Jesus was and is. As Herman Ridderbos aptly puts it "Not only do we know too little of the situation of the first Christian community (let alone that of

---

33. I am indebted both to Richard Burridge's fine study, *What Are the Gospels? A Comparison with Greco-Roman Biography* (Cambridge: Cambridge University Press, 1992), and the various essays in the collection entitled *The Gospels for All Christians: Rethinking the Gospel Audiences*, ed. Richard Bauckham (Grand Rapids: Eerdmans, 1998). While the Gospels have striking differences from many ancient biographies, they do undoubtedly have biographical elements and intentions.

the "Johannine" community) but the flight of the eagle (the traditional symbol of John) among the Evangelists covers far too much distance for us to view it only from the perspective of the situation of one church or one phase in the history of the church."[34] Needless to say, if these assertions are true, they call for careful attention to the text as it now stands, as a purposeful argument for the significance of Jesus' life, ministry, death, and resurrection. However, we need not foreclose the possibility that such study might well be suggestive for pondering once more the contexts that best explain the origins of the Gospel of John.

The avowed purpose of the Gospel is first and foremost to offer an interpretation of Jesus' life that will instill faith in its readers that he is the "Messiah, the Son of God" (20:31). Yet this summary statement cannot be isolated from the whole narrative that has preceded it, as is too often done when all attention is directed to the precise nuance of "Messiah" or the text-critical decision whether to read the present or aorist tense of the verb "believe." The purpose statement comes at the climax of a Gospel that opens with a description of that same "Son, who is in the bosom of the Father," who has "made God known" (1:18). Unless, then, one comes through the Gospel to an understanding of who that God is whom Jesus, the Son of God, has revealed, the Gospel will not have achieved its purpose.

To recover the theological framework of the Gospel, then, renders historical and exegetical conclusions more precisely and delineates Johannine theology more fully. Barrett charted the way, but Kysar's *Forschungsbericht* may be taken as evidence that the scholarly mainstream continues to balk at anything but a Christocentric course. The present study hopes to show that "Christocentric" is a misleading term for the Gospel of John. Barrett, Dahl, Dunn, Keck, and others have argued convincingly that Christology is indeed an aspect of theology and only in that perspective properly grasped. All these studies have themselves directed our attention to God, but none has actually pursued the suggested topic — "God" — at length. As noted above, Dahl articulated the desideratum as follows: "As the New Testament is a complex and multidimensional entity, the most appropriate form for dealing with its theology (both in the wider and narrower sense of the term) is not a comprehensive textbook but a monograph that con-

---

34. Herman Ridderbos, *The Gospel of John: A Theological Commentary* (Grand Rapids: Eerdmans, 1997), p. 11.

centrates upon one topic in such a way that it contributes to a better understanding of an aspect of the whole."[35]

The chapters that follow endeavor to concentrate upon one topic, the identity of God in the Fourth Gospel. They do so by treating issues and subjects that are essential to an understanding of that greater topic. The subjects for treatment in each chapter have arisen both from the Gospel itself and from concerns related to the identity of God, which are embodied in literature from the period in which the Gospel came to be in its present form, the first century of the present era. The case for inclusion of each topic to be discussed will, I hope, become apparent in due course. My aim in this study is to concentrate on the topic "God in the Fourth Gospel" in such a way that it contributes to our understanding of the Fourth Gospel, of NT theology, of theology itself, and of God.

35. Dahl, "Neglected Factor," p. 157.

ONE

The Meaning of "God"

> It seems to me that the early Christians, including the writers of
> the New Testament, wrestled with [the question of the meaning of
> the word "God"] more than is usually imagined. The word theos
> for Greek-speakers (and its equivalents in other languages spoken
> in the first century) was not univocal, and the early Christians
> made out a fairly thorough case for understanding it in a particu-
> lar sense.[1]

> Theos, though a basic term of Greek religion, has never been
> given a detailed semantic study. Scholars, in their eagerness to ex-
> amine what the Greeks thought about their gods, have generally
> not paused to consider the prior question — what does theos
> mean?[2]

These quotations urge us to reconsider what we have easily taken for
granted — the meaning of the word "god" (θεός) in general and, for the

1. N. T. Wright, The New Testament and the People of God vol. 1: Christian Origins and
the Question of God (Minneapolis: Fortress, 1992), p. xiv.
2. S. R. F. Price, "Gods and Emperors: The Greek Language of the Roman Imperial
Cult," JHS 104 (1984): 79.

17

present study, in John's Gospel. This question can be raised on several levels. On the one hand, we may have in mind a question about how we conceive of God, with what attributes, characteristics, or descriptive phrases. We may intend, on the other hand, a question focusing on the referent of the word "god" — that is, to which figure(s) does the word "god" refer? "God," it is assumed, means "a divine being" of some sort, and the question is merely to which being(s) the designation refers. Monotheists generally collapse the meaning and referent of "god," since "god" *means* "a divine being" but *refers* to the only such being. To say "God" thus implies much more than a particular *kind* of being, a deity as opposed to humans or animals; it rather identifies the one who is the sole member of the class *theos*. Not surprisingly, it is easy to fill the word "god" with those connotations typically attached to one's conception of a particular deity. The result is that the meaning of "god" is filtered through convictions about the nature and reality of the only god in whom people believe and whom they worship.

Such a confusion of meaning and referent has led to unfounded conclusions about the application of "god" to various figures in the OT, Judaism, and early Christianity. Maurice Casey, for example, argues that "the deity of Jesus is . . . *inherently* unJewish. The witness of Jewish texts is unvarying: belief that a second being is God involves departure from the Jewish community."[3] Yet Philo writes that Moses is "god" and that the Logos is "a second god" — and neither of these confessions necessitates "departure from the Jewish community." It depends entirely on how one construes the predication "is god" or, in Philo's case, even "is a second God." Casey assumes that either predication can only mean "there are two gods." Since behind the word "God" there stands some sort of concept as "unique, supreme being," to apply the statement "is God" to anyone other than the one God renders one a di-theist. Hence, what Casey actually finds unacceptable in first-century Judaism is the belief that there are "two gods." However, this is to beg the question whether monotheism — belief that there is only one God — can encompass the claim that a "second being is god," and what sort of predication is made by that statement. To answer that question one needs to determine what "is God" predicates.

As another example of the confusion of the meaning of "god" with the concept of god or convictions about God, take the following discussion:

---

3. Maurice Casey, *From Jewish Prophet to Gentile God: The Origins and Development of New Testament Christology* (Louisville: Westminster/John Knox, 1991), p. 176.

While all [these examples of ancient figures being called "god" indicate] the widespread use of the appellation θεός for certain persons, care should be taken not to read theological doctrine into statements that were often merely the product of obsequious flattery or profound respect.[4]

Yet on what grounds can the use of *theos* sometimes be deemed "*merely the product of obsequious flattery or profound respect*" while at other times, apparently, be thought to contain "theological doctrine" that *ought* to be read into certain statements? If the application of *theos* is at times the result of flattery or respect, how does one know that all instances of the word ought not to be read in this way? Moreover, given the fact that there were other terms and ways in which one could express "profound respect," on what grounds is the appellation "god" chosen rather than some other title, such as Lord, or some other description, such as "all powerful"?

Finally, confusion regarding "meaning of god" and "concepts about God" can be illustrated by the question of identity most frequently asked about Jesus: Does the NT call Jesus God? Once an affirmative answer is received, the inquirer then assumes that we understand who Jesus is: Jesus is God. However, the crucial question here is, What does the NT mean when it calls Jesus God? Those who assume that they know what it means to say "Jesus is God" do so because they have some idea of what "god" means. Since we know what "God" means, then we must know what it means to say "Jesus is God." Here, however, the logic breaks down, for those who confess that "Jesus is God" (usually) do *not* intend to posit an *equivalence* between "Jesus" and "God," where "God" designates the one and only God, Israel's God. Rather, they wish to make similar, if not equivalent, predications *about* that God and Jesus through the application to both of the word "god." Yet this simply begs the question, In what sense can the word "god" be applied to both Jesus and God? As N. T. Wright notes:

> The christological question, as to whether the statement "Jesus is God" is true, and if so in what sense, is often asked as though "God" were the known and "Jesus" the unknown; this, I suggest, is manifestly mistaken. If anything, the matter stands the other way around.

4. Murray J. Harris, *Jesus as God: The New Testament Use of Theos in Reference to Jesus* (Grand Rapids: Baker, 1992), p. 28.

I in no way wish to deny that the application of the term *theos* to Jesus is an important part of the consideration of both the identity of Jesus and of God in the Gospel of John. Yet in order to consider that question, it is crucial to ask a prior question — what does *theos* mean? S. R. F. Price asserts that there is general agreement that *theos* is not a name but a logical predicate,[5] but he asks: "What sort of predicate is *theos*? What were the conditions for its use?"[6] The question centers on the semantic contexts of the word *theos*, the formulations and predications in which it appears, and the conditions under which it is used to predicate something of an individual or being.

Thus, to say that *theos* is originally predicative leads to the question what that predication consists of, and whether *theos* predicates the same thing of all those beings to whom it is applied. To take a pagan example, we might ask whether "Zeus is god" makes the same predication regarding Zeus that "Caesar is god" makes with respect to Caesar. If not, what is the range of meanings possible for "god"? Even if the predications are identical, that does not yet tell us exactly what is being predicated. Do these statements, for example, indicate that Zeus and Caesar share some sort of nature? That they have similar powers? That both deserve reverence or worship? That both belong to a certain class of being? It is possible that what "god" predicates of someone differs from sentence to sentence, much the way that "the grass is green" differs from "this banana is green," where the former says something about the color of the grass and the latter about the ripeness of the fruit. Or, to take an example somewhat closer to home, Karl Barth could predicate "is the Word of God" of Jesus Christ, Scripture, and Church proclamation, but in each case the predication, though verbally identical, means something different.[7] The question is not whether these various assertions are true or false, but rather exactly what these sentences assert.[8]

In his study of the language used in the imperial cult, Price shows the

5. On this point see Herman Kleinknecht, "θεός," in *TDNT* 3:67; Price, "Gods and Emperors," pp. 79-95.

6. Price, "Gods and Emperors," p. 79.

7. For this example, see Nicholas Wolterstorff, *Divine Discourse: Philosophical Reflections on the Claim That God Speaks* (Cambridge: Cambridge University Press, 1995), p. 63.

8. See the discussion of univocal, equivocal, and analogical predication in William Placher, *The Domestication of Transcendence: How Modern Thinking about God Went Wrong* (Louisville: Westminster/John Knox, 1996), p. 28.

wide and diverse semantic field of *theos* in Graeco-Roman culture. Essentially, the term was used to designate a wide variety of (1) heavenly beings (in both Greek and Semitic language); (2) figures of exceptional power or status, such as kings; and (3) figures to whom one wished to show reverence.[9] Those persons long accustomed to the view that Judaism could be distinguished from neighboring religions by its "radical monotheism" will undoubtedly suspect that while Price's analysis will hold for pagan religion, it will not hold for Judaism and Jewish texts. Yet there are sources from Second Temple Judaism that use *theos, elim,* and *elohim* of other beings than the one God, but not in an unlimited sense and not without qualification. Those limitations and qualifications are instructive for understanding precisely the meaning of these terms.

The chief "qualification" is that *theos* and *elohim* or *elim* are typically applied only to figures for whom there is biblical precedent for doing so. For example, Philo expounds on God's declaration to Moses in Exodus 7:1 — "I have made you as God to Pharaoh" — in ways that are not clearly implied in the account in Exodus, but it is after all biblical usage that Philo expounds. Similarly, human judges are called *elohim,* even as they are called *theoi* in the Septuagint translation of the Hebrew (e.g., אֱלֹהִים = LXX θεούς; Exod. 22:27). In the Dead Sea Scrolls one finds angels spoken of as *elim* (אלים) or *beney elim* (בני אלים), the latter in keeping with Psalms 29:1 and 89:7.[10] Other passages from the Scrolls attest the use of *elohim* (אלוהים) for the angels, as is found in Psalms 8:6; 82:1, 6; 97:7; 138:1, and so on. By extension, Melchizedek, understood as the angel Michael, is spoken of as "your God" in a quotation from Isaiah 52:7 (11QMelch 2:24-25), and as an agent of God's judgment, in keeping with Psalm 82:1-2 and 7:8-9 (see 11QMelch 2:10-15). In this instance, while the Scrolls expand upon the biblical usage, they do not do so with unbridled license.

Even so, to observe this phenomenon in no way settles the question what *theos* predicates when applied to persons such as Moses or Melchizedek. Does *theos* predicate exactly the same thing when used of Moses

9. Price, "Gods and Emperors." On the difficulty of distinguishing between comparison and identification with God, see also A. E. Harvey, *Jesus and the Constraints of History* (Philadelphia: Westminster, 1982), p. 156.

10. For a discussion of the designations and titles used for angels in the *Songs of the Sabbath Sacrifice* and some of the other Scrolls as well, see Carol Newsom, *Songs of the Sabbath Sacrifice: A Critical Edition* (Atlanta: Scholars Press, 1985), esp. pp. 23-24.

and Melchizedek, of God and Moses, and so on? Precisely because the term seems to be used of a number of figures of different sorts, these questions arise. Of interest, then, is that certain adjectives or qualifying and explanatory phrases are almost always used in conjunction with "god" to show which "god" is in question or *in what way* a particular figure can be construed as "god." In other words, the word "god" does not always carry within it an understanding of how that term applies to the figure so designated. It certainly need not have implied a figure to be worshipped. Furthermore, when we consider the other options — such as Lord — available to a writer, we may learn something about the particular connotations of "god" from the instances and ways in which it is used as opposed to those alternate terms. Why, for example, do texts invariably say "God of our ancestors" rather than "King" or "Lord of our ancestors?" Why is it that "God" is so qualified by explanatory phrases, and what is the significance of those qualifications?

In this chapter, then, we focus on the word "god" itself and, more specifically, on the ways in which it is used. Naturally, the results of such an inquiry will spill over into, and themselves likely be produced by, certain religious convictions about and problems in conceiving God. For the purposes of this study, those texts that are of special interest are particularly texts of Greek-speaking Judaism that will help us to understand the contexts in which the Gospel of John finds its home. If construed quite narrowly, the question "How is *theos* used?" would eliminate Jewish texts written in Aramaic and Hebrew that are of relevance for understanding the Fourth Gospel and which we wish to include in our investigations. Yet Jewish texts written in Greek, including the LXX, would have been influenced and shaped by the Semitic terms for God. Thus, we will include texts not preserved or written in Greek, while taking into consideration the differences that may exist in the use of *theos* as opposed to *elohim* or other Semitic terms for "god."

Observations on the Use of "God"

As noted already, "god" (θεός) *is not a proper name, but a term that makes a predication about the person or reality so named.* The same holds true for the use of *elohim* in the OT, whatever its origin. Because in Hebrew, Greek, and English the respective terms *elohim, elim, theos,* and God are used both as names or designations of a specific figure and as labels for a class of be-ings, the point is often lost that "God" comes to be a name by the way it is used, much the way "Dad" or "Mom" functions for children as the name of their parent, even though these are not their given names and are used for many other persons. Other titles or designations for God, such as "Lord" or "Father," serve as appellatives for God, or as ways in which people ad-dress God. As is well known, according to the testimony of the OT, God has a name, typically rendered into English today as "Yahweh." However, the name was eventually not read, and it was pronounced only by the high priest on the Day of Atonement. In the LXX, the name itself was obscured through substitution, most often with *kyrios* (κύριος), but also several hundred times with *theos* (θεός).[11] Sometimes the LXX is expansionistic. In Deuteronomy 4:35, 39, for example, the translator replaces the Tetra-grammaton with "the LORD your God" (κύριος ὁ θεός σου). Some recensions of the Greek OT render the divine name by using various de-vices to substitute for it, such as putting the Tetragrammaton in Hebrew letters, in paleo-Hebrew script, or writing *IAO* in Greek characters. Need-less to say, the divine name took on a somewhat esoteric flavor.[12] Still, the fact that the high priest did pronounce that name, and that Greek equiva-lents (such as *IAO*) are present in the literature, suggest that its pronuncia-tion was not entirely lost.

The practices of rendering the Tetragrammaton in paleo-Hebrew script, or of using various devices to avoid writing it at all, are also attested from the writings of Qumran. For example, in 1QpHab 10:7 and 14, the Tetragrammaton appears in paleo-Hebrew script, and in 1QS 8:14 there is a citation of Isaiah 40:3, "In the desert, prepare the way of ****, straighten in the steppe a roadway for our God," where a series of four dots replaces the Tetragrammaton.[13] The Tetragrammaton can also be replaced by a tri-

---

11. Ethelbert Stauffer, "θεός," in *TDNT* 3:90; Harris (*Jesus as God*, p. 24, n. 10) gives the figure as 353.

12. On the question of the transmission of the divine name and the Tetragrammaton, see George Howard, "The Tetragram and the New Testament," *JBL* 96 (1977): 53-83; Martin Hengel, "'Sit at My Right Hand!' The Enthronement of Christ at the Right Hand of God and Psalm 110:1," in his *Studies in Early Christology* (Edinburgh: T. & T. Clark, 1995), pp. 156-57, esp. n. 81.

13. In the translation of Florentino García Martínez, the four dots are regularly ren-dered by asterisks. For other examples, see frags 1-2 and 9-11 of 4Q176 [4QTanh]; and 4Q462.

ple *yodh,* the elongated pronoun *hû',* the Greek form *IAO* (4Q120), or by God or Lord (CD 15:1). In short, the variety of alternatives suggest that a number of replacements for YHWH existed during the early years of the Christian Church.[14]

The oldest known prohibition against uttering the name of God when reading the Jewish Scriptures is apparently found in 1QS 6:27–7:2. Here we have the warning: "Whoever enunciates the Name (which is) honoured above all . . . shall not go back to the Community council." Josephus assumes that God's name was revealed to Moses during the episode of the burning bush, and that it is a name "of which I am forbidden to speak" (*Ant.* 2.275-276; cf. *J.W.* 5.438, "the hair-raising name"). Once he uses "the God who is" (θεός ὁ ὤν) where the Hebrew has "the Lord God of hosts" (LXX ὁ κύριος παντοκράτωρ), suggesting that ὁ ὤν was a standing designation for God in Hellenistic Judaism.[15] In the place of other circumlocutions, we have often "the Name," a surrogate for God found in the writings of Second Temple Judaism, rabbinic texts, Samaritan writings, and even the NT.[16]

The NT, and especially the Gospel of John, does refer to "the name of God," which by the first century had become a stock phrase for speaking of the power or authority of God. While there are a number of circumlocutions for God ("the Blessed," "Power," "the Most High"), the absolute form of "God" (with and without the article) appears quite regularly. The

14. See Joseph A. Fitzmyer, "The Semitic Background of the New Testament *Kyrios*-Title," in his *A Wandering Aramean: Collected Aramaic Essays,* SBLMS 25 (Missoula, Mont.: Scholars Press, 1979), pp. 115-42; George Howard, "The Tetragram and the New Testament," *JBL* 96 (1977): 63-83. Adolf von Schlatter (*Wie Sprach Josephus von Gott?* BFCT 1/14 [Gütersloh: Bertelsmann, 1910]) suggests that Josephus's writings show us that the less frequently YHWH is used, the *less frequently kyrios* is used. In rabbinic Judaism, "the place" is the most widespread designation for God, and in post-Mishnaic writings, we have "the holy one, blessed be he."

15. Martin Hengel states that eventually the Jews made a virtue out of necessity by arguing that not only was one forbidden to speak the name of God, but that the true God was "nameless" (*Judaism and Hellenism: Studies in their Encounter in Palestine during the Early Hellenistic Period,* 2 vols. [Philadelphia: Fortress, 1974], 1:266). In *4 Bar.* 6:13, God's name cannot be known. Cf. Apuleius, *On the Teaching of Plato* 1.5: "God is unnameable." According to *Jos. Asen.* 15:12, the names of all the heavenly beings written in the book of the Most High are unspeakable. However, as already noted, the name was pronounced by the high priest on the Day of Atonement, and *IAO* shows that they knew how to pronounce it.

16. For examples, see 11Q5 [11QPsᵃ] 18; 4Q380 1 i 5-8; 4Q381 24:7 ("Your Name is my salvation"); 11Q14 [11QBer] 3, 13.

NT also reflects the practice of not reading or speaking the name of God in its regular use of *kyrios* (κύριος) in quotations of the OT when YHWH stands in the Hebrew or κύριος in the Greek. Thus while there are no explicit prohibitions against speaking God's name in the NT, such as one finds in Josephus and the Dead Sea Scrolls, the name of God is never actually written.[17]

"God" (θεός) often makes a predication about a particular individual or being *in conjunction with a genitive referring to a person or persons*. In looking at Jewish texts in particular, we note that *theos* and its Semitic counterparts tend to attract a variety of descriptive phrases and adjectives. A simple example can be found in the *Shema* in Deuteronomy 6:4, where the Israelites are commanded, "Hear, O Israel, the LORD our God, the LORD is one.' YHWH (LXX κύριος) is the subject of the sentence, and YHWH is identified as "our God" (אֱלֹהֵינוּ; LXX ὁ θεὸς ἡμῶν). Curiously, the confessional form does not call YHWH simply "God," but rather "*our* God." Although it may be debated whether this formula assumes the existence of other gods, inasmuch as YHWH must be singled out from others, the pertinent point for our discussion is that the statement "YHWH is our God" offers a particular nuance that "YHWH is God" does not: it binds the speaker or writer to God in a relationship that he or she does not have to other would-be gods. The possessive form found in the *Shema* recurs often, as do other variations of it.

In texts of Second Temple Judaism, there are almost countless variations identifying God with an individual (usually a patriarch), several individuals together, or the nation of Israel as a whole. For example, we have the stock phrase "the God of our fathers" (*T. Sim.* 2:8; 11Q19 [11QTemple] 54:13; 1QM 13:7) or "God of our ancestors" (4 Macc. 12:17; *Fr. Man.* 1);

---

17. See the references in Hengel, "'Sit at My Right Hand!'" p. 156, n. 82; and Jarl Fossum, *The Name of God and the Angel of the Lord: Samaritan and Jewish Concepts of Intermediation and the Origin of Gnosticism*, WUNT 36 (Tübingen: J. C. B. Mohr [Paul Siebeck], 1985), for discussion of the "name of the Lord" as reflection upon Exod. 23:20-21. Alan F. Segal also argues that Exod. 23:20 and the exegetical traditions that grew up from it influenced Paul's attribution to Jesus of "the name that is above every name," and further concludes: "For a Jew this phrase can only mean that Jesus received the divine name Yahweh, the tetragrammaton YHWH, translated as the Greek name *kyrios*, or Lord" (*Paul the Convert: The Apostolate and Apostasy of Saul the Pharisee* [New Haven: Yale University Press, 1990], p. 62). Similarly the contention of the book of Hebrews that Christ has inherited "a more excellent name than [that of the angels]" (Heb. 1:4) surely reflects the tradition that there was a principal angel who was the bearer of God's own name in Exod. 23:20-21.

"the God of Abraham, Isaac and Jacob";[18] and "the God of Israel" (1QS 3:24; 1QM 10:8; 13:1, 2, 13 passim). Often an individual is singled out, and there are numerous instances of texts that identify God in relationship to one human being. Thus, for example, we find "the Lord, the God of Joseph" (*Jos. Asen.* 3:4; 6:7; 21:4); "Lord God of my father Israel" (*Jos. Asen.* 8:9); "O Lord God and King, God of Abraham" (Add. Esth. 13:15; 14:18); "the Lord Almighty, God of Israel" (Bar. 3:1, 4); "Lord God of my ancestor Simeon" (Jdt. 9:2); "God of my ancestor, God of Israel's heritage" (Jdt. 9:12); "Lord God of Daniel" (Bel. 41); and "Lord God of Shem" (*Jub.* 8:18). Rather than specifying individuals by name, sometimes the speaker refers to "our God," often in contrast to "their god" or "their gods," or invokes God with the personal "my God" (e.g., 1QS 11:15; 11Q19 [11QTemple] 54:14, 16; 55:10, 14; 1QH 17:23; Jdt. 6:2; *L.A.B.* 23:14). There are also generic sorts of predications, such as "god of the righteous" or "god of those who repent," in which speakers implicitly identify themselves with the category so named.

In all these cases, the genitive phrases could be paraphrased as "the God worshipped by . . ." The primary idea seems to be that God is identified or known in relationship to the people who honor or worship that particular deity. A designation such as "God of our ancestors" does not primarily direct one's attention to the past, conveying some notion such as "God is lord of history," but identifies the one whom "the ancestors" followed and worshipped. In calling on the god of one's forbears, one not only expresses one's faithful allegiance to the same god but perhaps also invokes the favor of God by appealing to the memory of heroes of the faith. This, at least, is Philo's point in arguing that God called himself "The God of Abraham and of Isaac and of Jacob" in order to give humankind a name that would encourage a relationship of trust and dependence (*Abr.* 51).[19]

---

18. *Mos.* 1.74-76; *Pr. Man.* 1; Matt. 22:32//Mark 12:26; Luke 20:37; Acts 3:13; 7:31-32. In the OT, the phrase "the God of Abraham, the God of Isaac, and the God of Jacob" occurs only in Exod. 3:6, 15-16; 4:5.

19. In his discussion of Exod. 3:14-15, Philo asserts that "God" is called "God of Abraham and God of Isaac and God of Jacob," since each is an exemplar of the attainment of wisdom, although each attained the virtue differently, namely, by teaching (Abraham), inherently (Isaac), and practice (Jacob). See the discussion by David T. Runia, "God of the Philosophers, God of the Patriarchs: Exegetical Backgrounds in Philo of Alexandria," in his *Philo and the Church Fathers: A Collection of Papers,* Supplements to Vigiliae Christianae 32 (Leiden: Brill, 1995), p. 209.

It is striking how often one encounters such identifying genitive phrases with "God." Because *theos* is a generic term, referring to a being or beings of a certain sort, the god in view needs to be identified, and this is regularly done by identifying that god in relationship to the people who claim allegiance to that deity. A text from 3 Maccabees illustrates this use of *theos:* the Jews destined for slaughter call upon "the Almighty Lord and Ruler of all power, their merciful God and Father" (5:7). Clearly the god in view is the one God, who is nevertheless frequently designated as "our God."[20] Similarly, in the Pentateuch, the phrase *El Shaddai*, which apparently posed something of a riddle to the Greek translators, is rendered by the Septuagint as "my God," "your God," or "their God."[21] So, for example, in Exodus 6:3, the LXX reads, "I appeared to Abraham, Isaac, and Jacob, being their God, but I did not manifest to them my name LORD." In the same vein, in commenting on this verse, Philo writes that

> no proper name of [God] has been revealed to any. "I was seen," He says, "of Abraham, Isaac and Jacob, being their God, and My name of 'Lord' [τὸ ὄνομά μου κύριος] I did not reveal to them." (Exod. 6:3)

As Philo goes on to say, God's "eternal name" is nevertheless "relative" and not "absolute" (*Abr.* 51), that is, it is given in relationship to the three patriarchs by reason of their virtue, so that human beings would have some way of focusing their aspirations. The possessive pronoun used with "God" shows the relationship of God to the patriarchs and encourages them to put their trust in this God.[22]

Because "God" needs to be made precise, authors typically predicate a relationship of God to a person, or persons. Clearly it is not enough to say "god"; one must specify how that God is known or identified, or by whom that God is honored. The promise in *Jubilees* 22:15 that "he will be God for you and your seed" illustrates the relational or functional connotations of

---

20. However, compare the prayers of the Eighteen Benedictions, in which the speakers address themselves to "our Father" and "our King." For rabbinic examples of "Lord of all," see Ephraim Urbach, *The Sages: Their Concepts and Beliefs* (Cambridge, Mass.: Harvard University Press, 1987), p. 696, n. 7.

21. Elsewhere, of course, there are other translations, including "Almighty," God (*theos*), Lord (*kyrios*), and various other combinations; see C. H. Dodd, *The Bible and the Greeks* (London: Hodder & Stoughton, 1954), p. 14.

22. Runia, "God of the Philosophers," pp. 209-10.

the word "god," for here the promise that God will be "God for you" might have been paraphrased by a formulation such as "God will be present with you" or "God will be a protector for you." Similarly, an almost paradoxical statement in *Jubilees* 25:21 contains the prayer "May God Most High be their God." By juxtaposing the absolute "God Most High" with the possessive "their God," the text indirectly reveals that "god" needs qualification both with respect to the relation of God to other deities and with respect to human beings. This leads us directly to our next point.

"God" often requires qualifying phrases, such as "God of gods" or "Most High God" in order to make clear to whom or what the word refers. Such phrases characterize God not only by relationship to human beings, as do phrases such as "God of Abraham," but by relationship to the other gods, although phrases such as "God of gods" or "God of the heavens," popular during the Persian period (Jon. 1:9; Ezra 1:2; cf. 1QM 18:7), beg the question of the existence of these gods. In Daniel, for example, in a text whose point is to assert the uniqueness and supremacy of Israel's God, Nebuchadnezzar says to Daniel, "Truly, your God is God of gods and Lord of kings" (2:47), thus identifying this god with relationship both to Daniel ("your God") and to other deities ("God of gods"). The phrase "God who made heaven and earth" distinguishes this god from those idols that are manufactured by human hands, as the prophetic tirades against idolatry make clear. Since Judaism emerged from and lived within a polytheistic environment, it needed to identify its god. It did so in relationship to its past and to other gods.

Calling Israel's God the "God of gods" raises the question of the status or existence of these other "gods." They may have been conceived of as divine or supernatural beings, whether beneficent or demonic. Clearly Jews and Christians alike believed in the existence of such entities. What is at issue in describing more precisely the nature or identity of these beings is their relationship to the Most High God. As Shaye Cohen notes, it is not belief in multiple heavenly beings that compromises monotheism, but rather the attribution of independence to them.[23] Indeed, many of the

---

23. Shaye J. D. Cohen, *From the Maccabees to the Mishnah*, Library of Early Christianity 7, ed. Wayne A. Meeks (Philadelphia: Westminster, 1987), p. 84. Similarly, Stauffer ("θεός," in *TDNT* 3:98) writes: "Theocentric thinking is safeguarded even in later Jewish conceptions of intermediary and angelic beings. Indeed, it reaches its full force in this thinking. We encounter a plenitude of hypostases in apocal. and Philo. . . . But they are not independent magnitudes alongside God. They cannot dispute His rank. They are subordinate to Him. They are

phrases that predicate supreme power of God — including "Most High God," "Lord God Almighty," and "Almighty God Most High" — do so by implying the supremacy of this God to other gods (3 Macc. 7:9; 4Q492 1:13; 3 Macc. 6:2; 11QBer 3, 6; 1QS 10:12). In each of these phrases, "God" is somewhat dispensable: "Most High" communicates the same thing as "Most High God."[24] The term "God" is not actually needed, but the qualifying phrases "Almighty" or "Most High" are. Hence in Judith's confession, "thou art God," God is further identified as "the God of all power and might" (9:14), thus demonstrating God's sovereignty over any competing powers. A text from Qumran identifies God as "the Great One, the Lord Eternal," leaving little doubt to whom the designation refers, even though "God" is not used (4Q529). Similarly, in Sirach 36:17 (LXX) we read "You are the Lord, the eternal God" (REB) or "You are the Lord, the God of the ages" (NRSV; 36:22). "God" needs particular qualification.

This point should not be exaggerated. One also finds adjectives, such as merciful, true, and just, without which the noun "god" would communicate little. Sometimes such descriptions are found in genitive phrases, such as "God of mercies," "God of revenge," or "God of salvation." Other designations for *YHWH*, such as King, Lord, or Sovereign, are often elaborately qualified.[25] "Lord" may often remain unmodified because it is understood to be a substitute for the divine name, and hence no further identification is needed. Certain phrases, such as "the living one" or "the divine one," can stand alone for the reader immediately knows to whom the phrase refers. In these instances, no qualification is needed because the description predicates what can only be predicated of God.

Still, *theos often attracts a variety of qualifying and descriptive phrases and adjectives to it.* Apparently the unadorned "God" simply does not say enough about the deity in question. As an example, we may cite the book of Sirach, where the absolute "God" is seldom used, and even "God" in

His instruments or deputies in creation and history." In contrast, Peter Hayman argues that "monotheism" actually misrepresents Judaism through at least the period of the Middle Ages since Judaism is better described as "monarchistic throughout. God is the king of a heavenly court consisting of many other powerful beings, not always under his control. For most Jews, God is the sole object of worship, but he is not the only divine being" ("Monotheism — A Misused Word in Jewish Studies?" *JJS* 42 [1991]: 15).

24. There are also forms such as "the Highest" (1QS 11:15).

25. For example, "supremely holy father" (2 Macc. 2:21, *OTP*); "King of great power, Almighty God Most High" (3 Macc. 6:2; Sir 50:17).

various combined forms appears rarely. More common are Lord and the Most High. Other epithets are also found, such as Mighty One, Almighty, Maker, Master, and sometimes these terms are used in combination with Lord or Most High.[26] As already noted, "god" is often used in conjunction with terms that show the relationship between the speaker or writer and god. The author beseeches the Lord as "God of my life" (Sir. 23:4) and elsewhere refers to God as "Master, God of all," implying the divine rule over all creation (36:1). When predicating the uniqueness of Israel's God, the form is "There is no God but you," similar to "You alone are God," rather than a bald assertion "You are God." That is, "God" implies a divine being or deity, and although Sirach acknowledges that only the Lord is such, nevertheless there are obviously others acknowledged by that designation. Since "God" is originally a predicate that refers to a class or type of being, it is often delimited by explanatory and exclusive phrases. There may be "many gods" — but there is only one "Most High," only one who is "God of Israel," or "God of my life." So also Abraham, in *Jubilees* 12:19-20, prays, "*My God*, the Most High God, you alone are God *to me*." Statements of God's uniqueness are frequently couched in terms of personal confession.

One can also compare the LXX translation of some instances of the Tetragrammaton with explanatory phrases. For example, where the Hebrew of Deuteronomy 4:35 reads, "Yahweh is God" (יְהוָה הוּא הָאֱלֹהִים), the LXX reads, "The Lord your God, this one is God" (κύριος ὁ θεός σου οὗτος θεός ἐστιν), replacing the name Yahweh with the phrase "the Lord your God," and the predication "is God" with the emphatic "this one is God." Thus, while the Septuagint seems to efface God's particular identity by leaving out the proper name, YHWH, it nevertheless maintains the specificity of the identification by speaking of "your God" who "is God." In this case the second predication, "this one is God," indicates that the one whom the Israelites claim to be *their* God is also, absolutely, God (θεός).[27]

---

26. For example, in Sirach one finds "the Lord God" (*kyrios ho theos;* 4:28); "the Most High" (23:18, 23); "Lord Most High" (47:5; 50:19); "the Lord, the Mighty One" (46:6); "the Most High Lord"; "the Holy One, the Most High"; and the particularly full "Almighty God Most High" (50:17). "God" appears in 23:4, where petition is made to the "Lord, Father and God of my life," a parallel designation to an earlier "Lord, Father and Master of my life" (23:1). In 36:1, there is an address to "Master, the God of all," and in 36:5, the author writes, "There is no God but you, Lord."

27. In 1 Kings 8:60 (= LXX 3 Kgdms 8:60) "YHWH is God" (יְהוָה הוּא הָאֱלֹהִים) be-

In Isaiah 44:6, the LXX uses *theos* for YHWH twice: "Thus says God [MT = יהוה], the King of Israel who saved him; God [יהוה] Sabaoth; I am the first and I am after these things. Except me there is no God" (cf. Isa. 45:5). Even though the less specific *theos* substitutes for the proper name, YHWH, there are so many qualifications that there is little question to whom *theos* refers. This one is "King of Israel," "God of hosts," "first and last," and the only God. It is not the statement "is God" that alone predicates the uniqueness of God. Hence an emphatic formulation such as "Truly the LORD is God; the LORD, he is God" (1 Kings 18:39) assigns to the predication "is God" the sense of exclusivism: there is no other God.

The translational practices of various Targums are also of interest, even in spite of the disputed dates of the traditions within them. In an analysis of divine titles in the Pentateuchal Targumim, Andrew Chester documents the frequent substitution of a form of the Tetragrammaton for *elohim*, a practice that avoids any possible misunderstanding of the referent of the noun.[28] As Chester notes:

> The particular problems posed for all the Targumim by אלהים are that it is a plural form, and besides meaning "God (of Israel)" it can also have the (potentially dangerous) meanings "(foreign) gods" or "idols," "angels," "judges"; thus also, as a general designation of deity, it was open to abuse particularly by (Jewish and non-Jewish) ditheistic groups. Hence אלהים used of the God of Israel is taken over as such in all the Targumim only where it is juxtaposed with יהוה, or used with a suffix in a genitival relationship; in other words where it is sufficiently well defined already. Only in a very few instances is it allowed to stand in absolute usage, without further definition, apparently as a title in its own right.[29]

However, as Chester notes, *elohim* is retained in constructions with pronominal suffixes, often plural, since the suffix identifies God with respect to a particular people and so avoids any possible misunderstanding about which

---

comes "the Lord is God, he is God" (κύριος ὁ θεός· αὐτὸς θεός); and in 1 Kings 18:39 (= LXX 3 Kgdms 18:39) "YHWH is God, YHWH is God" becomes "Truly the Lord is God, he is God" (ἀληθῶς κύριός ἐστιν ὁ θεός, αὐτὸς ὁ θεός).

28. Andrew Chester, *Divine Revelation and Divine Titles in the Pentateuchal Targumim,* Texte und Studien zum Antiken Judentum 14 (Tübingen: J. C. B. Mohr [Paul Siebeck], 1986).

29. Chester, *Divine Revelation,* p. 348.

god is in question. In any case, when either *el* or *elohim* is used together with the divine name, it indicates that the writer thinks that the category *elohim* is "exhausted in *Yahweh.*"[30] There are no *elohim* besides Yahweh.

In some instances, *theos* or *elohim* predicates *a God-given privilege or function of an individual, with the exact nature of that privilege or function determined from context.* In Psalm 45:7, *elohim* certainly refers to the king. Other passages seem to refer to the gods *(elohim)* of the heavenly council (Ps. 82:1, 6 [MT]) or to various sorts of human judgment (Exod. 21:6; 22:7-9). In these passages in Exodus, the Targums read "judges" for *elohim,* and later midrashim offer variations such as "the judgment seat of God." When *elohim* refers to heavenly beings, the LXX typically renders it as "angels" (ἄγγελοι, Ps. 96:7; Job 1:6) or "sons of God" (υἱοὶ θεοῦ, Deut. 32:43).

A particularly interesting translation crux occurs in two passages in Exodus, where God is reported as telling Moses, first, "[Aaron] shall speak for you to the people; and he shall be a mouth for you, and you shall be to him as God" (4:16), and then, "I shall make you God to Pharaoh" (7:1). At issue, of course, is what is implied in the declarations that Moses shall be "as God" to Aaron and to Pharaoh. The Hebrew at 4:16 reads "You shall be to him *as God*" (וְאַתָּה תִּהְיֶה-לּוֹ לֵאלֹהִים), which the LXX translates "you shall be for him in things pertaining to God" (σὺ δὲ αὐτῷ ἔσῃ τὰ πρὸς τὸν θεόν; so also the Vulgate). At 7:1 the LXX reads, "Behold, I have given you *as God* to Pharaoh," a literal translation of the Hebrew.[31]

Not surprisingly, none of the Targums allows the phrases "be to him as God" and "make you God" to remain unaltered; they exhibit instead a variety of interpretations. At both 4:16 and 7:1, *Tg. Onqelos* construes *elohim* as connoting the function of authority, reading, "See here, I have appointed you as a leader towards the Pharaoh" (7:1; cf. 4:16). *Tg. Neofiti* conveys something of the same sense at 7:1, which it translates, "See, I have made you lord and ruler to Pharaoh," while at 4:16 it reads, somewhat more enigmatically, "you shall be as one seeking instruction from before the Lord." *Pseudo-Jonathan* reads, "You shall be his teacher who seeks instruction from before the Lord" at 4:16. The author of *Pseudo-Jonathan* comes at the problem from a slightly different angle at 7:1, inserting the

---

30. Gottfried Quell, "θεός," in *TDNT* 3:82.

31. The difficulty of translating these phrases leads the NRSV to render them "and you shall *serve as God* for him" (4:16) and "I have made you *like God* to Pharaoh" (7:1). The question remains in what way Moses "serves as God" or is made "like God."

question "Why are you afraid?" and then continuing, "See, I have already made you (an object of) fear to Pharaoh as if (you were) his God." As Chester comments with respect to such passages, "In a number of instances where the sense of *elohim* is ambiguous or difficult the Targumim use various devices to avoid any possible confusion between God on the one hand and other supernatural beings or humans on the other."[32] Thus the Targums wish to avoid any implication that there is more than one God, as the application of *elohim* to Moses could perhaps lead some to believe. Further clouding the issue here is that *elohim* is a plural form, a fact that leads perhaps too easily to the suggestion that Moses is a god alongside God. Yet the Targumic substitutions are not simply an evasive maneuver but suggest positively that *elohim* conveys either authority (leader, lord, ruler, teacher) or reverence. In other words, although the Targums avoid the term *elohim* for Moses, they do not offer an arbitrary substitution for it, but rather one in keeping with their understanding of *elohim* and particularly of its meaning (master, sovereign) in context.

The same sort of tradition, emphasizing the superior power of God manifest through Moses, occurs in the Midrash:

> Yet God called Moses by His own name, as it says: "Behold, I have made thee as a God unto Pharaoh." God said to Moses: "The wicked Pharaoh made himself out to be a God," as it says: "My river is mine own, and I have made it for myself" (Ezek. xxix,3); let him, therefore, see thee and say: "This is God." (*Exod. Rab. [Va'e-a]* 8.1).

Philo likewise interpreted the text as the bestowal upon Moses of the same title with which God is named. Regarding this passage, Philo commented,

> For, since God judged him worthy to appear as a partner of His own possessions, He gave into his hands the whole world as a portion well fitted for His heir. . . . Was not the joy of [Moses'] partnership with the Father and Maker of all magnified also by the honour of being deemed worthy to bear the same title [προσρήσεως]? For he was named god and king of the whole nation. (*Mos.* 1.155-158; *Prob.* 42-44)[33]

32. Chester, *Divine Revelation*, p. 338.
33. On this passage see Wayne A. Meeks, "The Divine Agent and His Counterfeit in Philo and the Fourth Gospel," in *Aspects of Religious Propaganda in Judaism and Early*

Moses was granted these honors by God since, as "the lover of virtue and nobility," this was "the reward due to him." Because of his noble and virtuous deeds, such as hatred of impurity and evil, impartiality in judgment, and frugality, God named him friend (156) and heir (155) and went so far as to honor him with his very own title, "God." Moreover, Moses "entered into the darkness where God was," and, having thus participated in the divine realm, he was able to convey to others what is hidden from human sight (158; cf. *Mut.* 7; Exod. 20:21).

Philo is here clearly explicating, while also expanding upon, a biblical text. He adds to the biblical text the notion that Moses is "king" of the whole nation. "God" and "king" are epithets indicating both the function of ruling and the status of "friend" and "heir" of God. God's entrusting to Moses of authority over Israel leads to Moses' receiving the designation "god" (cf. *Sacr.* 10, for the same point). Philo applies the term "god" to Moses to make a point about the nature of Moses' commission from God and function in the world as God's emissary or mediator.[34] In any case, it is clear that, for Philo, Moses' status and function designated by the phrase "god of the whole nation" never implies a status independent of the "Father and Maker of all." Rather, it is precisely in relationship to that one that Moses may be designated "god." It is equally clear that for Philo the text of Exodus generates his musings regarding Moses' exalted role. Hence the larger context of Exodus, including the revelation but a few chapters before of God's name to Moses in the burning bush, must be assumed to be the framework in which Philo interprets this statement regarding Moses.

Christianity, ed. Elisabeth Schüssler Fiorenza (Notre Dame: University of Notre Dame Press, 1976), p. 47. As Meeks points out, for Philo, Moses is the intermediary *par excellence* between the divine and human (p. 47).

34. Larry W. Hurtado, *One God, One Lord: Early Christian Devotion and Ancient Jewish Monotheism* (Philadelphia: Fortress, 1988), p. 62; and Carl Holladay, *Theios Aner in Hellenistic Judaism: A Critique of the Use of This Category in New Testament Christology,* SBLDS 40 (Missoula, Mont.: Scholars Press, 1977), pp. 108-55. Philo does not assume that any human being may literally be thought of as God. Paul A. Rainbow ("Monotheism and Christology in 1 Corinthians 8:4-6," D.Phil. diss., Oxford University, 1987, p. 70) speaks of the "idealization" and "perhaps at least partial or incipient divinization of Moses," and also points to evidence that suggests "some degree of divinization" of figures such as Moses and the principal angel among writers such as Philo (p. 98). The awkwardness of characterizations such as "partial divinization" and "some degree of divinization" underscores the difficulty in interpreting passages where Philo (and others) attribute to figures other than God divine functions, titles, or attributes.

Philo also calls the Logos of God "god." In commenting on the statement "in the image of God He made humankind," Philo asks why God does not say, "in his own image God made humankind," but rather speaks of himself in the third person. Philo's response is that nothing mortal can be made in the likeness of the Most High One. Hence, human beings are made in the image of "the second God, who is his Logos" (*QG* 2.62).[35] Philo wants to maintain both the biblical affirmation that human beings are created "in the image of God" and the impossibility that the corruptible physical world can bear the "image" or form of the immaterial, incorruptible God.[36]

Philo's explanation indicates that he can distinguish, at least for heuristic purposes, between God and "the second god, the logos of God." The way in which he draws a line between "God" and the "logos" leads to the question whether there are in fact two gods. Although this might, at first glance, appear to be a theological rather than semantic question, Philo addresses the issue on the grounds of the use of the definite article with *theos*. Referring to Genesis 31:13 — "I am the God who appeared to thee in the place of God" (LXX: ἐγώ εἰμι ὁ θεὸς ὁ ὀφθείς σοι ἐν τόπῳ θεοῦ) — Philo distinguishes between the articular and anarticular use of "God" (ὁ θεός and Θεός):[37]

> He that is truly God is One, but those that are improperly so called are more than one. Accordingly the holy word in the present instance has indicated Him Who is truly God by means of the article saying "I am the God," while it omits the article when mentioning him who is improperly so called, saying "Who appeared to thee in the place" not "of the God," but simply "of God." Here it gives the title of "God" to His chief

35. Justin Martyr also calls the Logos a second god; see *1 Apol.* 63.15; *Dial.* 56.4; see also Origen, *Cels.* 5.39; Eusebius, *Praep. Ev.* 7.12, 320C; *Dem. Ev.* 5.4.9-14; and the discussion in G. L. Prestige, *God in Patristic Thought* (London: Heinemann, 1936), pp. 140-46.

36. Margaret Barker, *The Great Angel: A Study of Israel's Second God* (Louisville: Westminster/John Knox, 1992), p. 131: "Philo shows beyond any doubt that the Judaism of the first Christian century acknowledged a second God." However, Alan F. Segal argues that Philo's view of mediation here prevents the pure, eternal God from participating in the corruptible world (*Two Powers in Heaven: Early Rabbinic Reports about Christianity and Gnosticism*, Studies in Judaism in Late Antiquity 25, ed. Jacob Neusner [Leiden: Brill, 1977], p. 164).

37. Philo obviously misses the point that the LXX *topō theou* renders the Hebrew "Beth-El" quite literally.

Word, not from any superstitious nicety in applying names, but with one aim before him, to use words to express facts. (*Somn.* 1.229-230).[38]

Philo thus argues that the articular (ὁ θεός) denotes the one who is "properly called God," by which he apparently means "He that is truly God." The Word is "improperly so called" not because the manifestation spoken of here is of some deity other than the only true God, but because Philo consistently speaks of the theophanies of God in the OT as appearances of the Logos, not of *to on* (τὸ ὄν), the God who is.[39] Thus to call the Logos "god" expresses the facts: the Logos is not the unknowable high God but nevertheless truly a manifestation of the "One who is."[40]

In a related application of the term *theos,* Philo writes:

> In the first place (there is) He Who is elder than the one and the monad and the beginning. Then (comes) the Logos of the Existent One, the truly seminal substance of existing things. And from the divine Logos, as from a spring, there divide and break forth two powers. One is the creative (power), through which the Artificer placed and ordered all things; this is named "God." And (the other is) the royal (power), since through it the Creator rules over created things; this is called "Lord." (*QE* 2.68)

Here Philo labels one of the powers of the Logos — already a "second emanation," as it were, from God — "God." Elsewhere, Philo puts it this way: "The creative Potency [is] called God, because through this the Father who is its begetter and contriver made the universe, so that 'I am thy God' is equivalent to "I am the Maker and Artificer" (*Mut.* 29). That is to say, the power or means through which "the Father" creates is known as "God."

---

38. This is the translation of F. H. Colson and G. H. Whitaker in the Loeb Classical Library.

39. For the same point in the Church Fathers, see Hengel, "'Sit at My Right Hand!'" pp. 126-27.

40. Segal (*Two Powers,* p. 161; see the references there) refers to Philo's understanding of the Logos as "the hypostasized intelligence of God." For other passages in which Philo distinguishes between the application of the same word to God and the Logos, see *Somn.* 1.61-67, where Philo takes the two references to "place" in Gen. 22:3-4 ("Abraham came to the place of which God had told him: and lifting up his eyes he saw the place from afar") as referring respectively to the Logos (which can be attained) and "the other God," "Him Who is in very essence God," but who cannot be reached; *Leg.* 3.207-208; *Conf.* 146-147.

Philo thus uses *theos* not so much as a name or designation for the only God but, depending on the context as a way to refer either to the unknowable reality of that God or to the knowable manifestations of that same God. For Philo, "God" may refer to the manifestation of "the One who is," or to the power of the "One who is," or to "the One who is." Although one and the same divinity is in question, "god" predicates something different in each case. Clearly, however, Philo assumes a unity between τὸ ὄν and the Logos, since both may be spoken of as "God."[41] To illustrate the point, if one were to ask Philo, "Is the Logos 'God'?" he might answer, "Yes and no," or, "It depends what you mean." If he was asked, "Is the Logos 'the One who is'?" he would answer, "No, but the manifestation of the One who is and, hence, God." The distinguishing predication of the one true god is not the word "god" itself.

To be sure, Philo's discussion here depends largely upon his Platonism. He is concerned to maintain a distinction between the One who is, who is "truly" God, and who is immaterial, from the multiple manifestations of the powers of God in the physical world. Hence, the meaning of "god" in a specific context depends more on Philo's presuppositions about the possibilities of the manifestation of deity in the material world. Issues such as the incorruptibility, immateriality, and unknowability of God may not dominate the thought of many other Jewish writers of the first century, but what Philo's thought at least demonstrates is the way in which the term *theos* can be used to denote both the one true God, the Most High, and the manifestations of that God in visible and other forms. To designate that "visible" manifestation of God, Philo employs the concept of the Logos. While John does not share the particular philosophical range of questions and speculation troubling Philo, nevertheless he does also use "god" to speak both of the one unseen God and of the Logos, the Word of God, who became incarnate and manifested or made visible God's glory (1:14).

There are some other passages in Jewish sources that use the word "god" of a human being. In *Jubilees* 40:7 when Pharaoh establishes Joseph as second in command over all Egypt, Joseph is hailed as "*El, El wa*

---

41. A number of scholars have thought that one could explain the NT's use of *theos* for Jesus following Philo's distinction between the articular and anarticular use of *theos*. Both Origen (*Comm Jc.* 2.1-2, 17-18) and Clement (*Strom.* 3.81.5) use the argument. See Prestige, *God in Patristic Thought*, pp. 139-46. For an examination of the validity of the exegetical arguments, see Harris, *Jesus as God*, pp. 29-71.

Abirer."[42] Granted, this narrative represents the ways in which pagans, not Jews, honored Joseph, and it reflects the practice during the Hellenistic period of honoring kings as "gods." This may be little more than flattery, possibly even to be censured by the reader, although there is no editorial correction of the people's accolade. Yet if the label fits, it fits because its suits Joseph in his function of ruling over Egypt.

Similarly, in 11QMelchizedek, several lines from Psalms 7 and 82, which in the Hebrew refer to *elohim* (אלוֹהִים), are quoted with reference to Melchizedek. The lines that are applied to "Melchizedek" stress his role as God's agent for judgment of the peoples:

"Elohim will stand up in the assem[bly of God], in the midst of the gods he judges." (Ps. 82:1)

"Above it return to the heights, God will judge the peoples." (Ps. 7:8-9)

"How long will you judge unjustly and show partiality to the wicked?" (Ps. 82:2; 11QMelch 2:10-11)[43]

It is of course also possible that Melchizedek was understood to be the angel Michael, as a number of interpreters propose, and hence identified as one of the *elohim*, the heavenly beings or angels. Even so, he exercises the specific function of judgment.

A few passages from Josephus can be adduced here as well. In *Antiquities* 8.34, Josephus refers to Solomon as one who possesses "godlike understanding" (θείαν διάνοιαν) in his ability to understand the hearts and intentions of the two mothers disputing over whose baby had died and whose had lived, and to render a prudent verdict. Josephus also speaks of the prophet Isaiah as "a man of God and marvelously possessed of the truth . . . never having spoken what was false." While the English "man of God" could easily refer to Isaiah's prophetic status, nevertheless the Greek words *homologoumenōs theios* (ὁμολογουμένως θεῖος) point rather to the fact that Isaiah's possession of truth renders him in some way like God, possessing the characteristics of God.

---

42. Note the ascription of the title "Mighty God" *(el g'bur)* to the coming son of David in Isa. 9:5.

43. Translations are from Florentino García Martínez, *The Dead Sea Scrolls Translated: The Qumran Texts in English*, 2nd ed. (Leiden: Brill; Grand Rapids: Eerdmans, 1996).

The application of terms such as θεός and אֱלֹהִים to human beings ought to be counterbalanced by the handful of stories in the Bible and Jewish tradition in which certain kings, who demand to be worshipped, are punished or humiliated for their arrogance. In their presumptuous claim to the title or designation "god" they arrogate unto themselves a status or certain functions that do not rightfully belong to them as human beings. In the discussion in the Midrash on Exodus 7:1 ("I have made thee as God to Pharaoh") there follows a long passage concerning those kings who endeavored to usurp for themselves the prerogatives and status of divinity, including the prince of Tyre (Ezek. 28:2); Nebuchadnezzar, king of Babylon (Isa. 14:13; cf. Jdt. 3:8; 6:2); Pharaoh (Ezek. 29:3), and Joash (2 Chron. 24:17). Others who make presumptuous claims to divinity include Antiochus Epiphanes (Dan. 11:36-39),[44] Caligula (Philo, *Legat.* 22, 74-80, 93-97; Josephus, *Ant.* 19.4), Nero (*Sib. Or.* 5:33-35, 137-154, 214-221), and Herod Agrippa (Josephus, *Ant.* 19.345, 347; Acts 12:22). These individuals are rebuked for accepting or demanding veneration of some sort (Joash, Nebuchadnezzar, Caligula), for usurping divine prerogatives (Pharaoh), or for presumptuous arrogance and failure to acknowledge the supremacy and power of God. Josephus notes that Caligula "deified himself and demanded from his subjects honors that were no longer such as may be rendered to a man," and that, upon visiting the Temple of Jupiter, "he had the audacity to address Jupiter as brother." By contrast, God *grants* to Moses and, apparently, to Melchizedek, the name of God, coupled with specific functions, most notably rule and judgment, that are typical prerogatives of God. Whereas it is impious to seize such prerogatives, they can be exercised by God's authorization. Philo, for example, acknowledges God's unique causative role and the impiety of those who claim to exercise it:

> It becomes God to plant and to build virtues in the soul, but that the mind shows itself to be without God (ἄθεος) and full of self-love, when it deems itself as on a par with God (ἴσος εἶναι θεῷ); and, whereas passivity is its true part, looks on itself as an agent. When God sows and plants noble qualities in the soul, the mind that says "I plant" is guilty of impiety. (*Leg.* 1.49)[45]

44. Antiochus minted coins with the title *theos*. See Hengel, *Judaism and Hellenism*, 1:285.

45. Arthur Darby Nock writes, "*isotheos* is not *theos*" ("Deification and Julian," in *Essays on Religion and the Ancient World*, ed. Zeph Stewart [Cambridge, Mass.: Harvard Uni-

The soul exhibits impiety by failing to acknowledge its proper role with respect to God.

The condemnation of persons claiming divine honors or status was not limited to Jewish and Christian sources. The famous message from the oracle at Delphi, "Know thyself," was not an ancient call to personal introspection but a summons to recognize one's place in the grand scheme of things, to know that one was a human being, and not god. Apollodorus (1.9.7) refers to the impious behavior of a certain Salmoneus who "was arrogant and wanted to make himself equal to Zeus, and because of his impiety he was punished; for he said that he was Zeus."[46] According to Philostratus's life of Apollonius of Tyana, Apollonius was brought to trial before the emperor Domitian at least in part because people had called him a god (*Vita Apoll.* 8.5). Apollonius's defense against this charge mentions the general applicability of the term "god" to good persons; he demands to know whether the sorts of deeds he performed were calculated to induce people to pray to him, whether he issued decrees for them to assemble and sacrifice in his honor, or whether he pursued the course of action of those seeking "divine honors." Caligula's claim to divinity was censured by Roman as well as Jewish writers. Cassius Dio comments (59.4.2, 26.5, 28.5) that Gaius eventually ordered temples and sacrifices in his honor, that he impersonated the gods, and that he called himself "Jupiter Latiaris" (cf. Suetonius, *Cal.* 22).[47] These texts may also show the typical Roman reticence to accord divinity to the living emperor or human figures, a reticence not shared so firmly in the East, where Hellenistic patterns of attributing divine status and honors to the king were more typical.

This leads to a further observation. As A. E. Harvey comments, "'God' and 'divine' express the exceptional nature of the person so described. . . . Calling [a philosopher] 'a god' was a way of describing his exceptional powers and character: it did not imply that divine honors should be paid to him." Again, in eastern portions of the Roman empire, there was less reservation in paying divine honors to persons such as the emperor, even

versity Press, 1972], 2:841). The offense is not blasphemy. Similarly, Apollonius is said to have refused divine honors upon his arrival to Sparta because they might arouse envy (Philostratus, *Vit. Apoll.* 4.31).

46. Cited in Robert M. Grant, *Gods and the One God* (Philadelphia: Westminster, 1986), p. 105.

47. Harvey, *Jesus and the Constraints of History*, p. 156.

during their lifetime. Harvey also distinguishes between calling a figure "god" by virtue of that individual's distinctive or exceptional powers and the worshipping of that figure, and this distinction certainly applies in the texts that we have discussed in which figures such as Moses, Joseph, or Melchizedek are designated or called "god." Calling a figure "god" does not compromise commitment to monotheism; worshipping that figure does. As Harvey further notes:

> In the idiom of the readers for whom they [*sc.*, Jewish apologists such as Philo and Josephus] were writing, to call Moses (in some sense) divine was to insist on the altogether exceptional nature of his gifts and to imply that these gifts were from God. But it was not for one moment to suggest that Moses should be (or ever had been) acclaimed or worshiped as a god, or that his existence qualified in any way the unique divinity of the Creator of the world.[48]

Saul Lieberman makes much the same point:

> The ancients were much less sensitive to the term god than our modern society. Mortals are styled "gods" during their lifetime. The Jews living in a polytheistic society were very well aware of it. The term "small god" would be shocking to us, but it was not so to the ancient mind. As long as no worship is involved the "small god" remains a mere title.[49]

In this argument, the crucial measure of "deity" is the practice of worship of a specific figure. Even in religious systems with multiple deities, it still behooves human beings to recognize their proper place and not to overstep their boundaries to demand veneration and honors properly belonging to the gods.[50]

---

48. Harvey, *Jesus and the Constraints of History*, p. 157. This is the argument developed at some length by Hurtado in *One God, One Lord*.

49. Appendix 1, "Metatron, The meaning of his name and his functions" in Ithamar Gruenwald, *Apocalyptic and Merkavah Mysticism* (Leiden: Brill, 1980), p. 237. "Small god" (or "little Yahweh") appears for Metatron.

50. Wayne A. Meeks, "The Divine Agent and His Counterfeit in Philo and the Fourth Gospel," in *Aspects of Religious Propaganda in Judaism and Early Christianity*, ed. Elisabeth Schüssler Fiorenza (Notre Dame: University of Notre Dame Press, 1976), p. 43: "There was no nobler reward for the man of virtue than to be granted by the gods a share of their status; there was no more repugnant an act of *hybris* than, being man, to make oneself a god."

Yet it is clear that the claim to possess or exercise not merely "exceptional" but uniquely *divine* functions and prerogatives is tolerated little more than the demand for worship. This is clearly evident from the consistent Targumic rewriting of Exodus 4:16 and 7:1, as well as from Philo's long discussion of how and why "god" aptly applies to Moses. Although one could be granted particular prerogatives by God, appointed "as God" for a particular purpose and mission, one could never claim the title or presume to exercise God's rule and sovereignty without direct divine appointment. While there were appropriate applications of the term *theos* to human beings, such as Moses, the term could not be applied at will to any and every individual, nor for reasons other than the carrying out of a specific divine commission or mission. The application of the term *theos* to human figures takes on a different shape, particularly in Judaism and Christianity, where *theos* not only designates a certain kind of being, and additionally a set of functions and prerogatives, but also a particular Being.[51] This highlights yet another difference between paganism and Judaism, for both Greek and Roman religions had multiple gods and could envision the deification of certain individuals, usually particularly after their deaths, when they could also appropriately be accorded divine honors. Hence, the world of divinity was conceived of as something like a spectrum, ranging from Zeus the "father of gods and mortals," to human beings who could join the divine pantheon. In Judaism, however, the situation is rather different, where a marked distinction exists between the one God, God Most High, and all created beings. To name one of these created beings "God" will therefore mean that this being or figure must be interpreted not with reference to a shared attribute of "divinity," but rather in reference and with relationship to the one figure properly so designated, the one true God.

Summary Observations

By way of summary, we may lift out from the previous discussion certain important points. We note that the OT clearly understands *el* and cognates to denote what is heavenly as distinct from what is human. Thus, for example, Ezekiel 28:2 reads "You are human and not God" (וְאַתָּה אָדָם וְלֹא־אֵל); a

51. Quell, "θεός," in *TDNT* 3:83.

contrast between *el* (God) and *ish* (man) can be found in Hosea 11:9.[52]
These connotations also adhere to their Greek equivalents in Jewish and
Christian texts. When "god" is used without any descriptive or qualifying
phrases, it belongs in a category of terms that designate "heavenly beings"
and may, by extension, be applied to human beings. Here the phrase is used
not so much of identifying a person with God, but rather of comparing that
person with God, or with some characteristic or feature of God. When used
by way of comparing a human figure to God, the term clearly does not denote a heavenly being worthy of worship but rather isolates an action or
characteristic as worthy of the highest accolades, because that action or characteristic is either particularly distinctive of or best seen in God. Similar
terms are lord and king, although certainly by the time of the writing of the
NT "Lord" came to be regarded as an appropriate substitute for the name of
God, and it frequently renders the Tetragrammaton in the LXX.[53]

There are certain adjectives and qualifying phrases that serve to distinguish Israel's God from any other bearer of the designation "god." For example, Moses may be called "god," but he is not called "Lord God Almighty," "the Most High," "God of gods," or "the God of Abraham, Isaac,
and Jacob." These descriptive phrases leave little room for maneuvering,
even less than the use of the divine name, Yahweh, which is sometimes assigned to God's chief angel, at least secondarily or derivatively.[54] These
phrases are important, moreover, because they speak of certain activities,
notably creation, sovereignty, and judgment, which belong to God alone
and can be said to be given to human beings only by virtue of God's authorization. Therefore it is really the actions by which one usurped divine
honors or divine prerogatives that merited human or divine censure.

---

52. In Exod. 15:3 and Isa. 42:13, God is called a "man of war" (*ish milchama*); not surprisingly, perhaps, the LXX alters the text to *syntribon polemous*, "the one who crushes wars"
— but does this change intend to avoid the impression that God is a man, or that God is one
who wages war? *Tg. Onqelos* reads "The Lord is the Lord of victory in battles"; *Tg. Pseudo-
Jonathan* gives "The Lord is a hero who wages our wars in every generation"; and *Tg. Neofiti*,
surprisingly, has the most literal translation with "The Lord is a man making wars."

53. The Targums sometimes replaced terms for God with the Tetragrammaton. This
practice leads us to question the assertion that "Judaism was very careful to avoid the divine
name." So Stauffer, "θεός," in *TDNT* 3:91. Yet this holds true with respect to practices of
reading, not writing, the divine name.

54. The application of "Yahweh the Lesser" to Metatron or Yahoel is found in *3 Enoch* 7;
12:5; 48. See Segal, *Two Powers*, p. 197. For a different construal of the significance of the
designation "Yahweh the Lesser" or "Little Yahweh," see Barker, *The Great Angel*.

Josephus, for example, speaks of Claudius's edict allowing Jews the rights that Gaius would have denied them, including the right to refrain from calling Gaius "god." However, it is also clear that the central issue was that of worship of the emperor (*Ant.* 19.284). Thus, for example, in Philo's *Embassy to Gaius,* Philo asserts that Gaius claimed to be a god and longed to be acknowledged as such. When Philo and his compatriots defend themselves by saying "We sacrificed on your behalf," Gaius retorted, in effect, "Yes, but not *to me.*" Presumably the Jews would not have been happy to call Gaius "God" either, but the real problem was the implication that a person designated as "god" would receive veneration that the Jews allotted to one God alone (*Legat.* 357).[55] Gaius had usurped a privilege unique to God.

Part of the open-endedness of the term "God" is due to the fact that it does not refer only to Israel's God, even though this may be its most typical use in the texts we are examining. Both the Hebrew and Aramaic forms of *el* and *elohim* and the Greek *theos* are used as terms meaning "divine" or "heavenly" beings, "gods," and as the appellative for Israel's God.[56] *Theos* continues to serve both as a predicate, close or equivalent in meaning to "divine," and as an appellative, "the only one properly called God." Because the potential for confusion exists, some sort of explanatory phrase must be appended to "god," as illustrated by Paul's statement: "For although there may be so-called gods in heaven or on earth — as indeed there are many gods and many lords — yet *for us* there is *one* God, *the Father, from whom are all things and for whom we exist*" (1 Cor. 8:6). Through expansive additions, Paul thus excludes any possible misunderstanding as to which "god" he intends. Other words that might be substituted for god, such as "savior," "king," or "lord," would require similar restrictions, but some alternatives — the Most High, the Almighty, Maker of heaven and earth, or even Lord God — would not.

Yet "god" may be used as predicate in a variety of ways. On the one hand, to say "Yahweh is God" might mean that YHWH is divine, not human; that YHWH has a particular sort of power and sovereignty; that YHWH demands a certain sort of response from people; or even that

---

55. The centrality of worship even for pagans is noted by Price in describing the establishment of the imperial cult: "When a city came to pass a decree it was not concerned to debate the status of *theos* but to establish a cult of the emperor" ("Gods and Emperors," p. 82).

56. In Greek religion, *theos* is used both of a god and of Zeus.

"YHWH is the *only* God," as in the exhortation 'Know that the LORD is God!" The predication remains at least somewhat open-ended. On the other hand, "Yahweh is our God" suffers less from the same ambiguity. Such a statement implies that the speakers, whoever they might be, honor or venerate the one named "Yahweh." Similarly, "YHWH is the God of gods" and "YHWH is the Most High God" eliminate ambiguity: Yahweh reigns supreme. Because *theos* may serve to predicate divinity of a figure, but also and more commonly refers to Israel's God, "Lord" rather than "God" becomes the primary means of identifying or characterizing Jesus in NT confessions of faith.

One should not rashly exaggerate the number of instances in which "god" is used of human beings or other figures in Jewish tradition, which acknowledged multiple "heavenly" beings, such as angels and spirits.[57] Nor should one ignore the conditions, including the existence of biblical precedent and the focus on the exercise of specific functions, that attend the application of the term "god" to such figures. Whether or not one ought to apply the label "divine" to such beings depends entirely on how one construes the meaning of that term. Yet however many "heavenly beings" there might be, and whether they ought to be called "divine," what ultimately discloses their identity is not whether they are called "god" but what sort of honors or veneration they merit, what functions they exercise, and, perhaps most importantly, how they came to exercise those functions. Thus, when human beings or angels overstep their limits, demanding worship or exercising their authority by virtue of claims to divinity or kinship with the divine, the charges leveled against them typically do not refute their false claims to metaphysical status of divinity but rather rebuke them for their failure to keep to their own place. Thus Akiba's interpretation of Daniel 7:9 as allotting one throne to God and one to David (i.e., the Messiah) merits the censure "How long will you treat the Shekhina as profane!" (*b. Sanh.* 38b; *b. Ḥag.* 14a).[58] The apparent assertion that others, be-

---

57. On this point, see the comments of Martin Hengel, "Christological Titles in Early Christianity," in his *Studies in Early Christology* (Edinburgh: T. & T. Clark, 1995), p. 367: "It is, therefore, clear that the Christianity of the first century — like contemporary Judaism — was reluctant to transfer the term 'God' directly to a heavenly mediator figure, although it did not rule it out completely."

58. Similarly, in later legends the angel Metatron is punished for sitting down in the presence of God and hence giving rise to the misconception that there are "two powers in heaven" (cf. *b. Ḥag.* 15a). For discussion see Segal, *Two Powers*, p. 48.

sides God, exercise the divine prerogative to rule evokes the charge of blasphemy.

In brief, then, a more specific and descriptive characterization of a figure is attained through the delineation of certain functions or activities than through the application of the word *theos*. Although such an approach is often denigrated as leaving us with a "functional" rather than "ontological" Christology, in a world where multiple "gods" are thought to exist these deities are both identified and shown to be superior to others because of the powers they exercise and the functions they carry out. For "God" does not connote a "divine essence" that can be shared by a number of beings, even though there may be a number of beings who are called "god." In this sense, *theos* functions slightly differently than does the English term "deity." Although we use "deity" to refer both to God ("the Deity") and to a property (as in "the deity of Christ"), "god" does not refer to a characteristic or property the possession of which renders one "divine." Rather, "God" in biblical texts and Jewish thought either refers to the one and only God or, when used of a human figure, relates that figure to God by the exercise of some divine prerogative that is further exercised by God's authority. The term also refers, *but only with qualification,* to pagan deities, as in the phrase in Paul, "many so-called gods." The Greek term *theios* can be translated "divine," but it is not used in John and little in the NT (Acts 17:29; 2 Pet. 1:3, 4), and there is no Hebrew or Aramaic equivalent for it.

In his study of many of these same issues, Richard Bauckham draws the conclusion that "the God of Israel had a unique identity."[59] Bauckham further explains the concept of "identity," and his discussion is worth quoting at some length:

> The value of the concept of divine identity appears partly if we contrast it with a concept of divine essence or nature. Identity concerns who God is; nature concerns what God is or what divinity is. . . . That God is eternal, for example — a claim essential to all Jewish thinking about God —

---

59. Richard Bauckham, *God Crucified: Monotheism and Christology in the New Testament* (Grand Rapids: Eerdmans, 1998), p. 7. Although Bauckham's work came to my attention only after my own study was substantially completed, many of our conclusions dovetail at crucial points. I find his use of the phrase "divine identity" felicitous to describe my own reading of the historical evidence and of the Gospel of John and, hence, have borrowed the term here.

is not so much a statement about what divine nature is, more an element in the unique divine identity, along with claims that God alone created all things and rules all things, that God is gracious and merciful and just, that God brought Israel out of Egypt and made Israel his own people and gave Israel his law at Sinai, and so on. If we wish to know in what Second Temple Judaism considered the uniqueness of the one God to consist, what distinguished God as unique from all other reality, including beings worshiped as gods by Gentiles, we must look not for a definition of divine nature, but for ways of characterizing the unique divine identity.[60]

This description captures more aptly the approach and concerns of the literature of Second Temple Judaism to identifying and characterizing God than does the tired juxtaposition of "ontological" and "functional" categories.

There are, however, implications for the delineation of Christology as well, which we may indicate briefly. First, we should expect to find that NT Christology will be a *functional Christology*.[61] This most emphatically does not mean that NT Christology is a "low" Christology; quite the opposite. A "functional" Christology is a "high Christology," particularly when the functions exercised are seen as unique divine prerogatives. It is precisely the exercise of unique divine prerogatives that, when predicated of Jesus in John, lead to the harshest charges against him: in claiming to bestow life and to judge — two unique prerogatives of God — Jesus "makes himself equal to God." John addresses the charge by asserting that the Son does indeed exercise the unique and life-giving prerogatives of the Father because the Father has granted him this power (5:25-27). Second, we can expect NT Christology to be a functional Christology because of the monotheistic framework in which it is formulated. As we have seen, *theos* may refer to the one true God, and most typically does so, but it may also be used of other individuals. Yet it refers to other figures, human or heavenly, only when they are understood to exercise some sort of office or function on God's behalf and when assigned that office or function by God. Third, because Judaism is monotheistic, there is no "divine essence" that God may share with another. Attributes of "divinity," such as eternal existence, the power to create, and omniscience, belong to God, not to "divinity." If "di-

60. Bauckham, *God Crucified*, pp. 8-9.
61. See here also Bauckham, *God Crucified*, pp. 6-8, 40-42.

vinity" or "divine status" is predicated of a figure, it will necessarily imply a relationship to the one God. Fourth, then, we can expect NT Christology, just because it articulates its convictions in a monotheistic framework, to be *relational* in the sense that the task of NT Christology is to articulate the "open or hidden relationship to God, and of God to him" because "every statement about Christ implicates God."[62]

The Use of ΘΕΟΣ in the Gospel of John: Initial Reflections

We turn, then, to the Gospel of John to suggest how these observations help to illumine the meaning of "god" in the Fourth Gospel, as well as to begin to sketch the shape of the following chapters of this work. As we have seen from the previous analysis, Jewish authors referred to their God with a variety of designations for deity and descriptive phrases. There is first an acknowledgment that God has a proper name, even if that name is not spoken or is written in encrypted fashion. Second, in the Jewish texts examined, there are various forms of *El, elim,* or *elohim,* often in combination with genitives or in apposition (God Most High; God Almighty, etc.). In many of these instances, the qualifying and explanatory phrases become quite elaborate, or very specific, in linking God to a specific individual (Abraham, Isaac), group (Israel), characteristic attribute (mercy, justice) or activity (salvation, vengeance). Third, there are a variety of designations and epithets (such as "Heaven," "the Holy One," "King," etc.) that use neither the name of God, nor the designation "god" (*elohim* or one of its variants), nor the frequent Septuagintal reading of YHWH, Lord. These circumlocutions for God use some distinguishing characteristic, activity, or attribute of God in order to speak of God, and thus might be called instances of synecdoche, the designation of the whole by means of one of its constituent parts. Hence, it can be rather illuminating in unpacking the character and identity of God for a particular author or in a certain document to discern why a certain characteristic — mercy, justice, holiness — has been chosen to speak of God.

---

62. Paul W. Meyer, "'The Father': The Presentation of God in the Fourth Gospel," in *Exploring the Gospel of John: In Honor of D. Moody Smith,* ed. R. Alan Culpepper and C. Clifton Black (Louisville: Westminster/John Knox, 1996), p. 259; Leander Keck, "Toward the Renewal of New Testament Christology," *NTS* 32 (1986): 363.

The Gospel of John, and indeed the NT as a whole, demonstrates a remarkable spareness of descriptive language about God when compared to Hellenistic Jewish texts.[63] While there are references to the "name of God," there is no explicit mention of what that name might be, and one does not find any explicit prohibition against speaking the name of God. In fact, "the name of God" seems to have become a complete phrase, with no external referent. That is to say, when the NT speaks of the name of God it often does not refer to the Tetragrammaton. Rather, it uses "name of God" as equivalent to "authority" or "power" of God. In the Gospel of John, Jesus asserts that he has come in his Father's name (5:43) and that he works in "his Father's name" (10:25). He has come on the authority of the Father; hence he petitions the Father to glorify his name (12:28), to bring honor to himself because of the Son's mission. These formulations become recast as Jesus speaks of the mission that will be carried on in his name.

The absolute "God" appears very often in the NT, but "God" also appears in genitive phrases, echoing OT modes of speech such as God of the ancestors (Acts 3:13; 5:30; 22:14), of Israel (Matt. 15:31; Luke 1:68 [cf. 1:16; Acts 13:17; 2 Cor. 6:16; Heb. 11:16]); of Abraham, Isaac, and Jacob (Acts 3:13; 7:32; Matt. 22:32; Mark 12:26; Luke 20:37), as well as "our God" (Mark 12:29; Luke 1:78; Acts 2:39; 2 Pet. 1:1; Rev. 4:11; 7:12; 19:5) and "my God" (Luke 1:47; Rom. 1:8; 2 Cor. 12:21; John 20:17, 28). One also finds typical OT expressions such as "Lord of Hosts" (Rom. 9:29; James 5:4); "the Almighty" (2 Cor. 6:18; and often in Revelation); and "the Most High" (Mark 5:7; Luke 1:32, 35, 76; 6:35; 8:28; Acts 7:48; 16:17; Heb. 7:1). There are other descriptions of God as well, colored by Hellenistic terminology, which speak of God's eternity, deity, incorruptibility, and invisibility.[64] John often uses *theos* on its own, but he also uses it a few times with adjectives and descriptions:

63. According to Stauffer, "Hellenistic Judaism" (by which he means texts such as the LXX, 4 Maccabees, Philo, and Josephus) adopted the style of religious philosophy, including terms such as "deity," providence, and "the divine," in order not to seem uncultured ("θεός," in *TDNT* 3:90). Yet other terms more typically found in the Bible appear as well.

64. For example, "invisible nature" and "eternal power and divinity" (Rom. 1:20); "glory of the incorruptible God" (Rom. 1:23); "who alone has immortality and dwells in unapproachable light" (1 Tim. 6:16); "divine power" and "divine nature" (2 Pet. 1:3, 4). For the Hellenistic flavor of such terminology, see the statistics tabulated by Ralph Marcus, "Divine Names and Attributes in Hellenistic Jewish Literature," *Proceedings of the American Academy for Jewish Research* 3 (1931-32): 43-120.

the only God (5:44)
God the Father (6:27; cf. 8:41, 42)
the only true God (17:3)
my Father and your Father, my God and your God (20:17)
my Lord and my God (20:28; with reference to the risen Jesus).[65]

The relative scarcity of descriptions and epithets for God in the NT is likely due to the confluence of several factors: First, and most important, the Septuagint regularly translates various Hebrew words for God, including *elohim, el,* and *eloah,* as *theos.* In addition, it sometimes renders YHWH, when pointed with the vowels of *elohim,* and various epithets such as "rock," and "holy one," as *theos.*[66] As C. H. Dodd points out, however, *elohim* and *theos* or *theoi* are not perfect equivalents, since *theos* could still denote a being superior to a human being, whereas eventually by virtue of long association *elohim* had come to stand uniquely for the one God of Israel.[67] The regular use of *theos* in the Septuagint to refer to the one God of Israel clearly influences the NT writers, although they can still on occasion speak, as Paul does, of "many gods" *(theoi)* without thereby violating their monotheistic commitments.

In addition to references to the "name of God," and the use of "God" with various qualifying and explanatory phrases, there are also circumlocutions and other epithets used to refer to God. A particularly distinctive epithet for God in the Gospel of John is "the Father," which is used for God in John more often than in any other Gospel. Although John has no instances of the (Pauline) phrase, "Father of our Lord Jesus Christ," it does frequently have "the Father who sent me." God is identified most characteristically in relationship to Jesus, rather than in relationship to any of the patriarchs, heroes of the faith, or the people of Israel. In that relationship, the term "Father" figures most prominently. In John, Jesus does not speak of "God who sent me," nor does he in such formulations refer to God by any other term, such as Lord, King, Almighty, or Most High, or speak of

---

65. God, of course, is most typically referred to as "the Father," or "the Father who sent me," but this designation for God will be taken up below. As is well known, Ignatius often refers to Christ as *theos,* but it is noteworthy how often he uses the possessive pronoun in such constructions. For example, "our God" *(Eph.* proem; 15:3; 18:2; *Rom.* proem; 3:3); "my God" *(Rom.* 6:3).

66. See Dodd, *Bible and the Greeks,* pp. 3-24.

67. Dodd, *Bible and the Greeks,* pp. 5-8.

God in phrases such as "the God of Abraham, Isaac, and Jacob" or "the God of Israel." Instead, terms for God, as well as the entire understanding of God, must now be delineated with respect to Jesus. The consistent repetition of the designation of God as "the Father who sent me" not only underscores the identity of Jesus in terms of his relationship to God but also the reverse — God is most characteristically identified and named in relationship to Jesus.[68] Furthermore, when Jesus and God are defined in mutual relationship, the terms used to designate their relationship are "Son" and "Father." While the term "Father" for God has a history of usage independent of the Gospel, the virtual limitation of "Father" to the relationship of God to Jesus as Son moves toward a reshaping of the content of the word "God." What it means to know God is to know God as the Father of the Son, and this inevitably implies a reconceptualization of the identity of God. Hence, the Father-Son language of the Gospel of John is a prime example of the point that NT Christology is formulated primarily in relational terms, and that it articulates the relationship of Jesus to God and God to Jesus.

Descriptions after the pattern "God of . . ." feature prominently in OT and Jewish texts.[69] For example, we have "the God of Abraham" or "the God of Israel" or the "God of mercies," phrases that serve to distinguish and characterize the "god" in question with respect either to individuals or certain characteristics of God. In the Gospel of John, the closest parallel is the phrase "the Father who sent me," thus identifying God in relationship to Jesus with two strokes: God is "the Father" of Jesus; and is known by his specific activity of sending the Son. The implication is clear. If "God of Abraham" reveals a specific deity, now the phrase "the Father who sent me" spells out how the one of whom Jesus speaks is to be identified and known. There is another interesting pattern in John, and that is the regular occurrence of genitive phrases that speak of some entity, reality, or figure in relationship to God: for example, son of God, lamb of God, gift of God, bread of God, holy one of God, work of God, kingdom of God, glory of God, and

68. See Meyer, "'The Father,'" pp. 255-73.
69. Stauffer ("θεός," in *TDNT* 3:112) points out that it is common and natural to combine a substantive with the genitive of *theos*; for example, *pistis tou theou* (Rom. 3:3). He notes, however, that Paul prefers many combinations that invert this construction in ways reminiscent of the OT. For example, "the God of peace" (Rom. 15:33; 16:20; 1 Thess. 5:23; Phil. 4:9; 1 Cor. 14:33); "God of hope" (Rom. 15:13); "God of comfort" (2 Cor. 1:3); and "God of love" (2 Cor. 13:11).

so on.[70] Most of the genitive phrases that relate some entity to God serve to characterize Jesus or something that Jesus mediates, brings, or gives. God is repeatedly and regularly identified primarily in terms of the activity and work of Jesus. The verbs "send" and "work," used in close relationship to the sending of Jesus and "working" through Jesus, are key identifying characteristics of the God of the Gospel of John. In this sense, then, while one may speak of the Christology of John as functional, it is also true that the *theo*logy of John is "functional" in the sense that the identity and character of God are explicated in terms of the works and words of Jesus.

Thus it behooves the reader not only to pay close attention to the narrative of the Gospel, but also to be reminded how much of the understanding of "deity" implied the exercise of certain prerogatives and entailed certain activities appropriate to God. These activities included particularly God's creation and sovereign rule of the world. Hence, even when the word "god" is used with reference to some figure other than the one Most High God, it is typically because of the powers and authority delegated to that individual. The argument of the Fourth Gospel is that the distinctive divine prerogatives of creation and sovereignty have been delegated to and are being exercised by Jesus, that the conferring of these prerogatives upon Jesus rests on the relationship of the Father and the Son, and that therefore the Son may be known as "God." John makes his argument for the identity of Jesus, and simultaneously for the identity of God, by attributing to Jesus alone powers that are not routinely granted to any other agent or mediator figure. By concentrating these functions uniquely in Jesus, John thus denies the exercise of these prerogatives to other mediator figures. By making Jesus not only the one who exercises these prerogatives, such as the power to give life and to judge, but who also *has them "in himself"* (5:25-26), John places Jesus in a different category from all other figures who might be thought worthy or capable of exercising similar prerogatives. Consequently, John also maintains the imperative of honoring the Son even as one honors the Father (5:23).

Yet the very application of "god" to figures or entities other than the Most High God raises the question of the unity of God, as well as the relationship of God to the other heavenly beings or powers. So, for example, in

---

70. R. Alan Culpepper (*Anatomy of the Fourth Gospel: A Study in Literary Design* [Philadelphia: Fortress, 1983], pp. 113-14) also calls attention to the frequent use of "God" in genitive phrases, but he draws a different conclusion from this fact.

Jewish sources of the first century, titles such as "God of gods" posit the supremacy of YHWH to other gods. Ancient Israelite and Jewish monotheism clearly did not preclude belief in other heavenly beings, such as angels and spirits, but there is no contradiction between a plethora of supernatural beings and the unity of God so long as these beings are understood to be dependent upon and answerable to God. It is not their mere existence, but rather the suggestion of their autonomy, that threatens monotheism.[71]

The problem of God's unity is addressed in the Gospel of John in several ways. The issue is taken up with respect to Jesus' exercise of God's prerogatives and distinctive functions. God is known primarily as the one who creates, saves, gives life, and judges. When Jesus' adversaries accuse him of "making himself equal to God" (5:18), they charge him with usurping the divine prerogatives of working on the Sabbath. Jesus not only admits to the offense but heightens it by claiming to exercise the distinctive divine functions of judgment and giving life, activities that God does on the Sabbath. In defense of his action, Jesus responds that "the Son can do nothing on his own" and repeatedly asserts that he does only what the Father tells him to do and shows him to do. In other words, he argues for his dependence on God. Because the Son depends upon the Father for all he does, he does not engage in an independent or separate work but carries out the work of the one God. Hence, arguments for the Son's dependence on the Father are ultimately arguments for the unity of the Son with the Father. This is demonstrated most graphically in the oft-cited statement, "I and the Father are one" (10:30), which, in context, caps an argument about Jesus' power to "hold" his sheep as an exercise of the Father's power to "hold" those same sheep. Because the Father is the one, true, living God, the argument for Jesus' unity *with* God is tantamount to an argument for the unity *of* God. Indeed, as C. K. Barrett argues, the unity of the Father and Son "is emphasized in every possible way."

> It is baldly announced in the opening words of the Gospel: "In the beginning was the Word, and the Word was with God, and the Word was God" (i.1). It is stated in *moral* terms ("The Son can do nothing of himself, but what he seeth the Father doing: for what things soever he doeth, these the Son also doeth in like manner" v. 19), and in terms of *worship* (". . . that all may honour the Son, even as they honour the Father. He

71. Cohen, *From the Maccabees to the Mishnah*, p. 84.

that honoureth not the Son honoureth not the Father which sent him"
v. 23). It is stated in *metaphysical* terms ("I am in the Father, and the Father in me" xiv. 10f.), and as *revelation* ("He that hath seen me hath seen
the Father" xiv. 9; "No man hath seen God at any time; the only begotten
Son, which is in the bosom of the Father, he hath declared him" i.18).[72]

As we saw above, the epithet "God" can sometimes be ambiguous inasmuch as it could be applied not only to multiple deities but also in some
cases — especially in pagan settings — to certain human beings, of whom,
consequently, certain traits can be assumed. For example, human beings
who have been divinized in pagan thought have been made immortal. In
Jewish thought, the gap between human and divine cannot be bridged easily, if at all. Still, there are certain functions that are proper to God but can
be carried by human beings with the explicit authorization or empower-
ment by God; one example would be judgment. Furthermore, there are
certain prerogatives that belong to God alone and that, if usurped by human beings, lead naturally to the charge of arrogance and blasphemy.
Hence, if there is any "bridge" between divine and human identity or function, the bridge must be built and authorized by God. John argues that
God *has given* to Jesus certain uniquely divine prerogatives, such as the
power to give life and to judge (5:26-27). Even the predication that Jesus is
the incarnation of the Word of God assumes that the Word comes from
God.[73]

In Jewish thought, the particular and exclusive functions and prerogatives of God are central to delimiting God's uniqueness. From the foregoing survey, a few key elements may be singled out as determinative for
identifying God. God is identified, first, as the Maker and Creator of all
that is. God is the life-giving God. Because God is the Creator of all, God is
also supreme over all other beings, whether heavenly or human. Epithets
such as "Almighty" and "Most High" indicate God's supremacy over all
other figures and underscore the extent of God's sovereignty. As Creator
and Sovereign, God therefore merits worship and honor.

72. C. K. Barrett, "The Old Testament in the Fourth Gospel," *JTS* 48 (1947): 161-62.
73. Philo illustrates that "God" can be used to speak both of the unknown deity and the
visible manifestations of God, such as are embodied in the Logos. Both the Logos and "the
one who is" are "God" not because they share some essence in common but because the
Logos actually is a manifestation of the one true God, the presence of that unseen God, the
way in which that God is known.

Each of these key identifying marks of God plays an important role in the Fourth Gospel as well. For John the supreme manifestation of God's sovereignty comes through God's power to create and to give life. The prologue opens with echoes of Genesis and the creation of the world, here understood to have been accomplished through the agency of the Word. The life-giving God continues to bestow life to the world, as is manifested specifically in the signs of Jesus, as well as in the gift of the life-giving Spirit. Through these means God gathers together a people, who are "born from above" into a new life in a new family who acknowledge God as "Father" and address the risen Christ as "My Lord and my God!" These people are further distinguished by their worship of God "in Spirit and in truth," for "such the Father seeks to worship him." Those divine actions such as salvation, creation, and judgment are carried out through the agency of Jesus; human actions, such as worship, are likewise carried out through the same agency. When, in the climactic confession of the Gospel, Thomas addresses the risen Jesus as "My Lord and my God!" this formulation stands as the summary and elaboration of the work and person of Jesus through the Gospel. The direct confession of the risen Lord as God stands alongside and interprets, but does not eclipse, the narrative that points to his dependence upon and authorization by the Father. Like the prologue, then, the entire Gospel points both to the one who is "with God" and who "is God." The narrative of the Gospel demonstrates how the Father who seeks true worshippers finds them in the people who join in Thomas's confession of Jesus as "My Lord and my God." We turn, then, to the Gospel of John to assess the relevance of the foregoing discussion to the understanding of "God" in the Gospel of John.

TWO

The Living Father

The most common designation of God in John is "Father." John uses "Father" about 120 times, more often than all the other Gospels combined. By comparison, "God" (θεός) appears in John 108 times. Yet more revealing than the frequency of use is the pattern of the references. The first references to God as Father are found in the prologue (1:14, 18), where God is specifically the Father of the only Son (μονογενής), Jesus. Subsequent references to God as Father occur primarily in the words of Jesus, where Jesus refers to God as his Father or as "the Father." A few references are found in editorial comments, in which God is specifically named as the Father of Jesus (e.g., 5:18, "his own Father"; 8:27). John thus exemplifies the pattern of the other Gospels in limiting the address of God as Father to Jesus. Over 85 times we have simply "the Father" in the words of Jesus. Jesus speaks of "my Father" about two dozen times, and he addresses God simply as "Father" nine times (once, "Holy Father"). Once he speaks to his disciples of God as "your Father" (20:17). There are but one or two exceptions. In John 8, "the Jews" ask Jesus where his Father is (8:19), and subsequently argue that they have God as Father (8:41), a claim that Jesus disputes (8:42).

Given the frequency of the term "Father" in the Gospel, one might naturally conclude that it has simply become a substitute for "God," functioning as do a variety of epithets for God, such as "the Blessed" or "the Most High" or "the Almighty," in other NT texts, as well as in the literature of Judaism. Yet this is not the case. For example, formulations that refer to the

Son as being "sent" belong primarily to the Gospel's "Father" terminology; likewise, Jesus is said to do not "the will of God" but the "will of the Father." Similarly, believers are called "children of God" or those who are "born of God," but never "children of the Father" or those "born of the Father." Thus there are distinct patterns of usage that illumine the meaning of "Father" in the Gospel and suggest why it has become the most important term, other than *theos* (θεός) itself, to refer to God. It is these patterns of usage, and the particular formulations and contexts in which "Father" appears, that give shape and content to God's fatherhood in the Gospel of John. As the statistics cited above suggest, what is particularly telling in the depiction of God as Father is the way in which God's actions as Father are focused on Jesus himself. It is Jesus who speaks of, and addresses, God as Father. Jesus speaks but rarely even to his own disciples of God as their Father, and then only after the resurrection. In short, according to the Gospel it is the prerogative of Jesus to address God as Father, and to speak of God in these terms, because no else has that distinctive and particular relationship with God.

The pattern of the references to God as Father in the Gospel of John is illumined by the OT and Jewish literature. Of the characteristic descriptions of the activity or attributes of a father, and particularly of God as a father, three figure most prominently and importantly in John: (1) the father as the origin or source of life and, hence, as the "ancestor" who grants an inheritance to his heirs; (2) the father as a figure of authority, who is worthy of obedience and honor; and (3) the father as one who loves and cares for his children. In every case these characteristics or actions of God show the peculiar relationship of Jesus the Son to God the Father. We turn, first, to an examination of a number of texts from the OT and from Jewish literature to show the ways in which the portrayal of God as Father in them is appropriated in the Gospel of John.

God As Father in the Old Testament

"Father" is used of God in the OT only about a dozen times, where it reflects the role of the father in ancient Israelite society.[1] There are, however,

1. That the conception of God as Father is drawn from Israelite culture is contested on theological grounds by Karl Barth, Thomas F. Torrance, and others; see Thomas F. Torrance, "The Christian Apprehension of God," in *Speaking the Christian God: The Holy Trinity and*

many more passages that imply, without overtly stating it, that God has the character or role of Father, particularly in relationship to Israel. For example, passages that speak of God's "begetting" of Israel, or that portray Israel as the firstborn or beloved son of God, can be taken at least implicitly as suggestive of God's fatherhood. Yet we will not survey every such passage. Rather, we will simply attempt to establish the common patterns found in various OT passages.

The first aspect of "fatherhood," noted above, envisions the human father as the ancestor of a clan or family, and thus the one who gives an inheritance to his children; this aspect of fatherhood characterizes God as Father as well. While some passages of the OT speak of God's "begetting" in connection with the creation of all peoples (cf. Isa. 45:9-13), in general the "fatherhood of God" refers neither to God as universal Creator nor to some attribute or quality of God, but specifically to God's purposes and blessings for Israel (Isa. 63:16; 64:8; Jer. 3:19; 31:9) God is the Father of Israel as its founder, the ancestor of the "clan" of the Israelite nation insofar as he called it into being (Jer. 31:9; Deut. 32:4-6; cf. Deut. 32:18).[2] The Deuteronomist, for example, speaks of God as "the Rock that begot you" (32:18).[3] While the specific term "Father" is not used, the imagery of "begetting" does fit with other instances of the Bible's use of "father" for God, specifically in applying God's act of "begetting" to God's acts of redemption. Hosea contains one of the most cited passages portraying God's paternal love, although it does not specifically name God as "Father":

> When Israel was a child, I loved him,
>   and out of Egypt I called my son. . . .

---

the Challenge of Feminism, ed. Alvin F. Kimel Jr. (Grand Rapids: Eerdmans; Leominster: Gracewing, 1992), p. 130. Francis Martin (*The Feminist Question: Feminist Theology in the Light of Christian Tradition* [Grand Rapids: Eerdmans, 1994], p. 271) argues that the notion of God as Father could not have been borrowed from the patriarchal imagery for God of surrounding cultures because in those cultures the "father God" was "brutish, incompetent, ineffective, and generally inert." I have addressed some of these issues more fully in *The Promise of the Father: Jesus and God in the New Testament* (Louisville: Westminster/John Knox, 2000).

2. Rex Mason, *Old Testament Pictures of God* Regent's Study Guides (Oxford: Regent's Park College; Macon: Smyth and Helwys, 1993), p. 52; Joachim Jeremias, *The Prayers of Jesus* (Philadelphia: Fortress, 1967) p. 13.

3. The text also speaks of the "God who gave you birth," imagery used of the mother's role, rather than the father's. Because it is set in parallelism to "the Rock that begot you," it also refers to the creation, through acts of deliverance, of the people of God.

it was I who taught Ephraim to walk,
  I took them up in my arms;
  but they did not know that I healed them. (Hos. 11:1, 3)

Similar is the description of God's instruction to Moses in the book of Exodus, in which God commands Moses to "let my son go," rather than the more familiar "let my people go."

You shall say to Pharaoh,
"Thus says the LORD, 'Israel is my firstborn son . . .
Let my son go that he may serve me.'" (Exod. 4:22-23)

These passages portray God as a deliverer of Israel, the "firstborn" or beloved son or child. Other passages make explicit the link between God as Father and God as Redeemer.

Look down from heaven and see,
  from your holy and glorious habitation.
Where are your zeal and your might?
  The yearning of your heart and your compassion?
  They are withheld from me.
For you are our father,
  though Abraham does not know us
  and Israel does not acknowledge us;
you, O LORD, are our father;
  our Redeemer from of old is your name. (Isa. 63:15-16)

Similar, too, is Jeremiah's highly charged description of the "return" of the exiles, both to their land and to their God:

With weeping they shall come,
  and with consolations I will lead them back,
I will let them walk by brooks of water,
  in a straight path in which they shall not stumble;
for I have become a father to Israel,
  and Ephraim is my firstborn. (Jer. 31:9)

It is the relocating of the terminology of "begetting" (and "birth)" to the sphere of redemption that renders impossible any crudely imagined understanding of God's act of "begetting." Furthermore, the imagery serves to place the emphasis on God's initiative in the calling of Israel.[4] Even as a child plays no role in his or her own conception, or birth, neither does Israel figure in its own calling, a point that is further underscored by setting the image of God as Father in parallelism with the image of God as a potter:

> Yet, O LORD, you are our Father;
> > we are the clay, and you are our potter;
> > we are all the work of your hand
> Do not be exceedingly angry, O LORD,
> > and do not remember iniquity forever.
> Now consider, we are all your people. (Isa. 64:8-9)

The act of calling a people is ever the prerogative of God. However, as this passage also illustrates, the act of calling is pictured as an act of love and grace, and not as the tyrannical or arbitrary decision of an authoritarian despot. Indeed, it becomes the basis for the present appeal to God to forgive the sins of the people.

Just as a human father provides an inheritance to his firstborn son (Zech. 12:10; Mic. 6:7; Gen. 49:3; Exod. 13:15), so God provides Israel, God's "firstborn," with an inheritance (Jer. 3:19; 31:9; Isa. 61:7-10; 63:16). The inheritance is passed down from father to son — to *one son* — as an exclusive birthright. Some of the most poignant and memorable narratives of the OT pivot around the birth of an heir and the rights of inheritance that those heirs possess. One such account is the central narrative of God's promise of an heir to Abraham (Gen. 15 1-6), the births of Ishmael (Genesis 16) and Isaac (Genesis 21), and the conflict between their mothers, expressed particularly in Sarah's hostility to Ishmael's right to inherit (Gen. 21:10). Isaac's own sons, Jacob and Esau, are caught in the same conflicts. Jacob first dupes Esau of his birthright (Gen. 25:29-34) and then cheats his older brother of his rightful paternal blessing (Genesis 27). Similarly, Israel is portrayed as the firstborn son who has the rights of inheritance.[5]

Because of his love, God protects and provides for those who are his children. God is the "father of orphans and protector of widows" (Ps. 68:5; 27:10), who "gathers me up if father and mother forsake me" (Ps. 27:10).

4. Mason, *Old Testament Pictures of God*, p. 56.
5. In his book *The Death and Resurrection of the Beloved Son: The Transformation of Child Sacrifice in Judaism and Christianity* (New Haven: Yale University Press, 1993), Jon Levenson shows how frequently in the OT the younger son usurps the place of the older son in their father's affection and in receiving the blessing or inheritance due the older son.

This God has compassion "as a father has compassion for his children" (Ps. 103:13). This aspect of God's fatherhood, coupled with the imagery of God's initial "begetting" of Israel, also provides the basis for hope for the future.[6] As Father, God has not only "begotten" Israel but has compassion upon his sometimes wayward firstborn. Both in Jeremiah and in the last part of Isaiah, the exiles call upon God as Father in distress and hope for deliverance and return to the land (Jer. 31:9; Isa. 63:16). Interestingly, at Isaiah 63:16 and 64:8, the *Targum of Isaiah* translates "father" as "he whose mercies upon us are more than a father's upon sons," thus not only avoiding the anthropomorphic implication of God actually "begetting" offspring, but also highlighting one of the characteristic activities of God captured in the epithet "Father." As a Father to Israel, God is merciful, compassionate, abounding in steadfast love.

Although love, compassion, and pity are attributed to the ideal father, the final effect is not a sentimentalized portrait of that father. Father connotes a social relationship in which "father" and "children" are not equals; this is not a democratic relationship of peers. Fathers require obedience and honor. The command to "honor one's father and mother" (Exod. 20:12) has a parallel in the command to honor God, as the following passage from Malachi aptly shows: "A son honors his father, and servants their master. If then I am a father, where is the honor due me? And if I am a master, where is the respect due me? says the LORD of hosts" (Mal. 1:6).

The passage from Malachi further shows that fathers are also viewed as those who instruct and discipline the wayward. No matter how gracious and kind, the father remains a figure of authority and power to whom obedience and faithfulness are owed. In a number of passages where God is described as the Father of Israel the image underscores both God's call to obedience and, often, Israel's lack of it (Hos. 11:1, 3, 4; Jer. 31:9, 18, 20; cf. Prov. 3:11-12).[7] So Jeremiah upbraids the people for casually addressing God as "Father" and assuming him to be "the friend of my youth," while having "done all the evil that you could" (3:4-5). In Deuteronomy, we read this reproof:

Do you thus repay the LORD,
O foolish and senseless people?

6. Mason, *Old Testament Pictures of God*, pp. 65-66.
7. Mason, *Old Testament Pictures of God*, p. 68. Jeremias (*Prayers of Jesus*, pp. 11-12) states that the two aspects of God's fatherhood stressed in the OT are God's tenderness and "absolute authority."

Is not he your father, who created you,
who made you and established you? (Deut. 32:6)

Although Hosea does not explicitly speak of God as Father, nevertheless the prophet does speak of Israel as God's son who, in spite of all God's compassion, love, and mercy, refused to obey God (Hos. 11:1-8).

Even as Israel owes its Father obedience, they are in turn obligated to deal faithfully with others who name the same Father. In Malachi 2:10, the queries, "Have we not all one father? Has not one God created us?" serve as the basis for an appeal to faithfulness among members of the covenant community: "Why then are we faithless to one another, profaning the covenant of our ancestors?" Thus while "father" language assumes the authority of the father, the primary realm in which this is to be construed is not that of the relationship of the individual to God, nor is the relationship between Father and children to be understood primarily hierarchically. God's fatherhood relates primarily to the corporate entity of Israel, and within that framework implies the obligation of the children to each other.

One final aspect of God's fatherhood in the OT deserves mention. The covenant of God with Israel is sometimes focused in the promises to the king, with the relationship between God and the king depicted on analogy with the relationship of father and son. So, for example, God's promise to David, delivered through Nathan the prophet, is that God will establish the kingdom of David's son: "I will be a father to him, and he shall be a son to me. When he commits iniquity, I will punish him with a rod such as mortals use, with blows inflicted by human beings" (2 Sam. 7:12-14). Perhaps the most succinct expression of this father-son relationship between God and the king is found in Psalm 2:

"I have set my king on Zion, my holy hill."
I will tell of the decree of the LORD:
He said to me, "You are my son;
today I have begotten you.
Ask of me, and I will make the nations your heritage,
and the ends of the earth your possession." (Ps. 2:6-8)

God is not here explicitly referred to as Father, but he does address the king as "my son" and refer to his "begetting" the king, as well as to his willingness to give him all the nations as his inheritance. This application to the king shifts the focus from God as the Father of all Israel to God as the Father of one individual. However, insofar as the king also serves as the head and representative of a people, the corporate element of God's fatherhood is not necessarily eliminated. Such texts are, however, something of an anomaly when set against the rest of the OT passages.

In sum, in the OT the designation of God as "Father" pertains primarily to the relationship between God and Israel. Obviously individuals are implicated in these commands, but the injunctions focus on the relationship of the people to God and on their obligations to each other within the community. The one notable exception to the idea that God is the Father of the people, but not of individuals, is the relationship of God and the king, but even there the king functions as a representative of the people. As we turn to the literature of Judaism, we will find, not unexpectedly, that it is these biblical themes that are adopted and sometimes modified in portraying God as Father.

God As Father in Second Temple Judaism

In the literature of Second Temple Judaism there are texts that both characterize and invoke God as Father.[8] This simple fact is important to note, given the apparently common assumption that the NT view of God as Father was somehow novel, presenting God in a way hitherto unimagined. In the abbreviated survey of some of the literature of Second Temple Judaism offered below, we will see that in a variety of texts God was referred to or addressed as Father, and that such usage tended to be grounded in the special election of Israel by God.[9] Moreover, the notes of authority and mercy continue to be sounded as well. Since he is Father, God's authority is to be acknowledged in obedience; God's mercy may be depended upon in times

8. Texts that speak of God as the Father of an individual or portray an individual addressing God as Father include Wis. 2:16; 14:3; Sir. 23:1, 4; 51:10; 3 Macc. 6:3, 8; *Jub.* 19:29; 4Q460 5 i 5; 4Q382 55 ii 1-9; 4Q379 6 i 1-7; *Jos. Asen.* 12:8-15. Texts that speak of God as the Father of the nation include 1 Chron. 29:10 (LXX); Tob. 13:4; Wis. 11:10; 1QH 17:35; *Ant.* 2.152; 3 Macc. 2:21; 5:7; 7:6; *Jub.* 1:25, 28; *Apocr. Ezek.* frag. 2.

9. Dieter Zeller, "God as Father in the Proclamation and in the Prayer of Jesus," in *Standing Before God: Studies on Prayer in Scriptures and in Tradition with Essays in Honor of John M. Oesterreicher*, ed. Asher Finkel and Lawrence Frizzell (New York: KTAV, 1981), p. 119.

of distress or need. These texts thus show themselves beholden to the picture of God as Father in the OT. There are, however, some variations and developments, and we shall note these in due course.

The book of Tobit contains this description of God as Father:

> "Blessed be God who lives forever,
>   because his kingdom lasts throughout all ages.
> For he afflicts, and he shows mercy. . . .
> Acknowledge him before the nations, O children of Israel;
>   for he has scattered you among them.
>   He has shown you his greatness even there.
> Exalt him in the presence of every living being,
>   because he is our Lord and he is our God;
>   he is our Father and he is our God forever.
> He will afflict you for your iniquities,
>   but he will again show mercy on all of you." (Tob. 13:1-5)

This passage places "Lord" and "Father" in parallelism, underscoring the authority of the Father. Other functions or actions traditionally associated with God as the Father of Israel are here as well: God disciplines, but God also shows mercy. We may also refer to 3 Maccabees in this category, for there, when the Jews were prepared to be trampled by elephants, they called upon the "the Almighty Lord and Ruler of all power, their merciful God and Father" (5:7). Because God is "Almighty" and "Ruler of all power," he is able to deliver; because he is Father, his mercy may be sought. In this same document, God is spoken of as the one who "oversees all things, the first Father of all, holy among the holy ones" (3 Macc. 2:21; cf. 6:8, 28; 7:6). God is "first Father," a phrase that implies the role of generation, source, or origin; and he "oversees all," a phrase that implies his sovereignty. While this passage seems to speak of God as "Father of *all*," the explanatory phrase that follows, "holy among the holy ones" limits the extent of God's "fatherhood" to the righteous.

Jubilees also speaks of God as a Father to Israel. God's fatherhood is primarily manifested in God's authority to command and the Israelites' willingness to obey, a state of affairs that will be realized only when God creates a new spirit for the Israelites: "And they will do my commandments. And I shall be a father to them, and they will be sons to me. And they will all be called 'sons of the living God.' . . . I am their father in up-

65

rightness and righteousness. And I shall love them" (*Jub.* 1:23-25).[10] Later in the same book, Abraham offers this prayer for his son Jacob: "May the Lord God be for you and for the people a father always, and you be a first-born son" (19:29).

Until recently, the sole text quoted from Qumran as providing evidence that God was thought of or addressed as "Father" in that community was 1QH 17:35-36, "You are Father to all the sons of your truth," a text that again manifests the corporate understanding of God's fatherhood. In more recently published scrolls, however, there are additional references to God as Father, and these references include direct, personal address to God in prayer (Heb. אבי).[11] In 4Q372 1:16-17, we read Joseph's prayer: "My father and my God, do not abandon me in the hands of gentiles, do me justice, so that the poor and afflicted do not die." The author of this prayer calls upon God's care, faithfulness, and justice for preservation from "the gentiles." The speaker has a particular sense of God's goodness to the elect, here construed as the community of the faithful within Israel.

Another document that contains several references to God as "Father" is the *Testament of Job* (first century B.C. or A.D.), in which the references are to be found above all in prayers (33:3, 9; 40:2-3; possibly 47:11; 50:3).[12] Similarly, in the book of Sirach, a document from the second century B.C., we find personal and individual invocations to God as Father in prayers for assistance and mercy (Sir. 23:1, 4).[13] In these prayers, the individual petitioner addresses God as "Lord, Father and Ruler of my life" and "Lord, Father and God of my life" and so lodges all three designations for God in the personal sphere. God is conceived of as Lord, Father, and God of "my life." The use of "Father" for God, particularly in Sirach, stands alongside the frequent affirmation of God as "Maker" of the individual (47:8; see

10. In *Pss. Sol.* 17:26-32, Messiah brings together for God a holy people who are all "children of God."

11. These texts thus would require the revision of Jeremias's argument that there are no extant Palestinian materials that show an individual addressing God as Father. Although these texts do not use *abba*, they do show an individual directly addressing God as "my Father."

12. Bruce Chilton notes that the locution appears to be conventional ("God as 'Father' in the Targumim, in Non-Canonical Literatures of Early Judaism and Primitive Christianity, and in Matthew," *Judaic Approaches to the Gospels*, International Studies in Formative Christianity and Judaism 2 [Atlanta: Scholars Press, 1994], pp. 57-60).

13. As R. P. Spittler notes, "'Father' is used of God . . . as the Father of individuals at least since Ecclus 23:4 (cf. 23:1)" ("Testament of Job," *OTP* 1:855, n. 33g).

also 10:12; 32:13; 33:13). Although God is thus identified as the Maker of
the individual, Sirach's vision clearly encompasses God's creation of the
world, as well as his providential superintendence of its workings. God is
the Creator (15:14; 17:1; 18:1; 24:8; and passim), who filled the earth with
good things, including life and health (16:30; 34:20; 39:25); there is no
other God (36:5) than the Lord who is God of the ages (36:22), who lives
forever (18:1).

What we do not have in Sirach is a corresponding universalizing sense
of God as "Father." Although terms such as Lord, God, and Maker apply to
God in both the universal and the individual sense, "Father" appears to be
used only in relationship to individuals. However, that statement must be
qualified in light of the command, found elsewhere in Sirach, "Be a father
to orphans, and be like a husband to their mother; you shall then be like a
son of the Most High, and he will love you more than does your mother"
(Sir. 4:10). These texts conceive of God as the Father of Israel, or, perhaps
more specifically, as the Father of all righteous Israelites.[14] In this regard,
the text from Wisdom of Solomon 2:13-20 may be noted, where the un-
righteous person "boasts that God is his father" (2:16), whereas the truly
righteous child of God will be delivered by God.

In Josephus and Philo we find another tendency. Josephus designates
God as "Father" in order to portray him as the source or creator of all living things. Although Josephus does refer to God as the "Father of Israel"
(*Ant.* 5.93, "Lord and Father of the Hebrew race"), he more typically has in
view the universal application of the title, as for example in referring to
God as "Father and source of the universe, as creator of things human and
divine" (*Ant.* 7.380). God is "the Father of all" (*Ant.* 1.230; 2.152), the "universal Father who beholds all things" (*Ant.* 1.20). In such epithets,
Josephus echoes the Homeric characterization of Zeus as "Father of gods
and human beings" (*Il.* 15.47), rather than the more typical OT designation of God as the Father of Israel or the Father of the righteous.[15]

The use of "Father" to designate God's role as the "source of the universe" and creator of all things is found also in Philo. God is the sole
uncreated — hence eternal — being, and thus he necessarily is the source

14. Henry J. Wicks, *The Doctrine of God in the Jewish Apocryphal and Apocalyptic Literature* (New York: KTAV, 1971), p. 344.

15. In the *Sibylline Oracles,* God is several times referred to as one who begets; hence,
"the great Begetter" (3:295); "the one who has begotten all" (3:550); "the immortal begetter"
(3:604).

of the life of the world (*Her.* 206). God is Creator and Maker of all (*Spec.* 1.30; *Somn.* 1.76; *Mut.* 29; *Decal.* 61); the "first cause" (*Somn.* 1.67);[16] as well as Father;[17] and Parent (*Spec.* 2.198). Because God created all that is, God is therefore the Father of all human beings: "Created things, in so far as they are created, are brothers, since they have all one Father, the Maker of the universe" (*Decal.* 64–65). God's fatherhood therefore pertains to the creation of the world, rather than to the salvation of specific persons, whether that be construed corporately, as the people of Israel, or individually, in terms of specific righteous individuals.[18]

There are two distinct ways of construing the fatherhood of God in these texts of Second Temple Judaism. On the one hand, Josephus and Philo link together the ideas of God as Creator and as Father, thus allowing and assuming the universal scope of God's fatherhood. God is Father of all because God is Creator of all.[19] On the other hand, a second group of texts tend to speak of God as "Father" only in relationship to the faithful. Yet whether God is understood to be Father of all, or the Father of the faithful, the conviction that God is the origin and source of existence provides the rationale. Where God is appealed to as the Father of all the living, it is because God is the origin of their existence, the source of their life. Where God is appealed to as the Father of Israel, it is because God has called them into being, created them, and established them as a people. By extension, this understanding applies when God is taken to be the Father of the righ-

---

16. See *Decal.* 52: "The transcendent source of all that exists is God."

17. The Father: *Spec.* 2.198; *Opif.* 74, 75; *Mut.* 29; "Father of all things, for he begat them," *Cher.* 49; "Father and Maker," *Opif.* 77; "Father and Maker of all," *Decal.* 51.

18. In rabbinic literature, God is the Father both of the nation and of righteous individuals. God loves and educates, cares for, and protects them. There is an emphasis on God's mercy. In a noteworthy parallel to Luke 6:36, the *Tg. Ps.-J.* on Lev. 22:28 reads, "My people, children of Israel, as our Father is merciful in heaven, so you shall be merciful on earth." Israelites call to their Father in times of peril for assistance, for rain, or for forgiveness. There is also an emphasis on obedience to the will of the Father in heaven (*Tg. Onq.* Deut. 32:6; *Tg. Ps.-J.* Deut. 32:6; *Song Rab.* 2:16 §1; *m. 'Abot* 3:14; *Num. Rab.* 17 (on Num. 15:2); *Mek. Exod.* 14:19; *Exod. Rab.* 46.4-5 (on Exod. 34:1); *m. Soṭah* 9:15; *Tg. Ps.-J.* Exod. 1:19). For discussions of these and other passages, see Zeller, "God as Father," and Mary Rose D'Angelo, "*Abba* and 'Father': Imperial Theology and the Jesus Traditions," *JBL* 111 (1992): 611-30.

19. Perhaps another text that belongs in this camp is 3 Macc. 2:21, which speaks of God as "the first Father of all," but also immediately after as "holy among the holy ones." In the NT, several texts reflect the view that as "Father" God is the source of all that is (1 Cor. 8:6; Eph. 2:18; 3:14-19; 4:6; 5:20; 6:23).

teous within Israel. Whichever view is adopted, however, all authors agree
that because God is Father, he is owed obedience and honor. Indeed, for
Philo and Josephus, God's fatherhood becomes the ground to call all people to obedience and worship. Several other themes run throughout many
of these texts. Not only is God as Father understood to be the source of life,
but God is also understood to be the one who bestows an inheritance upon
those who are his children. In the collective "our Father," as well as in the
sectarian appropriation of "fatherhood," the idea of a peculiar and exclusive relationship between a father and his heir may also be applied to the
community. As Father, God is understood to exercise mercy and discipline
toward his children, whom he also cares for and delivers. Typically, then,
God is addressed as Father in petitions when people are in peril or need.
With this background in mind, we turn to examine the use of Father in the
Gospel of John.

God As Father in the Gospel of John

The Father seeks true worshippers (4:23); works (5:17, 19-20); loves the
Son (5:20; 10:17; 15:9; 17:23, 26); shows the Son what he is doing (5:20);
raises the dead and gives life (5:21); gives authority to the Son to have life
(5:26) and execute judgment (5:27); gives his works to the Son (5:36); sent
the Son (5:37, 38; 6:29, 39, 57; 8:16, 18, 26; 11:42); testifies to Jesus (5:37;
8:18); set his seal on the Son of man (6:27); gives true bread from heaven
(6:32); gives "all" to the Son (6:37; 13:3; 17:2, 7); "draws" people to him
and teaches them (6:44-45, 65); judges (8:16); instructs Jesus (8:28); is
with Jesus (8:29); seeks Jesus' glory (8:50, 54); knows the Son (10:15); con-
secrated the Son (10:36); hears the Son (11:41); honors those who serve Jesus (12:26); glorifies his name (12:28); will come and "make his home"
with believers (14:23); will send the Holy Spirit (14:26); prunes the vine
(15:2); loves the disciples (16:27; 17:23); glorifies Jesus (17:1, 24); "keeps"
what has been given to the Son (17:11, 15); and sanctifies believers in the
truth (17:17). From this list, two things are of particular note: (1) The actions of God as Father are distinctly and peculiarly concentrated toward
and through Jesus the Son. What the Father gives and does, the Father
gives and does through the Son. (2) God's activity with relationship to the
Son is all-encompassing and comes to expression in statements regarding
God's life-giving powers and activity in past, present, and future.

When these Johannine statements are set against the context of the foregoing survey of God as Father in the OT and Jewish literature, we find that Jesus is the Son who receives life from the Father and in turn gives it to others (5:25-26); who receives the Father's inheritance (8:31-38); who alone manifests the obedience to which God calls his children (8:39-50); and who receives the Father's love. Indeed, the mutual love of the Father and the Son lies at the heart of their relationship (3:35; 5:20; 10:17). While the Gospel does speak of God's love for the world (3:16), it does so only once, just as only once does Jesus speak to his disciples of the Father's love for *them* (16:27). Similarly, the vocabulary for "children" remains distinct: Jesus is always called "Son" (*huios;* υἱός), whereas believers are always designated "children" (*tekna;* τέκνα).[20] While there are many "children" of God, there is only *one* Son. That there is no other Son obviously has implications for understanding what it means to designate God as Father. This distinction between the nature of Jesus' filial relationship to God and that of believers is further underscored by Jesus' single reference to God as "your Father" when speaking to the disciples, as well as by the fact that this reference occurs only after the resurrection (20:17).[21] Again, those who have faith are said to be *born of* God, and hence are properly the children of God, but Jesus is the one who *comes from* God, the Son of God. Thus there are two ways of construing relationship to God as Father, embodied in and through two different terms, "children" and "Son." Strikingly, the one who is uniquely Son is never said to be "born" of God. Rather, the Son comes from God and is related to God in a direct manner.

The conviction that God is uniquely and distinctly the Father of Jesus undergirds the predications in the Gospel that link Father and Son together. Their "kinship" as Father and Son becomes the basis for a number of claims made for Jesus, including his authority to judge, to give life, to mediate knowledge of the Father and to reveal him, to do the works and will of the Father, and therefore to receive honor, as even the Father does. The assertions that are made regarding the Father and Son depend more on the kinship that exists between parent and child, father and son, than

20. This distinction is maintained in the Gospel and in 1 John. It is not found, however, in Paul or the other literature of the NT.

21. See also Paul W. Meyer, "'The Father': The Presentation of God in the Fourth Gospel," in *Exploring the Gospel of John: In Honor of D. Moody Smith*, ed. R. Alan Culpepper and C. Clifton Black (Louisville: Westminster/John Knox, 1996), p. 260.

on any specific attribute of a father. That is, in John it is not a particular characteristic of God that shapes understanding of God as Father, but rather the fundamental reality that a father's relationship to his children consists first in terms simply of giving them life. What it means to be a father is to be the origin or source of the life of one's children. For John, this pertains particularly to the way in which the Father has given life to the Son, and through the Son has mediated life to others, who become "children of God" (1:12; 11:52; see 1 John 3:1-2). It is probably not accidental that there is no text in either the Gospel or epistles of John that speaks of believers as "children of the Father" or of being born "from the Father." There are texts that come close. 1 John 3:1 reads, "See what love the Father has given us, that we should be called 'children of God.'" Yet the Johannine tradition enshrines a genuine distinction not only in the terminology for Jesus as *Son* of God, or the Son of the Father, and believers as *children* of God, but also in the terminology used of God in each instance. The obverse of the uniqueness of Jesus' filial relationship to God is the uniqueness of God's paternal relationship to Jesus. After all, Jesus speaks not of "our Father" but of "my Father" and "the Father who sent me."

Indeed, John so emphasizes the unique character of the relationship between the Son and the Father that it is not unreasonable to ask whether it is even possible to talk about God as Father apart from talking about Jesus as the Son. On this point, Paul Meyer writes, "The unity of Father and Son, a prominent motif in the evangelist's Christology, seems to preclude any talk about God apart from the Son, or at least to render highly problematic any venture to devote a separate chapter on Johannine theology to 'the Father.'"[22] Although the very emphasis on the unity and inseparability of Father and Son offers a real challenge to the discrete delineation of the Father apart from the Son, it does so only if the question is framed somewhat as follows: "What does the Fourth Gospel say about the Father apart from what it says about the Son?" To phrase the question that way, however, already suggests that the question is misconstrued, for it is only in relation to the Son that God is "Father." It is not merely the designation of God as "Father" but the corollary reference to Jesus as "Son" that delineates the meaning of each.[23]

22. Meyer, "'The Father,'" p. 255.
23. As Meyer makes clear in his very fine essay, "'The Father.'"

The relationship of father and son implies at one and the same time an indissoluble unity and a clear separateness: for while a son is not his father, no other human relationship connects people in quite the same way as does the relationship of a parent to a child, for this is a relationship in which the very being of the one comes from the other, and in which neither has their identity as "father" or "son," "parent" or "child," without the other. Although the language of "intimacy" is often used to speak of the relationship between Jesus and God, this characterization of the relationship between parents and children owes more to Romanticism than to biblical concepts of paternity.[24]

Put differently, the idea of "kinship" or "relationship," rather than emotional intimacy, grounds the understanding of the father's relationship to a son. When Jesus calls God "Father," he points first to the Father as the source or origin of life, and to the relationship established through the life-giving activity of the Father. Yet once again these terms apply differently to those "born of God," and to Jesus as the only Son of God. Since he is the Son, Jesus' very life and being are to be found within the Father. He has life because "the living Father" (6:57) gives it to him; in fact, he has "life in himself" just as the "Father has life in himself" (5:26), a remarkable statement that simultaneously affirms that the Son derives his life from the Father and yet has life in a distinct way, as the Father has it. We shall return to discuss these statements below, for they are essential to understanding John's delineation of God as Father and Jesus as Son. As Father, God is the source of life, the one who lives and gives life to others. That God is the sole source of life, the creator of all that is, is a foundational tenet of Jewish monotheism. Thus before we continue our discussion of God as Father in John, we turn briefly to an examination of the OT understanding of "the living God" and the implications of the phrase, and then also to the use of the phrase in several Jewish texts, which show the link between God as "living" and God as the source or creator of all life. In coining the phrase "the living Father" John actually joins two very similar ideas into one: as the living one, the Father is the source of the life of his Son.

---

24. This point is made by A. E. Harvey, *Jesus and the Constraints of History* (Philadelphia: Westminster, 1982), p. 158.

The Living God

The phrase "the living God" is found in the OT in that form (Deut. 5:26; Jer. 10:10), as well as in variations, such as "the everlasting God" (Isa. 40:28) and "the living God and the everlasting King" (Jer. 10:10).[25] God is the Everlasting God (Gen. 21:33; Isa. 40:28; Hab. 1:12), the One who is "from everlasting to everlasting" (Ps. 90:2; 93:2). Related to these assertions is the oath formula, "As Yahweh lives," or "As I live, says Yahweh."[26] All these expressions are grounded in the simple assertion, "Yahweh lives" (Ps. 18:46), which means, according to the book of Daniel, that "Yahweh lives *forever*" (Dan. 12:7; Deut. 32:40; cf. Isa. 43:12; Ps. 41:14; 106:48).

In biblical polemic, the epithet "living God" contrasts the Lord who creates with "dead idols" made by human hands (1 Sam. 17:26, 36; 2 Kings 19:4, 16; Jer. 23:36; Deut. 5:26; Josh. 3:10; Ps. 42:2; 84:2; Isa. 40:18-20; 41:21-24; 44:9-20, 24; 45:16-22; 46:5-7). "[Idols] are the work of the artisan and of the hands of the goldsmith. . . . they are all the product of skilled workers. But the LORD is the true God; he is the living God and the everlasting King" (Jer. 10:8-10). Rather than a created artifact, the living God is the creator and source of life (Ps. 36:9; Jer. 2:13; Ezek. 37:1-6). While there are numerous texts, then, in which the actual phrase "living God" does not occur, the affirmation of God as Creator, and creator of all that is, points to the same notion of God as the living source of all life.

Various biblical metaphors make the same point in a different manner. Yahweh is called "the fountain of living waters" (Jer. 2:13; 17:13) or the fountain of life (Ps. 36:9). Even the designation that God is "from everlasting to everlasting" (Ps. 90:2; 93:2; 145:3) rests on the fundamental assumption that God lives, and that God's life is qualitatively different from that of human beings precisely in its eternity. As a polemic found in the prophetic strands of the Bible, the emphasis on God as "living" serves to

25. According to Paul A. Rainbow, the identification of God as "living" and/or "true" is one of ten features of explicitly "monotheistic speech" in Graeco-Roman Jewish language. As Rainbow points out, such phrases as "living God" or "true God" are often linked with other formulas that posit the uniqueness of Yahweh and generally imply that other gods do not exist or simply cannot be compared with the one God. See Paul A. Rainbow, "Monotheism and Christology in 1 Corinthians 8:4-6," D.Phil. diss., Oxford University, 1987, pp. 44-46.

26. See Hans-Joachim Kraus, "Der lebendige Gott. Ein Kapitel biblischer Theologie," *EvT* 27 (1967): 169-99.

protect the uniqueness of God and to provide the basis for the demand of Israel's undivided loyalty and worship.

Thus the designation of God as the "living God" or as creator of all that is stands in the service of the argument for monotheism.[27] Perhaps no section of the OT states this as clearly as do the arguments of Isaiah 40–55, in which the uniqueness of God and God's creation of the world are linked together and provide the basis for the tirade against idolatry that also figures prominently in these chapters. The oft-echoed refrain of these chapters of Second Isaiah, "I am the LORD, and there is no other," is repeatedly linked to God's creation of the world, as well as God's continued sovereignty over it: "For thus says the LORD, who created the heavens (he is God!), who formed the earth and made it (he established it; he did not create it a chaos, he formed it to be inhabited!): I am the LORD, and there is no other" (45:18). Here God is characterized not only as Creator but as sole creator of the world (44:24) and of all that is (40:28; 45:7), as he is also in other formulations, such as: "The LORD is the everlasting God, the creator of the ends of the earth" (40:28) and "I am He; I am the first, and I am the last. My hand laid the foundation of the earth, and my right hand spread out the heavens" (48:12-13; cf. 42:5; 44:24; 45:11-12). These passages again join the affirmation of God's everlasting being, expressed now in terms of "the first and the last," with the creation of the world. Elsewhere Isaiah reads, "I, the LORD, am first, and will be with the last" (41:4), to which the LXX adds, "and for the coming times I am," which posits God not only as Creator but also as sovereign throughout history (see also 44:6; 40:18, 23; 43:10, 11; 44:8; 45:5, 6, 14, 18, 21, 22; 46:9; 48:12). This monotheistic emphasis portrays God as the sole creator of all that is, as well as "the God of world history who can therefore act as its lord."[28] God always is, and of "none other" can such predications be made.[29]

On the whole, these points are assumed rather than argued in much of the literature of Second Temple Judaism. Numerous texts could be ad-

27. On this point, see now especially Richard J. Bauckham, *God Crucified: Monotheism and Christology in the New Testament* (Grand Rapids: Eerdmans, 1998), p. 7; and Rainbow, "Monotheism and Christology in 1 Corinthians 8.4-6," pp. 57-65.

28. Andrew Lincoln, "Trials, Plots, and the Narrative of the Fourth Gospel," *JSNT* 56 (1994): 21.

29. These divine assertions in Isaiah appear in the LXX in various forms, but often in the Greek with ἐγώ εἰμι ("I am"); these formulations are discussed further in the following chapter.

duced to show that belief in God's eternal existence is commonplace. For example, Tobit blesses "the God who lives forever" (13:1). A prayer from 2 Maccabees addresses God as "creator of all things" and goes on to describe God as "alone" bountiful, just, almighty, and eternal (2 Macc 1:24-25). In 3 Maccabees God is spoken of as "the living God of heaven" (6:28), and in the Greek additions to Esther, as "the most mighty living God" (16:16). In the apocryphal book Bel and the Dragon, Daniel defends his refusal to worship Bel as follows: "I do not revere man-made idols, but the living God, who created heaven and earth and has dominion over all flesh" (Bel 5, 6, 24, 25). Elsewhere, different terms are used, such as "eternal" or "everlasting," sometimes with the definite article, as in "the everlasting One," thus distinguishing eternal existence as the unique identifying characteristic of God (αἰώνιος; 2 Macc. 1:25; Bar. 4:8, 10, 22, 35; 3 Macc. 6:12). The *Sibylline Oracles* speak often of God as "immortal" and "imperishable" (2.214-220, 284, 318, 330).

One of the clear corollaries of belief in the uniqueness of the living God, or in God's eternal existence, is the affirmation of God as creator of the world.[30] Consequently, where some variation of the phrase "living God" or "everlasting God" is absent, one often finds instead a description of God as Creator, or as the source of all life. Sirach explicitly joins together God's eternal existence with God's creation of the world: "He who lives forever created the whole universe" (18:1). For Philo, of course, God's eternity is the self-evident truth about God; God is "the One who is" (ὁ ὤν). God is the source of the life of the world (*Her.* 206); Creator and Maker (*Spec.* 2.30; *Somn.* 1.76; *Mut.* 29; *Decal.* 61); planter of the world (*Conf.* 196); Father; Parent (*Spec.* 2.198); "Cause of all things" (*Somn.* 1.67);[31] and Fountain of life (*Fug.* 198).[32] That God creates all that is rests on the assumption that God is the only ungenerated being. For Philo, in other words, God is the "unmoved mover." Eternal existence and creation go together. To be sure, Philo has interpreted these biblical themes in light of his Platonism, but nevertheless they are biblical themes that he both affirms and develops.

30. One of the frequent conclusions drawn from this affirmation is that God alone is to be worshipped. These texts are taken up and discussed at greater length in Chapter 5, "The Worship of God."

31. See *Decal.* 52: "The transcendent source of all that exists is God."

32. "God is the most ancient of all fountains . . . God alone is the cause of animation and of that life which is in union with prudence; for the matter is dead. But God is something more than life; he is, as he himself has said, the everlasting fountain of living."

Similar views are found throughout Josephus's writings. Josephus writes that God is "the beginning and middle and end of all things," who created the world "not with hands, not with toil, not with assistants of whom He had no need" (*Ag. Ap.* 2.190-192; cf. *Ant.* 8.280, "the beginning and end of all"). In fact, Josephus argues that the etymology of the Greek word Zeus shows the proper understanding of deity, for the name comes from the fact that "he breathes life (ζῆν) into all creatures" (*Ant.* 12.22). Once Josephus asserts that "the only true God is ὁ ὤν" ("the One who is"; *Ant.* 8.350). Josephus likewise assumes that the God of Israel is "the God who made heaven and earth and sea" (*Ag. Ap.* 2.121, 190-192; see also Jdt. 9:12; *Jub.* 2:31-32; 12:19; 16:26-27; 22:4; 2 Macc. 1:24; 7:28). In describing the zealous piety of the Essenes, Josephus states that they pray before and after meals in order "to do homage to God as the bountiful giver of life" (*J.W.* 2.131).

One could easily multiply texts that assume God's eternity and, particularly, God's creation of all that is in order to show that for Jewish authors of the period the uniqueness of Israel's God was lodged in God's creation of all the world. God is "the Lord God who gives life to all things" (*Jos. Asen.* 8:4), the "creator of all things" who, in his mercy, gives "life and breath" (2 Macc. 1:24; 7:23). Precisely in this life-giving activity, God is unique. Echoing the words of Isaiah, one of the Scrolls from Qumran reads, "You are the living God, you alone, and there is no other apart from you" (4Q504 5:9).

As already noted, the stock characterization of God as "the living God," so crucial to parts of the OT and Jewish texts, does not occur in John, although the variant "the living Father" does. The occurrence of the phrase "living Father," rather than "living God," is not simply an incidental variant attributable to Johannine style or preference. Rather, the epithet embodies within it the conviction that, as the eternally existent, living God, God alone is the source of all life, an aspect of God's activity that is illuminated by an image drawn from the human sphere of paternal relationship, particularly since that life is bestowed through the Son. The affirmation that God is "Father" cannot be separated from the affirmation that God is the source of life, nor from the conviction that the life of the Father has been given to, and comes to human beings through, the Son. Consequently, within the Gospel of John, the commonplace that God is the living God appears within polemic contexts (chs. 5 and 6) precisely as the warrant for the claims about the life-giving work of Jesus, the Son. John is not interested in the Unmoved Mover but in the living life-giver.

Indeed, the Johannine emphasis on God as "the living Father" goes a long way toward explaining the prominence of the theme of life in the Gospel.[33] Taken together, the ideas of God as "Father," and hence the source of life, and of God as the living God, the creator of all that is, account for the belief that God gives *life* through the Son who, by definition, derives his life from the Father. A father gives life to his son; indeed, a son by definition is one who has life from his father. So also, the Father gives life to his Son; the Son by definition has life from his Father. Therefore, through him life can be given to others as well. These virtually tautologous statements can be unpacked by looking briefly at the fundamental assertion that the Son has life *even as* the Father has it, and that through faith in the Son one *has* life in the present.

"As the Father Has Life in Himself"

By now it will be evident that a central conviction of the OT and of first-century Judaism was that God is the living God who has created all that is. Against this backdrop, we may examine some of the foundational theological statements of the Fourth Gospel: "Truly, truly, I say to you, the hour is coming, and now is, when the dead will hear the voice of the Son of God, and those who hear will live. For as the Father has life in himself, so he has granted the Son also to have life in himself" (John 5:25-26). According to these verses, those who hear the voice of the Son of God will live, because the Son "has life in himself" even as the Father does. The parallel clauses in these verses assert life-giving prerogatives of both the Father and the Son. These predications are striking, for in biblical thought the power to give life is attributed to God alone. As the eminent Johannine scholar C. K. Barrett comments, "This expression, denoting *exact parallelism* between the Father and the Son, is the key-note of this paragraph." The question remains, however, wherein this "exact parallelism" consists. Barrett himself explicates it as "the complete continuity between the *work* of the Father and the *work* of the Son."[34] Hence the emphasis is on the functional unity

33. John Ashton calls "life" the core or central symbol, around which all other symbols cluster (*Understanding the Fourth Gospel* [Oxford: Clarendon, 1991], p. 219, n. 28).

34. C. K. Barrett, *The Gospel According to St. John,* 2nd ed. (Philadelphia: Westminster, 1978), p. 260 (emphasis added).

of Father and Son. Raymond Brown asserts that the life in view is not the inner life of the Godhead but rather the "creative life-giving power exercised toward human beings."[35]

On this view, the Gospel is not addressing the question of the nature of the relationship or of the unity of Father and Son; rather it is characterizing the unity of their work. The Father's work and prerogative are to grant life, and, because he grants this prerogative to the Son, the Son participates in the Father's work. These assertions are clearly true, for in this passage, as throughout the Gospel, there is a concerted effort to argue that the work of the Son is indeed the very work of the Father, and that the Father does his work through the Son. Hence the most famous of all the Johannine assertions regarding the unity of the Father and Son, namely, "I and the Father are one" (10:30), actually refers in context to Jesus' promise that the Father and Son are one in the work of preserving the sheep of the fold from loss or harm. "I give them eternal life, and they shall never perish, and no one shall snatch them out of my hand. My Father, who has given them to me, is greater than all, and no one is able to snatch them out of the Father's hand" (10:28-29).

The remarkable assertions in 5:25-26 continue. The life-giving prerogative does not remain external to the Son; the Son does not receive the power to give life as a commission to be undertaken. Rather, the Son *partakes* of the very life of the Father: the Son has life in himself. Therefore, when Jesus *confers* life on those who believe, they also participate in and have to do with the life of the Father because the Father has given the Son to have life *in himself*, even as he has it.[36] Such predications assume and are dependent upon the conviction that there is but one God, one source of life. Jesus is not a second deity, not a second source of life, standing alongside the Father. Rather, the Son confers the Father's life, which he *has in himself*.[37] Hence the formulation assumes the unity of the life-giving *work* of Father and Son, but it also predicates a remarkable status of the Son,

35. Raymond E. Brown, *The Gospel According to John*, 2 vols., Anchor Bible (Garden City, N.Y.: Doubleday, 1966, 1970), 1:215.

36. See Kenneth Grayston, *The Gospel of John*, Narrative Commentaries (Philadelphia: Trinity, 1990), p. 51.

37. "Just as the Father as Creator and Consummator possesses life, he has given that possession also to the Son, not merely as the executor of incidental assignments but in the absolute sense of sharing in the Father's power" (Herman Ridderbos, *The Gospel of John: A Theological Commentary* [Grand Rapids: Eerdmans, 1997], p. 198).

one which is not made of any other mediator figure, either in John or in the literature surveyed above. The Son 'has life in himself.' Yet the statement does not stand on its own. Precisely in holding together the affirmations that the Son has "life in himself" with the affirmation that he has "been *given*" such life by the Father, we find the uniquely Johannine characterization of the relationship of the Father and the Son. The assertion that the Father has given this prerogative to the Son shows that the Gospel has in view neither an ultimate dualism of power tantamount to di-theism nor an arbitrary attribution of life-giving power to the Son as one possible agent through whom the Father might choose to confer life. The Father gives life to and through the *Son*.

The one verse in which the phrase "living Father" appears underscores again the relationship of the Father as one who gives life, and the Son as the one who receives it: "As the living Father sent me, and I live because of (διά) the Father, so whoever eats me will live because of (διά) me."[38] As in 5:26, Jesus speaks of his God-given authority and capacity to grant life.[39] Unless Jesus' life were granted to him from the Father, he would have no life; unless he came from the "living Father," he would be unable to confer life. The two assertions of this verse offer analogous, although not parallel, affirmations about the way in which Jesus and the believer receive life. Just as the Father has life and gives life to the Son, so the Son has life and gives life to those who have faith.[40] Jesus lives because of the Father's determination that he should have life in himself (cf. 5:21, 24-27), even as believers live because of Jesus' determination that they should have life. There is a difference, however, for believers always have a mediated life, never "life in themselves." They cannot pass on their 'life" to others; they have no offspring or heirs. If others live, it is because they receive the Father's life through the Son. Furthermore, although those who believe are said to be-

38. One might expect the use of διά plus the genitive in order to convey the idea of "source," as in 1 John 4:9, "God has sent his only Son into the world that we may have life through him" (δι' αὐτοῦ). Yet, as Brown points out, the context seems to indicate the "chain of sources of life," as is also implied by John 5:26 (*John*, 1:283).

39. See Barnabas Lindars, *The Gospel of John*, New Century Bible Commentary (Grand Rapids: Eerdmans, 1972), p. 270.

40. Ernst Haenchen, *A Commentary on the Gospel of John*, Hermeneia, 2 vols. (Philadelphia: Fortress, 1984), 1:296. Rudolf Bultmann translates, "As (i.e., correspondingly as) I have life because of the Father, so too he who eats me will live through me," thus effacing the parallelism (*The Gospel of John* [Philadelphia: Westminster, 1971], p. 236, n. 8).

come "children of God" who are "born of God" (1:12-13) or born "from above" by the power of the Spirit of God, the terminological distinction between them as *children* who are born of God and Jesus as the *Son* who comes from God remains.

These assertions assume that God is the living and life-giving Creator, who exercises sovereignty over all life, from creation to final redemption. The work of creation, the universal sovereignty over creation, and its expected final redemption are all carried on in the Gospel through the Son, and they are all expressed in terms of life. At the outset, in the prologue of the Gospel, we read the affirmation: "All things were made through [the Logos], and without him was not anything made that was made. In him was life" (1:3-4). These verses underscore the presence and agency of the Logos in creation. That same word "became flesh" in Jesus of Nazareth, and so when he acts and speaks, the dead come forth from their tombs (5:28-29). His words are "spirit and life" (6:63); in fact, he is life (11:25; 14:6). God grants the gift of life through Jesus, and Jesus' life-giving works also anticipate the final resurrection at the last day, which he himself effects (6:39, 40, 44, 54; 11:24; 12:48). In short, the life-giving work of the Father in the Son does not refer to a single event but to the all-encompassing creative and sustaining work of God, which has past, present, and future reference points.

"Realized Eschatology" in the Gospel of John

It is against this backdrop that we must interpret John's statements regarding "life" and "eternal life." Those statements speak of "passing from death to life" and of "eternal life" as a present reality. So, for instance, Jesus says, "Truly, truly, I say to you, he who hears my word and believes him who sent me *has eternal life*; he does not come into judgment, but has passed from death to life" (5:24). Statements such as these have led to a characterization of John as embodying a "realized eschatology." Simply put, realized eschatology refers to the belief that the blessings of the future era, such as eternal life, fellowship with God, joy, and peace, are now available. For some interpreters, then, John's realized eschatology basically reinterprets the future hope in terms of a present existential reality known in the quality of the present life.[41] Some have suggested that John's emphasis on "real-

41. Bultmann, "ζάω," in *TDNT* 2:871-72.

ized eschatology" comes from his effort to deal with the problem of the delay of the parousia. Since Christ did not return as anticipated, John reinterpreted the promises of and for the future as embodied in the person of Jesus.[42]

John's realized eschatology is frequently interpreted as a consequence of Johannine Christology.[43] Because Christ has come to the world, and because he brings "eschatological salvation," then salvation, construed as eternal life, is truly present in the world. To some extent, these interpretations are all predicated on the assumption that John has reinterpreted a primarily temporal schema of present and future, relocating the quality of life generally thought to be a future hope into the present experience of believers. John's eschatology is thus a variation of the NT's "inaugurated eschatology," in which the blessings of the future age are thought to be present at least *in nuce*. The difference, then, is that John highlights the present realization of those future blessings: according to some, putting more emphasis on the present than the future, and according to others, quite drastically reinterpreting the future hope in terms of present experience and realities. He does so, on this theory, because of his belief that all the blessings of the future are embodied in the person of Jesus. Realized eschatology is in fact a function of Christology.

Often the argument that John contains a "realized eschatology" includes the assertion that John transmutes the hope for a future *resurrection* into a present and spiritual experience of the believer, or that passages that refer to a future resurrection fit rather poorly with John's emphasis on the present possession of "eternal life."[44] Rudolf Bultmann, for example,

42. Brown, *John*, 1:lxxxv.

43. Paolo Ricca, *Die Eschatologie des vierten Evangeliums* (Zürich und Frankfurt a. M.: Gotthelf-Verlag, 1966), pp. 82, 90, 92, 98, 128; Josef Blank, *Krisis: Untersuchungen zur johanneischen Christologie und Eschatologie* (Breisgau: Lambertus-Verlag, 1964), pp. 15, 38, 125; Rudolf Schnackenburg, *The Gospel According to St. John*, 3 vols. (vol. 1: New York: Seabury, 1968; vol. 2: New York: Seabury, 1980; vol. 3: New York: Crossroad, 1982), 2:353, 355, 426-27; Ernst Käsemann, *The Testament of Jesus: A Study of the Gospel of John in the Light of Chapter 17*, ET (Philadelphia: Fortress, 1968), p. 16. The judgment that John's eschatology is essentially a function of his Christology is disputed, for different reasons, by David E. Aune (*The Cultic Setting of Realized Eschatology in Early Christianity* [Leiden: Brill, 1972], p. 86) and Dale C. Allison (*The End of the Ages Has Come: An Early Interpretation of the Passion and Resurrection of Jesus* [Philadelphia: Fortress, 1985], pp. 52-59).

44. Bultmann, *Gospel of John*, p. 261; *Theology of the New Testament*, 2 vols. (New York: Scribner's, 1951, 1955), 1:37-40; cf. Haenchen, *John*, 1:88-89, 253-54.

thought that the passages in the Gospel that refer to future resurrection or the "last day" were added by a later redactor since they clash with John's reinterpretation of the future in existential terms. Along these lines, Ernst Käsemann argued that the Johannine community gives evidence of "an enthusiastic piety which affirmed a sacramentally realized resurrection of the dead in the present."[45]

Yet the rich and full OT and Jewish understanding of God as the sole source, creator, and giver of *all* life compels us to reconsider the adequacy of such interpretations of John's "realized eschatology." Convictions regarding God's creation and sovereignty, which are expressed through the Father-Son relationship in the Fourth Gospel, provide the framework for John's interpretation of traditional eschatological language and realities. "Life" is first of all a theological reality. Life is the foremost characteristic, unique prerogative, and gracious gift of God. Properly speaking, then, the "realized eschatology" of the Gospel is as much a function of the Gospel's theology as of its eschatology or Christology. Or, perhaps better, the Gospel's "realized eschatology" can be said to be "Christological" insofar as and because it is first "theological." Johannine realized eschatology formulates in temporal terms the fundamental belief of the *Father*'s life-giving activity through the Son. Thus when the Johannine Jesus says, "Truly, truly, I say to you, whoever hears my word and believes him who sent me, *has eternal life;* they do not come into judgment, but *have passed from death to life,*" he underscores the enactment of the Father's life-giving power through him.[46] The statements also accord with John's definition of eternal life: "This is eternal life, that they may know you, the only true God, and Jesus Christ whom you have sent" (17:3). Eternal life consists of knowing that one, true, life-giving God, who sent the Son, Jesus Christ, who embodies and mediates the life of the living Father. To be gathered into the life of one is inevitably and simultaneously to be caught into the life of the other.

The assumption that John dispenses with the future resurrection would mean that he has significantly altered the view of "resurrection" found elsewhere in the documents of the NT or in the Judaism of the pe-

---

45. Käsemann, *Testament of Jesus,* p. 15; cf. pp. 20, 75.

46. Ridderbos, *Gospel of John,* p. 198. See also the comment by George W. Nickelsburg: "[John's] radicalization of eschatology is tied to Jesus' function as the revealer who brings life (1:4 and *passim,* also in the many life-related metaphors, e.g., bread and water)" ("Resurrection (Early Judaism and Christianity)," in *ABD* 5:690).

riod. In these texts, the dead are raised, not "spiritually" or metaphorically, but bodily. It is of course possible that John has done just that: radically re-interpreted the meaning of "the resurrection," but the data of the Gospel do not bear out the assumption that John has collapsed the future resurrection into a present quality of life, even a divinely given life. One finds in John an affirmation of the gift of the Father's life through the Son as well as the promise of being "raised up" at the last day. What one does not find in John is the assertion of the gift and presence of life couched in terms of the presence of *resurrection*. John does not speak of being "raised up" with Christ (cf. Eph. 2:6; Col. 3:1). Language of being raised up remains reso-lutely attached to the future, to "the last day." Resurrection overcomes death and so seals the believer in life eternally. It is that life, construed as fellowship and union with God, that is present for those who believe. Be-cause the resurrection is future, and because believers will be raised up "at the last day," the implication is clearly that the "life" one has in the present is as much promise as possession. The full possession of life awaits the promise of the resurrection. The belief in the future resurrection cannot be viewed as a vestige of a future eschatology that John retained even though it fit poorly with his preferred 'realized eschatology." Father, the future resurrection brings to fruition what the Father offers through the Son, the gift of life.[47]

The importance of the future resurrection to John's eschatology can be demonstrated by paying close attention to some of the passages often understood to be most supportive of and amenable to the argument that John has recast the future resurrection into a present experience or reality. In John 5, there are two statements that refer to the life-giving work of the Son:

"Very truly, I tell you, the hour is coming, and is now here, when the dead will hear the voice of the Son of God, and those who hear will live." (5:25)

"Do not be astonished at this; for the hour is coming when all who are in their graves will hear his voice and will come out — those who have done good, to the resurrection of life, and those who have done evil, to the resurrection of condemnation." (5:28-29)

---

47. See also Ridderbos, *Gospel of John*, pp. 199-200.

At first glance, these two statements seem to be restatements one of the other. There are, however, several telling differences. First, while both statements assert that "the hour is coming," the statement in John 5:25 adds, "and is now here." The hour for "the dead" to "hear the voice of the Son of God" and so to "live" is "now here." Second, the statement in 5:25 speaks of "the dead," while the statement in 5:28 more graphically refers to "those who are in their graves." Finally, the statement of 5:25 avers that the "dead will live," while in 5:28-29 those who are in the graves will come out, either "to the resurrection of life" or "to the resurrection of judgment." These differences are not incidental. What is in view in 5:25 is specifically the situation of present *believers*, who in hearing the voice of the Son of God receive the life "which he has in himself" (5:26). The one who has such life speaks the words that are spirit and life (6:63). Through the work of the Spirit, those who have faith receive that life as well, as they enter into the new life of the Spirit and into fellowship with God (3:3, 5-8; 17:3). They have passed from death to life because they have entered into fellowship with the very source of life, God himself, through hearing the word of the one who brings God's life into the world in and through his very person. The situation envisioned in 5:28-29 lies yet in the future. The hour has not yet come for the *resurrection* of *all* those who are in their graves. The word resurrection refers specifically to the raising of all the dead, those who have faith in the life-giving Son and those who do not. Thus the promise of "resurrection" in 5:28-29 differs from the promise of "life" in 5:25. "Life" refers first to that which is received in the present by those who have faith, while resurrection refers to that which is received in the future. While the promises regarding life in 5:25 envision a time that is coming and is *now here*, the promise regarding resurrection in 5:28-29 envisions a time that is coming but is *not* here.

Jesus' great statement, "I am the resurrection and the life," maintains the same distinction between "life" and "resurrection." In 11:25-26 Jesus explains the meaning of "resurrection" when he says, "he who believes in me, though he die, yet shall he live." The point is not that even though one will experience physical death, one nevertheless maintains a sort of spiritual life with God, but rather that the one who experiences physical death will live again. Death will be overcome through the resurrection to life.[48]

48. Alf Corell, *Consummatum Est: Eschatology and Church in the Gospel of St. John* (London: SPCK, 1958), p. 148.

Jesus' assertion that he is "life" is explicated by the statement "whoever lives and believes in me shall never die."[49] Since, in light of the previous statement, this verse cannot have in view physical immortality, some interpreters have understood it to refer to an immortality of the human spirit.[50] But in light of the Gospel's description of eternal life as fellowship with God, as a participation in the life of the Father through the Son, the verse seems rather to mean that not even physical death can sever that fellowship. Those who are presently alive in God will not experience death as a threat to that fellowship and participation in eternal life.[51] For this reality, which extends from the present into the future, the Gospel uses the term "life."

The assumption of a future resurrection is underscored by the connection that John draws between Jesus and believers. Jesus presents his own resurrection as the basis for the resurrection to life of his followers, "Because I live, you also will live" (14:19). Granted, this verse has been variously interpreted as referring to the resurrection, the parousia, or the whole series of events set in motion by Jesus' resurrection, including the ascension, the coming of the Spirit, and the parousia.[52] In the course of the narrative, however, the promise of Jesus anticipates his own *resurrection*. Hence, Jesus promises that, because he will be raised, so too the disciples will be raised to life, and this promise is fulfilled in the narrative in Jesus' resurrection appearances to the disciples. "Because I live, you shall live" refers to Jesus' resurrection, as well as to that of believers. Thus in the statement, "Because I live, you also will live. On that day you will know that I am in my Father, and you in me, and I in you" (14:19-20), the temporal

49. C. H. Dodd, *The Interpretation of the Fourth Gospel* (Cambridge: Cambridge University Press, 1953), p. 365; J Ramsey Michaels, *John*, New International Biblical Commentary (Peabody, Mass.: Hendrickson, 1989), p. 202; George R. Beasley-Murray, *John*, 2nd ed., Word Biblical Commentary (Nashville: Nelson, 1999), pp. 190-91. "Resurrection" and "life" are not equivalent, as some have held, e.g., Bultmann, *Gospel of John*, p. 403; Schnackenburg, *St. John*, 2:331; Jürgen Becker, *Das Evangelium des Johannes*, 2 vols., ÖTKNT 4/1 (Gütersloh: G. Mohn, 1979, 1981), 2:359-61.

50. J. H. Bernard, *The Gospel According to St. John*, 2 vols., International Critical Commentary (Edinburgh: T & T. Clark, 1928), 2.388.

51. Beasley-Murray, *John*, p. 191; Aune, *Cultic Setting*, pp. 120-21.

52. For a representative discussion of the latter view, see Brown, *John*, 2:645; for interpretation as the "demythologizing" of the parousia, see Bultmann *Gospel of John*, p. 620; for a primary reference to the resurrection, see Barrett, *John*, p. 464 (who nevertheless sees a reinterpretation of the parousia in these verses), and Ridderbos, *Gospel of John*, p. 505.

phrase "on that day" "marks the great transition to be effected by Jesus' resurrection."[53] Although Jesus returns, through his resurrection, to the life he has always had with God, it is through resurrection that such a return occurs. Death cannot rob him of life; he returns to the life he had with God. He has been raised to life; he now lives with God. The resurrection appearances attest to these realities. Similarly, death cannot rob the believer of eternal life; resurrection raises the believer to the permanence of life with God.

In John's "realized eschatology" what is present is not "the future" but rather the life-giving presence of the living God. John's "realized eschatology" ought to be construed as the articulation of his convictions about the sovereignty of the living God rather than as the reinterpretation of an unsatisfactory temporal schematization of "present" and "future."[54] John's eschatology is "realized" because John presses the point that the knowledge and presence of God are manifested through and made accessible in the presence of Jesus Christ. To paraphrase with an eye on the rest of the Gospel, Jesus is the means through which God grants life to human beings, but the resurrection seals the believer in that life. The present tense of John's statements regarding the possession of eternal life in no way eliminates the need for the resurrection. What it means to have "life" in the present is to have the genuine knowledge of and relationship to God, but to hold it as promise anticipating the resurrection.

John has often been understood to dissolve any so-called "tension" between the "already" and "not yet," between the present and future, in favor of his emphasis on the present reality of the salvation and blessings of God. Yet even though "tension" may not quite capture the flavor of Johannine eschatology, there clearly is a definite "space" between the here and now and the future. This may also be seen in Jesus' own journey to the Father — and his promise to the disciples that they will be where he is. Since he is returning to the Father, to the place and position that he had before the creation of the world, and since in that position he alone has seen the Father, the implication is that the disciples too have the promise

53. Ridderbos, *Gospel of John*, p. 505.

54. "The resurrection and life he grants encompass both present and future because *he* encompasses both as the One in whom the Word reveals itself, the Word that was with God in the beginning and by whom all things were created and who is therefore also the Son of man in whose hands the Father has put the future government over all things" (Ridderbos, *Gospel of John*, p. 398).

of the vision of God.[55] In this present life, because the Word of God has become incarnate, there is genuine knowledge of God; in seeing the Son, one sees the unseen Father. Yet the full vision of the unseen Father remains a future hope (see 1 John 3:1-2). Similarly, through the words and deeds of Jesus, one knows God and so has eternal life (17:3). Yet just as the Incarnate Word is fully God, yet not the entire fullness of God, and just as one sees the Father in the Son and yet does not see the Father in fullness, so too the life that the Word grants to human beings is fully the life of God, but not yet the complete fullness of that life. It awaits the resurrection. The very language of eternal life presses logically toward this end: life with the one who is the very origin and source of all life, the living and life-giving God.

The "I am" Sayings of the Fourth Gospel

In connection with the assertions that in John life comes *from* the Father and *through* the Son, we would do well to examine briefly the "I am" statements of the Fourth Gospel.[56] In several of these statements Jesus apparently asserts not that he offers or mediates God's life but rather that in some way he is the source of life, the eternal "I am." I would contend, however, that on closer examination of these statements in context, they will not overthrow, but rather support, the basic contentions of this chapter: that in offering the gift of life Jesus exercises a unique divine prerogative, and that the exercise of this prerogative attests to the unity that Jesus has with God as the Son of the Father.

We may begin with those "I am" sayings whose predicates speak of Jesus as "life." In chapter 6, Jesus asserts "I am the bread of life," and "I am the living bread." As the Son of man, he can give "food which endures to eternal life" (6:27). However, he is able to give such food "because on him has God the Father set his seal." Jesus' Father gives "the true bread from heaven." The bread of *God* comes "comes down from heaven and gives life to the world" (6:33). As has been pointed out above, those who come to Je-

---

55. This point is taken up more fully in the following chapter.

56. For a recent and thorough study of the "I Am" sayings see David Mark Ball, *"I Am" in John's Gospel: Literary Function, Background, and Theological Implications*, JSNTSup 124 (Sheffield: Sheffield Academic Press, 1996).

sus are given to him by the Father (6:37), whose will it is that they should have eternal life and be raised at the last day. God feeds people with the bread of life.

Embedded in the great Tabernacles discourse of chapters 7–10 we find, twice, "I am the light of the world," as well as the saying about Jesus as the good shepherd who comes to give his sheep life. Each of these sayings can, at first glance, be taken to point to Jesus, rather than through Jesus to God. As the world's light, Jesus extends and expands the light brought through Torah primarily to Israel (7:37–8:1). He heals the blind man. Furthermore, he will lay down his life so that his sheep may know fullness of life. This he does of his own volition (10:17-18). Yet, again, attention to context will show that the light Jesus brings enables people to know God (8:19; 9:39) because he is from the world above (8:23, 26-27, 38, 42; 9:30-31, 33) and does the works and will of God (9:3; 10:18). Indeed, the healing of the man born blind is not the work of Jesus but the work of God (9:3): through Jesus, God brings light to the world, and "light" in the Fourth Gospel is "the light of life," that is, the light that confers or leads to life. By their form, the "I am" sayings appear to call attention to Jesus, for the emphasis in these Greek formulations falls on the personal pronoun "I" (*egō;* ἐγώ) By their content and context, however, these sayings point to God, who is the source of all life.

In two of the "I am" sayings, Jesus says explicitly that he is "life." Yet these two sayings require interpretation, for simply to say that John has reinterpreted the hope for resurrection and eternal life in a radically Christological sense does not greatly illumine their meaning, or explain *how* that life is appropriated. Because we have already discussed John 11:25-26, here we may glance quickly at the saying found in 14:6, "I am the way, the truth, and the life." The second half of the statement — "no one comes to the Father but by me" — explains the first half, the "I am" saying. The next verse continues by way of explanation, "If you had known me, you would have known my Father also." That is, Jesus is the way to the Father because he mediates knowledge of the Father.[57] Therefore, he is also the mediator of truth and life. Both the exclusive nature of Jesus' claim and his function as the mediator of knowledge of God and so of life come to the fore.

The absolute "I am" sayings of the Fourth Gospel. Yet what of the other,

---

57. See Barrett, *John,* p. 458; Brown, *John,* 2:628; Beasley-Murray, *John,* p. 252.

more enigmatic "I am" sayings of the Gospel, those absolute formulations that have no predicate, but in which Jesus seems to use OT language reserved for God? After all, God is revealed to Moses with the words "I am that I am." Do not the absolute "I am" statements suggest that Jesus is more than a mediator of the knowledge of God, more than a mediator of God's life? In order to answer these questions, we will take a closer look at the three absolute "I am" statements found in chapter 8 (8:24, 28, 58).

One pressing issue in the interpretation of the "I am" sayings of the Fourth Gospel has to do with their background. The issues are wide-ranging and cannot be adequately or fully surveyed here. The most likely candidates for interpreting the "I am" sayings are generally assumed to be either the divine pronouncements of Isaiah or the revelation to Moses of the divine name. Thus the translations of these passages, and the traditions that sprang up around their interpretation, are of particular interest. We note, first, that the LXX translation of Exodus 3:14 reads "I am the One who is" (ἐγώ εἰμι ὁ ὤν).[58] This understanding of God's self-revelation has an analog in the divine declarations of Isaiah 40–66, where "I am Yahweh" (אֲנִי יהוה) is regularly translated "I am" (ἐγώ εἰμι), suggesting a revelation of God as the one who simply is. Although Josephus once uses the phrase *to on* (τὸ ὄν) as a description of God, the phrase is not typical of him. Philo echoes the LXX at this point, repeatedly referring to God either as "the One who is" (ο ὤν) or, more frequently, "that which is" (τὸ ὄν). Expounding on Exodus 3:14, Philo comments:

> Thus in another place, when he had inquired whether He that is has any proper name, he came to know full well that He has no proper name, and that whatever name anyone may use for Him he will use by license of language; for it is not the nature of Him that is to be spoken of, but simply to be. Testimony to this afforded also by the divine response made to Moses' question whether He has a name, even "I am he that is" (Ex. 3:14).' (*Somn.* 1.230-231)

---

58. Brevard S. Childs (*Biblical Theology of the Old and New Testaments* [Minneapolis: Fortress, 1992], p. 356) laments that the patristic use of the LXX translation of Exod. 3:14 to formulate God's identity in terms of a philosophical concept of ontology constituted an interpretative move "foreign to the Hebrew Bible." However, the renderings of Exod. 3:14 in the LXX and Philo show that already in the first century God's self-revelation was understood in terms of God's unique existence.

Elsewhere Philo glosses "I am who I am" with the rendition "My nature is to be, not to be spoken of" (*Mut.* 11). Again, however, because human beings need titles with which to address others and God, God allows them to use the title of the Lord God "as though it were His proper name" (*Mut.* 12). Yet since God has no proper name, a substitute for it is given to Moses and human beings in the theophany of the burning bush (*Mut.* 13–15). God cannot be named; God can only be known as the One who is (*Somn.* 1.230; *Deus* 62). Philo also comments that the title "the Existent One" of Exodus 3:14 truly characterizes the One who is, who "alone has veritable being" (*Det.* 160). Indeed, "to speak of God as 'not being' at some former time, or having 'become' at some particular time and not existing for all eternity is profanity" (*Decal.* 58). Philo so emphasizes God's eternal being that one writer has commented that for Philo "God is just existence."[59] In fact, the one true God is "not apprehensible even by the mind, save in the fact that He is" (*Deus* 62).

The Targums interpret the revelation of God's name in Exodus 3:14 along a different line. Both *Tg. Neofiti I* (and its marginal variants) and *Tg. Onqelos* preserve the enigma of God's self-identification by retaining the Hebrew rather than the Aramaic in rendering "I am who I am." Still, *Tg. Neofiti* offers an elaborate paraphrase as explanation of the meaning of the phrase, "And the Lord said to Moses: 'I AM WHO I AM.' And he said: 'Thus shall you say to the children of Israel: "The one who said and the world came into existence from the beginning; and is to say to it again: Be, and it will be, has sent me to you."'" There are two marginal readings in *Tg. Neofiti* at this point. One paraphrases "'I have existed before the world was created and have existed after the world has been created. I am he who has been at your aid in the Egyptian exile, and I am he who will (again) be at your aid in every generation.' And he said: 'Thus you shall say to the children of Israel. I AM sent me to you.'"[60] *Tg. Pseudo-Jonathan*, however, reads "And the Lord said to Moses, 'He who said and the world was, (who) said and everything was.' Then he said, 'Thus you shall say to the children

---

59. Ephraim Urbach, *The Sages: Their Concepts and Beliefs* (Cambridge, Mass.: Harvard University Press, 1987), p. 40. Some examples of Philo's emphasis on the existence of God can be found in *Det.* 160; *Mut.* 10–12, 17; *Somn.* 1.230-231. Cf. also *4 Ezra* 8:7; *4 Macc.* 5:24; *Liv. Pro.* 21:8; *Wis.* 13:1).

60. The other reads, "The Memra of the Lord (said) to Moses: 'He who said to the world, "Be," and it came into being, and who will again say to it: "Be," and it (will be).' And he said: 'Thus shall you say to the children of Israel: "WHO I AM has sent (me)."'"

of Israel, "I-am-who-I-am-and-who-will-be has sent me to you.""[61] Alan Segal contends that these Targumic traditions are related to the rabbinic polemic against "two powers in heaven." They intend to show that the One who was present with Israel in all its trials, and will always be present, is none other than the one true God.[62] Indeed, these Targumic renderings offer something of a counterpoint to Philo's rather rarified view, interpreting God's eternal being in existential terms as God's eternal, redeeming presence with Israel. *Tg. Pseudo-Jonathan* also links the revelation of the divine name with the creation of the world.

This brings us to the absolute "I am" statements of the Gospel. In John 8, where the theme of life surfaces again, we see that Jesus participates in the life of God and therefore in God's purposes of giving life to the world. Life is contrasted sharply with death (8:21, 24). Whereas it is Jesus' mission and intention to bring life (8:51-52), it is the intent of his opponents, those who are "from below," to bring death, especially to Jesus himself. Jesus, in fact, makes the bold promise that he can give eternal life (8:52). The Jews correctly understand that Jesus is making a claim about the kind of life that he lives, but they misunderstand the statement when they construe it in terms of chronological age: they hear him saying that he existed prior to Abraham. He must indeed be older than 50! Yet Jesus is making a claim to have quite another *kind of life* in himself, and that is eternal life, divine life, the very life of God. This fact has been established for the reader earlier in the Gospel, with Jesus' claim "As the Father has life in himself, so also he has given it to the Son to have life in himself" (5:26). Therefore, Jesus can confer it upon them.

Thus the contrast between the Son and Abraham (8:58) is between the kinds of life that they have. "Before Abraham was [came into being, was born], I am [exist, am alive, continue to live]." Abraham's life has a beginning point, but that of the Son does not. His existence is like that of God. He is "greater than Abraham" and the prophets precisely because "they died" (8:52-53), but the Son *is*. There may be a reference to the divine "I

61. Translations of *Tg. Neofiti 1* and *Tg. Pseudo-Jonathan* are from *Targum Neofiti 1: Exodus,* trans. with introduction and apparatus by Martin McNamara, M.S.C., with notes by Robert Hayward, and *Targum Pseudo-Jonathan: Exodus,* trans. with notes by Michael Maher, M.S.C., Aramaic Bible, vol. 2 (Collegeville, Minn.: Liturgical Press, 1994).

62. Alan F. Segal, *Two Powers in Heaven: Early Rabbinic Reports about Christianity and Gnosticism,* Studies in Judaism in Late Antiquity 25, ed. Jacob Neusner (Leiden: Brill, 1977), p. 51.

am" of the OT in the claim of 8:58, but it is allusive or indirect. Jesus does not say "I am the I am."[63] It is not until he makes the claim "to have seen Abraham," that is, to share in an eternal kind of life, that the people react: now he is claiming to have what God alone has. Thus the link between Jesus' statement and the divine OT "I am" is through the middle term, life. Jesus claims to share in God's kind of existence, eternal existence, existence that does not "come into being" but that simply "is" (8:35; 1:1, 2). This life he has from the living Father (6:57; 5:26; 10:18).

In thus using the absolute "I am," Jesus does not simply appropriate to himself a "name" for God, but he does use language that is particularly redolent of the passage in Exodus 3:14 when he utters the "I am" as the climax to his discourse about his authority to bestow life. Furthermore, the "I am" of the Gospel may be even more allusive of the similar phrases in Isaiah, where the emphasis falls both on God's eternity and on God's unique identity as creator of all and sovereign over all. Both the biblical and later Jewish interpretative traditions make clear that the interpretation of God's name, revealed in the incident of the burning bush, was inextricably linked to God's life-giving power, in terms of past and future creation of life. It is just this claim to have such life that leads the crowds to charge Jesus with blasphemy, for he appropriates to himself a unique divine identity and function in claiming to have been before Abraham and to be able to confer, through his word, eternal life.

"The Father Who Sent Me"

On the lips of Jesus, God is repeatedly designated not only as Father, but as "the Father who sent me." This description underscores the distinctiveness of Jesus' relationship to God as "Father" in several ways. First, the expression highlights the unique way in which God is the Father of Jesus. God is "the Father who sent *me*." When John the Baptist is said to be "sent by God," the designation "Father" is conspicuous by its absence. The only other figure sent by the Father is the Paraclete, the Holy Spirit. Second,

63. Philip B. Harner (*The "I Am" of the Fourth Gospel: A Study in Johannine Usage and Thought,* Facet Books 26 [Philadelphia: Fortress, 1970]) concludes that while the "I AM" of Exod. 3:14 "can hardly be considered a direct source for an absolute use of *ego eimi* in the Fourth Gospel . . . we should not entirely exclude the I AM of Exodus 3:14 as part of the more general background for the Johannine usage of *egō eimi*" (p. 17).

the very use of the participial form (ὁ πέμψας με πατήρ), by designating the Father as *the one who sends*, makes the Father the subject and initiator of the Son's activity[64] and once again identifies the Father by means of his action with respect to the Son. Third, the emphasis on God as the Father who has "sent" the Son introduces a new element into the description of the relationship of Father and Son. Not only is God "Father," but God is "the Father who *sent* me." The language of *sending* reflects a view of the Son as an emissary or agent who is sent by another to carry out a task or fulfill a commission. Indeed, the Son is identified primarily in terms of the one sent to carry out that mission and the Father as the one who sends the Son.[65]

In his study of Jesus, A. E. Harvey argues that there were three defining aspects of a son's relationship to his father in ancient Jewish thought: (1) the obedience of the son to his father; (2) a son's apprenticeship to his father, and a father's instruction of his son; and (3) the son as an agent of his father.[66] The first two points correlate with our findings in the survey of the role of the father in the OT and Jewish literature, where the father was understood to be (1) worthy of honor and obedience, and (2) charged with the instruction and discipline of his son. We shall discuss these characterizations of the Father-Son relationship in John below. Thus, we begin with the third point, that a son is the agent of his father. This point did not arise in our earlier overview of the role of the Father, because while a son may be one who ably serves as an agent or emissary of his father in transacting business, the father is not equally identified as one who authorizes his son to carry out certain commissions.[67] A father may do so; but this

64. David A. Fennema, "Jesus and God According to John: An Analysis of the Fourth Gospel's Father/Son Christology," Ph.D. diss., Duke University, 1979, p. 4.

65. Ashton (*Understanding the Fourth Gospel*, p. 314) distinguishes between the Gospel's language of *mission*, reminiscent of the sending of prophets in the OT, and the nonreligious language of *agency*. With respect to the latter, Ashton comments: "Here for the first time we appear to have an authentic tradition capable under the right conditions of generating the high christology according to which the man who has listened to the words of Jesus has heard the voice of God and, more strikingly, in Jesus' own words to Philip, 'He who has seen me has seen the Father.'"

66. In *Jesus and the Constraints of History*, pp. 159-63, Harvey makes the third point, the agency of the son, programmatic for understanding Jesus. We shall take up the discussion of "agency" in greater detail in the following chapter.

67. Ashton, *Understanding the Fourth Gospel*, p. 318, argues in a somewhat different direction when he asserts that sons are "rarely *sent*" by their fathers.

scarcely constitutes a distinguishing characteristic of a *father*. It is, therefore, all the more significant that whereas on numerous occasions John
states that God, or the Father, has sent Jesus, he never speaks of Jesus as
"the sent one" or "the one sent by the Father." The fact of Jesus' being sent
has not become crystallized into a title or name. Yet often the participial
phrase "the one who sent me" is appended to "the Father," so that the Father becomes identified primarily with and through the act of sending the
Son. As Paul Meyer comments,

> There is not so much a *Gesandtenchristologie* [a Christology of the one
> who is sent] in the Gospel as there is a *Sendertheologie* [theology of the
> one who sends]. . . . The language of "sending" is *theo*logical language
> that undergirds Christology but refuses to be absorbed into it.[68]

At this point, John's formulations stand somewhat in contrast with the
oft-quoted formulation from rabbinic writings, "The one who is sent is
like the one who sent him." Rather than predicating the virtual equality of
the one who is sent with the one who sends, John tends to stress that the
one who sends is greater than the one who is sent. So, for example, in John
13:16, Jesus asserts, "Truly, truly, I say to you, a servant is not greater than
his master; nor is he who is sent greater than he who sent him." Such affirmations are often read in light of another affirmation in John, "The Father
is greater than I" (14:28). While such formulations in the Gospel are typically labeled as examples of John's "subordinationism," the label is at best
misleading, inasmuch as it conceives of the relationship of Father and Son
primarily in hierarchical terms. Since John stresses the function of the Father as the one who gives life to his offspring, rather than the role of the
Father as the one who instructs or disciplines, statements such as "the Father is greater than I" ought not to be read against a backdrop of patriarchal hierarchy. The Father is the source of the Son's life; it is as the origin of
the Son's very being that "the Father is greater than I." This is clear even
from the context of that statement, in which Jesus asserts that he *returns* to
the Father, because the Father is greater; that is, he has his origins in the
Father (14:28). In the Fourth Gospel, then, the emphasis on the Son as the
"agent" who is sent actually serves to shift attention to the Father who
sends the Son.

---

68. Meyer, "'The Father,'" p. 264. See also Bultmann, *Theology of the New Testament*,
2:34.

The case is much the same in considering the theme of a son's obedience to his father. While maintaining the typical view that a true Son is one who "does the will of the Father," John nevertheless stresses rather dramatically the harmony of the Son's will with the Father's, interpreting the Son's obedience as an enactment of the Father's will, rather than as submission or acquiescence to it. For although the Son is often said to "do the will" (4:34; 5:30; 6:38, 39) or to "do the works" of the Father (5:36; 10:25, 37), the word "obey" is never actually used. Jesus receives and carries out the Father's commandments (12:49; 14:31; 15:10). Yet this does not imply that the Johannine Jesus has no will, rather that it is fully in harmony with that of the Father.

Few passages in John illumine as fully the character of the Son's "obedience" as do Jesus' statements regarding his death: "For this reason the Father loves me, because I lay down my life, that I may take it again. No one takes it from me, but I lay it down of my own accord. I have power to lay it down, and I have power to take it again; this charge I have received from my Father" (10:17-18). Here Jesus speaks of his death in terms of a "charge" that he received from his Father, a "charge" that encompasses his resurrection as well (10:18). Yet the passage simultaneously stresses Jesus' sovereignty: he lays down his life freely, not by force (10:18). Indeed, the emphasis on his own initiative sounds a steady drumbeat throughout these two verses: "*I* lay down my life"; "*I* take it again"; "*I* lay it down of my own accord"; "*I* have power to lay it down"; "*I* have power to take it again." The climactic statement, "this charge I have received from my Father," stands out almost as a surd element, for now Jesus' sovereignty over his own life, death, and resurrection is attributed to the *command* of the Father. However, the dialectic is resolved in the peculiarity of the Father-Son relationship in John, in which the Father not only gives the Son his life but grants it to him to dispose of it as he will — or, as the Father wills. A direct line runs from these statements to the recasting of Jesus' prayer prior to his death as a declaration of his intent to do the Father's will, rather than as a petition that the Father remove the cup. The Son's obedience to the Father does not establish their unity, nor is it an obedience construed in terms of submission to an alien command. Rather, the Son's "obedience" is the expression of the will of the One who sent him.

The connection between "fatherhood" and "works" becomes programmatic particularly in the heated debates of John 8. Beginning especially with 8:31, a bitter controversy is recounted between Jesus and his opponents about their origins and heritage. Jesus grants the Jews their claim that they are offspring of Abraham (*sperma;* σπέρμα, 8:37). They are physically descended from Abraham, but physical descent is not the ultimate criterion in determining their true relationship either to Abraham or to Jesus' own Father. What is important is conduct: to show themselves to be Abraham's children (*tekna;* τέκνα, 8:39), "the Jews" ought to do what he did.[69] Similarly, Jesus honors God, who is his Father (8:49), but because "the Jews" do not honor the Son, nor hear his words, even though he comes from and speaks of God, then they do not have God as their Father (8:44, 49). They do not do the will of God; hence, God is not their Father.

At first glance, this treatment of the Father-Son imagery seems to tend in a rather different direction from that previously delineated, for here sonship is determined not by kinship or descent but by obedience. This argument, however, is set in a discourse that begins with the assertion that Jesus is the free Son of the house, the only rightful heir of the Father's inheritance, the one who is not destined for death (8:31-36). As "the Son of the house" (8:35), Jesus is the heir of the Father; he has life from the Father and can bestow it on others; he alone is obedient to the Father. All the elements of genuine sonship are embodied in him, but his mission is to set others free so that they can enter into the Father's inheritance through him. The exclusivity of Jesus' sonship actually becomes the means through which others may receive the life and freedom that characterizes the true "children of God."

Ultimately it will be through Jesus' death and resurrection that others are empowered to enter into such a relationship. The command of the risen Jesus to Mary makes clear the new situation: "Jesus said to her, 'Do not hold on to me, because I have not yet ascended to the Father. But go to my brothers and sisters and say to them, I am ascending to my Father and your Father, to my God and your God'" (20:17). This is the first use of "brothers and sisters" (*adelphous;* ἀδελφούς) to refer to Jesus' disciples, and the first and only reference to God as "your Father" in a positive way (contrast 8:41, 42, 44). Still there is no reference in John to God as "our Father" in which Jesus includes the disciples together with himself in such

---

69. Ridderbos (*Gospel of John,* p. 312) denies that this discourse deliberately contrasts offspring (σπέρμα) and children (τέκνα), conceding the first but denying the second to Jesus' disputants. Rather, Ridderbos asserts that the terms are used interchangeably, but that being Abraham's seed is attributed to the Jews "in the natural sense" but denied in the "spiritual sense." In the end, however, the point seems to be much the same.

address. The differences between the relationship of Jesus to the Father and of the disciples to the Father remain, but, through the life-giving work of the Son, the disciples — and others — enter into the relationship of kinship granted to them by the Son. Not surprisingly, after Jesus' resurrection, his disciples are referred to with the familiar NT designation *adelphoi* ("brothers and sisters"; 21:23), a term that plays an important role in 1 John as the basis for the call to unity and love (1 John 3:13-16).

Finally, we come to the third characteristic of sonship enumerated by Harvey, the aspect of receiving instruction from the father as an apprentice, a theme that, when seen from the vantage point of the father, puts the emphasis on instruction and, to a lesser extent, on discipline. The element of the Father's discipline or correction of his Son is absent from John. Similarly, the note of learning in apprenticeship does not capture the tenor of the Johannine depiction of Father and Son. The Son is never said to learn; rather, he speaks what he hears from the Father, and he does what he has seen the Father doing. The Gospel does speak of the Father as "teaching" the Son (8:28), and Jesus also asserts that his teaching is not his own but comes to him from God (7:16-17). Perhaps one may wish to call this "apprenticeship," for a son learns by imitation to model what he sees his father doing. Yet given the absence of the idea of Jesus' "learning," as well as the heightened emphasis on the Son's doing and speaking what he has seen and heard, the picture that emerges is closer to the view of a prophet who becomes a mouthpiece of God, or a "seer" who has a vision or heavenly journey and reports what has been seen. However, as we shall see in a subsequent chapter, John does not credit Jesus' doing and speaking to the work of the Spirit, as though he were an inspired prophet, but rather to the unique relationship of the Father and Son, perhaps best summarized in these pithy statements of John 5: "Jesus said to them, 'Very truly, I tell you, the Son can do nothing on his own, but only what he sees the Father doing; for whatever the Father does, the Son does likewise. For the Father loves the Son, and shows him all that he himself is doing'" (5:19-20). Similarly, Jesus has made no journeys to heaven, but rather has come from God. Herman Ridderbos's summary at this point is worth quoting at length:

> It is clear that in "seeing" and "hearing" we are dealing with neither just a "program" that the Father has given the Son once for all to carry out nor with incidental ad hoc instructions, but with the continuing agreement of the Son's speech and action with the Father, agreement rooted

97

in his oneness with the Father (cf. 1:1a) and in the absolute authority bestowed on him as the beloved Son (cf. 3:35; 5:21ff). Hence it can be said that the Son speaks and acts in accord both with what he *has* seen and heard from the Father and with what the Father *will* show him.[70]

The father-son relationship thus becomes the theological grounding for the predications of the authority and work of the Father given to and embodied in the Son. This is not to say that the imagery of father-son necessarily generated all aspects of John's Christology; clearly other categories enter into the picture as well. Yet John has made it central. It plays a dominant role not only in terms of sheer statistics but also in terms of its power to shape the way in which other imagery is taken up and used. Because the Son has the Father's life, Father and Son are one, and those who know the Son know the Father. The Son, who has the life-giving prerogatives of the Father, is "equal to God" (5:18). The Father has placed "all things" into the hands of the Son (3:35; 13:3; cf. 15:15; 16:15); the Father has given "all judgment" to the Son (5:22). As the Son of the Father, the one whose very identity is constituted by the life-giving work of the one designated as Father, Jesus embodies and confers God's creative and sustaining work. Consequently, God's identity as "Father" expresses itself first in the specific and distinctive relationship to Jesus, the Son. That God is "Father" is not some "ontological" predication in and of itself that can be separated from speaking of the Father's relationship to the Son, in whom the Father's life is embodied.

"The Father Loves the Son"

One of the features of "fatherhood" in the OT and Jewish literature and of God as Father was that of a father's care for his children. Both in Matthew and Luke, Jesus speaks to his disciples of the mercy, provision, forgiveness, and care of God the heavenly Father for them. Curiously, none of the Synoptic Gospels ever speaks explicitly either of God's love for Jesus or for his disciples. Jesus of course calls upon people to love God, to love their neighbors as themselves, and to love their enemies. He also speaks of loving him (Matt. 10:37). Yet even in contexts where one might expect Jesus to speak

70. Ridderbos, *Gospel of John*, p. 192.

of God's love for humankind or the disciples, such a note is explicitly missing. For example, according to Luke, Jesus speaks these words: "Love your enemies, and do good, and lend, expecting nothing in return. Your reward will be great, and you will be children of the Most High; for he is kind to the ungrateful and the wicked. Be merciful, just as your Father is merciful" (6:35-36). While Jesus commands his disciples to "love your enemies," he speaks of the "the Most High" as "kind" and of "your Father" as "merciful." The words of Matthew 5:46-48 reflect a similar pattern. There Jesus commands his disciples to "love your enemies" because even tax collectors "love those who love them." Instead, Jesus' disciples are to show the indiscriminate love of the one who "makes the sun rise on the evil and the good," and so to be perfect, as their heavenly Father is perfect. Obviously while the implication is that God's way of loving ought to be imitated by the disciples, it remains the case that in none of the Synoptic Gospels does Jesus ever speak directly of God's love for the disciples. In the announcement at Jesus' baptism, "You are my beloved Son" (Mark 1:11), one finds the sole Synoptic reference to Jesus' being loved by God. In the comment in Mark that Jesus looked at the rich young man and "loved him," one finds the only statement that Jesus is said to love anyone (Mark 10:21). In short, love is what people express towards God, towards their neighbors, and towards their enemies, but it is it not used explicitly of God's posture towards human beings, and only once of God's relationship to Jesus, once of Jesus' posture towards an individual, and never of Jesus' attitude towards God. This is not to say that the Synoptic Gospels deny these attitudes to God or Jesus, only that explicit statements to that fact are simply lacking.

By contrast, the Father's love for the Son and the Son's love for the Father, as well as the Son's love for the disciples and their love for him and for each other, are programmatic in John. Given the centrality of the relationship of the Father and Son, the emphasis on their reciprocal love is scarcely surprising. For as we have seen, "father" and "son" point to the relationship of God to Jesus in terms of a familial metaphor, with all the privileges and obligations entailed by it, including the rights of inheritance and the obligation of honor and obedience on the part of the son. While the primary characteristic of the Father-Son relationship is the life that constitutes their relationship, that relationship is further characterized in John in terms of love. Even as the life of the Father is given to the Son and so through him to others, so too the love of the Father is bestowed on the Son and through him to others. Again we note the striking concentration of the Father's activity, here expressed as the fundamental relationship of love, in and through the Son. The Father loves the Son (3:35; 5:20; 10:17), so much so that the Father has "given all things into his hands." The Father will love those who love Jesus (14:21, 23; 16:27). Because Jesus has made God known to his own, the Father's love for the Son is said to be in them (17:26). Even as those with faith receive life from the Father through the Son, and so are taken up into the relationship of the Father to the Son, so do they participate in the relationship of mutuality and love of the Father and the Son.

Thus the relationship between Father and Son is the reality in which those who have faith participate and dwell. This is the relationship or reality in which one finds "life," and whose fundamental commitment can be summarized in terms of "love." Love is not one of many possible attitudes or actions that the Father may express towards the Son, the Son towards the Father and believers, and so on. Rather it is the fundamental way of relating among those who find their very life and existence determined by the relationship of "father" and "son" to each other. The Father gives the Son life, who in turn gives it to others, and much the same may be said of love. There are, however, striking differences. Most notably, while Jesus commands his disciples to love one another as he has loved them, there is no similar command to give or extend life to each other. Yet both the Father's love and life are embodied in the Son and through him in the community gathered around him. The command to love each other extends the relationship of Father and Son, expressed both as life and love, and it is through the experience of the Father's love and life in the Son that those of faith participate in the reality of that relationship. This is not a life that floats abstractly above the real life of women and men in the world. It is life that is embodied, quite literally, in Jesus and his followers. In this way it can indeed become life for all the world.

THREE

Knowledge of God

How God is known is a question raised repeatedly, both explicitly and im-plicitly, in the Gospel of John. The final verse of the Gospel's prologue throws down the gauntlet in the form of the bold claim that although no one has ever seen God, the Son has made the Father known (1:18). Knowl-edge of God is thus possible through the Son. Questions regarding the knowledge of God surface as the point of contention between Jesus and his adversaries in the debates of chapters 7 and 8, in which Jesus asserts that he knows God and denies that his opponents do (7:29; 8:19, 55). All such claims occur more than once in the Gospel: Jesus asserts that he knows God (10:15; 17:25); that knowing God is vitally linked to knowing him (14:7), a knowing that can be equated with "eternal life" (17:3) and that the world has not known God (17:25). Clearly the issue is not whether God can be known, for not only is this point assumed, but without that as-sumption the subsidiary questions of how knowledge of God is attained and who may attain it would obviously not even be entertained.

That God can be known is not self-evident in the contexts that have shaped the Gospel of John. First among those contexts is the OT, in which one finds narratives of a variety of encounters with the divine. There are theophanies, such as the burning bush and the appearance to Moses on Si-nai, and visionary experiences, such as those of the prophets Isaiah and Ezekiel. These encounters are described primarily, although not exclu-sively, in visual terms. The human subject sees God, in some manifestation

101

or another. These phenomena are also auditory: Moses hears a voice from the bush; God speaks to him on Sinai. In these accounts, the experience of "seeing God" forms the basis for receiving some sort of commission or revelation from God. Through these sorts of encounters the human subject may come to know God, or at least to know something of God's will and purposes, and impart something of that experience or the instruction that was received to others. Other "encounters" with God are described primarily in auditory terms: one hears the voice of God, one receives the word of the Lord. In one way or other, whether directly or indirectly, God can be heard and seen; God can be known. Yet the recurring refrain, particularly among the prophets, is actually a lament of the failure of God's people to know and worship him (e.g., Jer. 10:25; Ps. 79:6). While God is said to know Israel, rarely do we find in the OT passages that speak confidently of human knowledge of God. It is easier to find statements that speak of the failure to know God, of ignorance of God.[1] Typically ignorance of God manifests itself either as idolatry, the worship of false gods, or as the pursuit of unethical and immoral behavior. Yet the assumption remains that God can be known and, indeed, should be known by his people. They have turned, however, from knowing, worshipping, and obeying their God to the pursuit of false deities. The problem of knowing God lies primarily with the human subject.

Yet the issue of knowing God in the OT is more complex. In the book of Job, for example, the difficulty comes in comprehending the ways of God. To some extent this may be a problem within the human subject, but the issue is not simply that human beings cannot grasp the ways of God. Circumstances and events may render comprehension of God's ways difficult, but ultimately God's ways so transcend human understanding that God cannot finally be completely grasped by the human subject. Knowledge of God is not phrased so much in terms of hearing or seeing God as in terms of understanding the purposes of God.

The difficulty in discerning and understanding God's will and actions is reflected in later Jewish and Christian apocalyptic literature. While this literature often reflects faith in the certainty of God's judgment and justice, it is also shot through with anguish over God's apparent delay in coming to the aid of his people. Circumstances in the world raise a huge question

---

1. See the discussion of C. H. Dodd, *The Interpretation of the Fourth Gospel* (Cambridge: Cambridge University Press, 1953), pp. 151-69.

mark against human ability to know God or, worse, to trust in God's ultimate justice. The apostle Paul wrestled with the ultimate mystery of the ways of God in trying to come to grips with God's purposes for Israel, the Church, and the world (cf. Rom. 11:33-35). Similarly, in speaking of rabbinic understandings of God, Shaye Cohen writes: "Whatever feelings the Jews had about God's elusiveness and ineffectiveness were caused not by his transcendence or remoteness but by the incomprehensibility of his actions. Why does a moral God allow evil to flourish?"[2] In one way or another, the problem of knowing God is not lodged ultimately in the will of the human subject, but rather in the mysterious and inscrutable ways of God.

For at least one Jewish writer contemporaneous with the NT, the problem of the knowledge of God presented itself on different terms. In the writings of Philo one finds extensive wrestling with the question of whether the immaterial Most High God may be known by human beings. Philo distinguished the unknowable reality of the Most High God and the genuine but distinct manifestations of that God through his Logos. Through the Logos God can be comprehended by human beings, but the Most High God, whom Philo elsewhere refers to as "the One who is" or even "that which is," cannot be known in his ultimate being. Philo thus wished to make a point about the nature or being of God — the Most High God cannot be seen or known — and about human knowledge of God — God is known through a "secondary" manifestation or self-revelation. Obviously for Philo, as well as for other Jewish and Christian thinkers influenced by Middle Platonism, the problem of the knowledge of God takes into account both the immateriality and the transcendence of God, as well as the nature of human knowledge of such a God. While human beings may attain to genuine knowledge of God, it is not direct apprehension of the ultimate being of God.

In short, the basic question of the knowledge of God is multifaceted and includes within it a series of questions related to it and to each other. The first is simply *whether* God can be known. If one gives an affirmative answer to that question, obviously an answer to the question *how* God may be known is already assumed within it. Even the question of how God is known may be phrased in one of two ways. One may have in mind primarily the question of revelation or manifestation: How is God made known?

---

2. Shaye J. D. Cohen, *From the Maccabees to the Mishnah*, Library of Early Christianity 7, ed. Wayne A. Meeks (Philadelphia: Westminster, 1987), p. 86.

In the biblical witness, God is revealed or made known in a variety of ways, including theophanies, visions, through intermediary figures such as prophets and angels, and the law. Clearly these are rather different means of God's self-manifestation. Formulated in this way, the question, "How is God made known?" focuses primarily on God's revelatory actions or the means of divine revelation, without necessarily specifying in what that knowledge will consist and how it will be made known. Hence, an integrally related question concerns the ways in which human beings recognize and discern divine revelation. The Bible speaks of hearing and seeing God, referring both to literal sensory experience and to the faculties of understanding and discerning. Knowledge of God includes, but is not limited to or fully encompassed in, sense perception.

To speak aptly of the knowledge of God, then, one must take into account both God's revelatory activity and human perception of it. John's contention is *that* the Son has made the Father known. However, such a statement does not yet make it transparent *how* the Son reveals the Father, and in what ways the Son mediates or makes possible knowledge of God. While John asserts that Jesus speaks the words of God and does the work of God, the Gospel pushes further in claiming that Jesus so fully embodies the Word of God that to see him is to see the manifestation of God's glory; to see the Son is to "see" the Father. That assertion not only heightens what is at stake in "seeing" Jesus but also leaves unanswered the question of how one sees God in Jesus. Even so, it is clear that the disciples of Jesus do not see God as he does, for whereas the Son sees the Father directly, others see the Father in and through the Son.

Knowledge of God is not limited to "seeing" alone, for John also speaks of "hearing" God's voice. Again, distinctions are drawn between the ways in which Jesus, his disciples, and their contemporaries hear God. Jesus has heard and continues to hear God speak. Everyone who "has heard and learned from the Father" comes to Jesus, showing that they have been "taught by God" (6:45). This affirmation is quickly followed, however, by the assertion that no one "has seen the Father except the one who is from God; he has seen the Father" (6:46). Hence, there is a distinction between "hearing" and "seeing" God. While those who have responded to Jesus may be said to have been *taught* by God, no one except Jesus has seen God (1:18; 5:38-39; 6:46). In the only instance in John where God is portrayed as speaking directly, the crowds who hear God's voice think that they have heard thunderings of an angel (12:28-30).

John's assertions regarding "seeing" and "hearing" God thus concentrate the revelation and knowledge of God in Jesus. Yet even that formulation must be qualified, for elsewhere the Gospel assumes that God has been present and revealed to Israel by various means — through Scripture, the workings of miraculous deeds in the wilderness, and particular prophets and persons.[3] God's work and revelation have not been limited to Jesus, although they are now concentrated in him. The Fourth Gospel does not deal with Philo's problem of how an immaterial Spirit could be present to and with a material world, but it does deal with the question how an unseen God may be "seen" and known, a question not unrelated to Philo's pondering how human beings may know the transcendent God. Both Philo and John answer that question with recourse to the mediating work of the Logos of God. Nor is John's problem precisely the apocalypticists' problem of the incomprehensibility of the work of the sovereign God. The problem is closer to that of the prophets: God should be, but is not, known by his people.

In this chapter we shall take up the related questions of how God is revealed and the ways in which human beings appropriate such revelation. We shall explore first the Johannine statements regarding "hearing" and "seeing" God. Under the influential shadow cast by Rudolf Bultmann, they have been played off against other. John Ashton even speaks of the "sight/hearing antithesis" that one finds in John.[4] "Hearing" has long been elevated to supreme rank, while "seeing," at least when used with reference to the signs of Jesus, has been denigrated as an inferior way of knowing God. However, a closer look at the evidence of John suggests that this evaluation ought to be turned completely around. The higher good, one to which Jesus alone may lay claim and that lies in the eschatological future for all others, is the good of *seeing* God. Hearing is in no way inferior to seeing, but it never attains the status of eschatological destiny for those of faith.[5]

Following a discussion of this claim regarding the role of "seeing" and "hearing" in John, we shall explore some of the most significant ways in which the Fourth Gospel understands the manifestation of God's presence

3. So also D. Moody Smith, *The Theology of the Gospel of John* (Cambridge: Cambridge University Press, 1995), p. 82.

4. John Ashton, *Understanding the Fourth Gospel* (Oxford: Clarendon, 1991), p. 521.

5. This is true of the Synoptic Gospels as well; so the beatitude reads "Blessed are the pure in heart, for they shall *see God*."

in the world. The primary categories to be considered are those that deal with various agency figures. The category of agency has been important both for studies of first-century Judaism and for the Christology of the Fourth Gospel, where figures such as the *shaliach* (agent) figure, personified Wisdom and Word, and even angelic revealers have been thought to provide the primary categories for the depiction of Jesus' role and person in the Gospel of John. As we shall see, while John concentrates the functions of nearly *all* agency figures — prophet, Messiah, Son of Man, Torah, Wisdom, Word, interpreting angel — in either Jesus or the Paraclete, it is those intermediary figures identified as personified attributes of God, such as Word and Wisdom, rather than human mediator figures such as prophets or legal agents that best account for the development and articulation of Johannine Christology.[6] That this is so accords with John's rendering of *seeing* both as the means of knowing God and as descriptive of the ultimate human encounter with God. At the conclusion of the chapter, then, we shall ask what light the previous examination has shed on John's understanding of "knowledge of God."

"God's Voice You Have Never Heard"

In his discussion of the Gospel of John in his *Theology of the New Testament*, Rudolf Bultmann included a chapter entitled simply "Faith," with its first subsection called "Faith as the Hearing of the Word."[7] That subtitle discloses Bultmann's argument that in John "hearing" the word is the central and preferred way of coming to faith. Indeed, Bultmann virtually collapsed "faith" and "hearing," contending that since Jesus and his word are identical, one can rightly speak either of faith in Jesus or of faith in his words. Bultmann furthermore subsumed all Jesus' works, including the signs of Jesus, under Jesus' words or, better, under Jesus' word. Thus one

---

6. At this point I agree with the thesis of Richard Bauckham (*God Crucified: Monotheism and Christology in the New Testament* [Grand Rapids: Eerdmans, 1998]) that figures such as Wisdom and Word are included within the unique identity of the God of Israel, whereas intermediary agency figures, such as angels, exalted patriarchs, and prophets are not, and that it is the first that are formative in the development of early Christology. This is certainly the case for the Gospel of John.

7. Rudolf Bultmann, *Theology of the New Testament*, 2 vols. (New York: Scribner's, 1951, 1955), 1:70-74.

can also speak of "seeing," but what is intended is the perception of faith; the sensory act of perception is not primarily in view. Although Bultmann asserted that hearing and seeing are identical terms, and that both can be used for "believing," it is clear both from the reduction of Jesus' works to his word and from the section heading — "faith as the hearing of the word" — that Bultmann interpreted John as giving pride of place to hearing, relegating "seeing" to a secondary status. Hence Bultmann spoke of the signs of Jesus as "concessions" to faith and of faith based on signs as unreliable. Along these lines, Jesus' rebuke of Thomas's confession upon seeing the risen Lord, coupled with Jesus' benediction on those who have not seen and yet believed, is taken to show the superiority of faith that does not rest on the "crutch" of seeing.

Bultmann's interpretation of the role of seeing in John has been highly influential, so that it is rather widely held that John does indeed prefer hearing to seeing, the word to the sign, faith arising without sight to faith arising from sight. Bultmann's interpretation takes it cue from various statements in John that underscore the centrality of hearing the word of Jesus. Those who hear Jesus directly, rather than through any intermediary, come to faith in him: "We have heard for ourselves, and we know that this is truly the Savior of the world" (4:42). Jesus speaks, and those who hear receive life: "The hour is coming, and is now here, when the dead will hear the voice of the Son of God, and those who hear will live" (5:25). In fact, "hearing" the voice of Jesus can be used in metaphorical descriptions of discipleship: "My sheep hear my voice. I know them, and they follow me" (10:27). To hear Jesus can virtually be equated with coming to him in faith. Those who hear the word of Jesus have heard or received the testimony of the Father (5:37). Conversely, those who have been taught by God, who have "heard and learned from the Father," come to Jesus (6:45). In other words, hearing and believing or trusting are virtually synonymous terms.

By contrast, those who do not "hear" the word of Jesus have not heard the voice of God; and those who have not heard the voice or teaching of God do not "hear" the word of Jesus. The connections between hearing the word of Jesus and the voice of God are sometimes difficult to trace. On the one hand, because Jesus speaks the words of God, his words can virtually be collapsed into God's word. To hear the one is to hear the other. Typical of such statements in the Gospel of John are the following: "The one who sent me is true, and I declare to the world what I have heard from him" (8:26); "I have made known to you everything I have heard from my Fa-

THE GOD OF THE GOSPEL OF JOHN

ther" (15:15). On the other hand, certain passages convey the sense that only if God grants insight does one then hear or understand the word of Jesus. Hence, God's instruction or teaching enables Jesus' word to be heard and understood, but it is not simply to be equated with it (6:45).

The possibility of "not hearing" also remains: "Anyone who hears my word and believes him who sent me has eternal life; he does not come into judgment, but has passed from death to life" (5:24). The failure to "hear" the word of Jesus, that is, to understand and accept it, is tantamount to a failure to hear the word of God (8:47). Most emphatically, Jesus denies that his contemporaries hear the voice of God, or even that they have ever heard it: "And the Father who sent me has himself borne witness to me. His voice you have never heard, his form you have never seen" (5:37).

This leads to a few observations about "hearing" in the Gospel of John. First, Jesus is said to speak only what he hears from the Father, a point that recurs in the Gospel. While this could suggest that Jesus repeats what he has heard from God, much of Jesus' discourse in the Gospels actually consists of material that has to do with his own person and role. It is not so much that Jesus repeats assertions that he has heard from God as that the content of his own self-testimony is identical with God's testimony to him (5:32; 8:18). His revelatory speaking is authorized by God. Those who accept Jesus' testimony and words thus have accepted God's witness to him. They have also accepted Jesus' testimony to God, to statements about his relationship to God, to God's judgments and promises made through Jesus, and so on.

Second, "hearing" is a means to some other end. Through hearing the word of Jesus one comes to receive eternal life; through hearing the voice of God one comes to know the truth of Jesus' words. Those who hear the voice of Jesus follow him in discipleship. When hearing is equated with obedience or believing, it leads to eternal life. At some places in John, hearing seems to be spoken of as though it were an end in itself, particularly when Jesus denies that his contemporaries have heard God's voice or God's word, a failure that clearly merits God's judgment. Even in such cases, however, hearing God's word is not an end in itself but the means by which one receives life rather than death.

Third, when the emphasis falls on hearing God's voice or God's word, the categories by which Jesus may be comprehended most naturally cluster around prophet, teacher, witness, or agent figure. God is thus made known primarily through words, whether written or spoken, and is comprehended indirectly — through what the prophet, teacher, or witness writes or speaks about God. One may object that John connects knowledge of God more closely with knowledge of Jesus when he speaks of the *identity* of Jesus' words with God's words. Yet that identity is an identity of word or witness, and, in that sense, knowledge of God through the word of Jesus remains indirect, mediated, and a means to the end of receiving life.

Fourth, while Jesus rebukes his contemporaries for their failures to both *see* and *hear*, the text of judgment from Isaiah 6, also quoted by the other three Gospels, limits the rebuke to seeing alone. Isaiah's word of judgment reads as follows:

> And he said, "Go, and say to this people:
> 'Hear and hear, but do not understand;
> see and see, but do not perceive.'
> Make the heart of this people fat,
>   and their ears heavy,
>   and shut their eyes;
> lest they see with their eyes.
>   and hear with their ears,
>   and understand with their hearts,
>   and turn and be healed." (Isa. 6:9-10)

This passage from Isaiah virtually equates hearing and seeing.[8] All three Synoptic Gospels quote this passage, albeit in some abbreviated form. Even so, all three Synoptics cite the passage from Isaiah so as to maintain the parallelism between hearing and seeing John alone eliminates the references to "hearing" in his citation of Isaiah 6:9-10, shaping the passage to interpret the failure of Jesus' contemporaries to respond to the signs that Jesus has done among them (12:40). They have failed to see Jesus' glory, a glory made known through the signs done among them, a glory that Isaiah "saw" (12:41). The placement of this passage at the climax of Jesus' public ministry underscores all the more the central role of *seeing* and the judgment on those who have failed to *see* God's glory in Jesus. Elsewhere, then,

---

8. So does a similar word of judgment in Deut. 29:2-4: "And Moses summoned all Israel and said to them: 'You have seen all that the LORD did before your eyes in the land of Egypt, to Pharaoh and to all his servants and to al his land, the great trials which your eyes saw, the signs, and those great wonders; but to this day the LORD has not given you a mind to understand, or *eyes to see, or ears to hear.*'"

Jesus rebukes his contemporaries because they have "seen me and yet do not believe" (6:36). For the will of God is that "every one who sees the Son and believes in him should have eternal life" (6:40).[9]

Finally, John reflects a pattern, found also in the OT, of distinguishing between the word of the Lord that is heard and the vision of God that is either denied, or granted only partially. So, for example, Moses may be said to speak to God "face to face" (Exod. 33:11), but he is not permitted to see God face to face, for "no one shall see me and live" (33:18-23). Instead, Moses is granted a vision of God as he "passes by." Similarly, according to Deuteronomy, when the people gathered to receive the law, they heard his voice but "saw no form" (4:12; cf. 5:4). This becomes the explanation for the command against making idols and images (4:15-18). In these passages, then, while it is possible to speak with God and hear the voice of God, seeing God is either not possible at all or possible only in a limited or partial way. Precisely because the vision of God is restricted in some way, it is also a superior means of experiencing or apprehending God.

In the Gospel of John there is a clear echo of these passages in the assertions that no one has ever seen God (1:18) or God's form (5:37; 6:45-46). There is, of course, one exception, and that is the Son, who has seen the Father and hence can make him known. The vision of God is thus restricted to the Son alone. Precisely here lies the essence of the contrast between seeing and hearing God in John, a contrast summarized in John 6:45-46: "Everyone who has heard and learned from the Father comes to me. Not that any one has seen the Father except him who is from God; he has seen the Father." These verses allow that while others have heard the Father, only the one from God, the Son, has actually seen him. This leads us, then, to a fuller discussion of seeing God in the Gospel of John.

"God's Form You Have Never Seen"

As just indicated, the Fourth Gospel limits "seeing God" to Jesus alone (1:18; 6:45-46). This distinguishes Jesus not only from his contemporaries,

---

9. See also the link between hearing and seeing in 14:7 ("If you had known me, you would have known my Father also; henceforth you know him and have seen him") and 14:17 ("even the Spirit of truth, whom the world cannot receive, because it neither sees him nor knows him; you know him, for he dwells with you, and will be in you").

who are said never to have seen God (5:38-39), but also from his disciples, who have not seen God either, although they have seen the Son. Even so, Jesus' vision of God is qualitatively unique, of a different sort than that vouchsafed the disciples, for they see the Father in the Son, rather than seeing him directly as the Son does. The distinctive and unique character of the Son's vision of God emphasizes the primacy of place given to "seeing God."

As one who has seen God, Jesus appears at first glance to be ranged alongside certain ancient worthies, such as Jacob and Moses, who, according to various passages in the OT, have seen God. In Genesis 32:30 (MT 32:31), Jacob is described as having seen God "face to face." Moses, too, is said to have spoken with God "face to face" on more than one occasion (Exod. 33:11; Deut. 34:10), and God is said to be known as a God who is seen "face to face" (Num. 14:14; Deut. 5:4). The seventy elders of Israel "saw the God of Israel" (Exod. 24:9-11). In Isaiah 6, Ezekiel 1, and Daniel 7, visions or visionary experiences of God are described that became the basis of later descriptions of seeing God in the literature of apocalyptic and mystical Judaism.[10] Perhaps not surprisingly, then, certain ancient writers such as Philo explained that "Israel" meant "the one who sees God." However, Philo qualified that statement by stating that one sees God as "through a mirror," that is, not directly (*Fug.* 213). In other words, in spite of the assumption that Israel "sees God," Philo explained the vision as an indirect vision, thus softening the anthropomorphism of the biblical text and preserving the immateriality and transcendence of God.[11]

Yet the tendency to reread passages that refer to a direct vision of God is already present in the biblical text, offering something of a counterpoint to assertions and accounts of seeing God. For example, although one reads of Moses and the elders of Israel seeing God (Exod. 24:9-10), later in the same narrative Moses is denied a vision of God's face on the grounds that no one can see God and live (33:21-23). What Moses therefore asks, and is denied, is a kind of encounter with God granted to no human being. Similarly, in Deuteronomy we read that the people of Israel never saw the form of God (4:12-15; 5:4), even though Moses is described as conversing regularly with God "face to face." Later readers and interpreters of the text would have had

10. See Christopher Rowland, "The Visions of God in Apocalyptic Literature," *JSJ* 10 (1979): 137-54; and Jey J. Kanagaraj, *"Mysticism" in the Gospel of John*, JSNTSup 158 (Sheffield: Sheffield Academic Press, 1998).

11. For further discussion of Philo and the vision of God, see Donald A. Hagner, "The Vision of God in Philo and John: A Comparative Study," *JETS* 14 (1971): 81-93.

to account for the apparent disparities within it. In John's Gospel, the Son alone has the kind of *vision* of God that Moses was denied in Exodus 33:21-23; the Son alone has *seen* God "face to face." Because the statement in the prologue that "no one has ever seen God" is followed immediately by the implicit assertion that the only Son is "in the bosom of the Father," this second statement may well imply that to be "in the bosom of the Father" is to have precisely that unprecedented face-to-face vision of God.

The Targums also interpret various biblical texts so as to prevent literalistic or anthropomorphic readings of them. They solve the problem of the apparent contradiction between passages that assert that no one can see God and live, and passages that present certain individuals as doing just that, by leveling them to the common experience of seeing the glory of God, or the glory of God's presence. No one, however, sees God face to face. According to *Targums Onqelos, Pseudo-Jonathan,* and *Neofiti I,* Jacob does not see God "face to face" (Gen. 32:31) but rather sees an angel or angels of the Lord face to face. In *Tg. Onqelos,* the elders of Israel do not see God but perceived "the Glory of the God of Israel" (Exod. 24:10).[12] God tells Moses that he may not see "the face of My Presence" (Exod. 33:20). Thus, even though the vision of God "face to face" is actually denied, the Targum still strives to avoid the anthropomorphism in speaking of God's face and renders instead "the face of My Presence."[13] Elsewhere *Tg. Onqelos* simply substitutes "presence" for "face" (e.g., Exod. 33:14, 15). At Numbers 14:14, *Tg. Onqelos* renders the description of God as one who is known "face to face" as follows: "The inhabitants of the land have already heard that You are the Lord, whose Shekhina rests among this people, who with their own eyes have seen the Shekhina of Your Glory, O Lord." What is seen is not God but God's Shekhina or, in other Targums, the glory of the Shekhina.[14] In the *Tg. of Isaiah,* Isaiah's vision is presented not with the

---

12. *Tg. Neofiti* has "they saw the Glory of the Shekinah of the Lord," and *Tg. Pseudo-Jonathan* specifies that Nadab and Abihu of the seventy, apparently excluding Moses, "saw the glory of the God of Israel."

13. *Tg. Neofiti* 33:23 asserts that what Moses will be allowed to see is "the Dibbera of the Glory of Shekinah," but what it is not possible for Moses to see is "the face of the Glory of my Shekinah."

14. *Tg. Pseudo-Jonathan* is nearly identical at this point. *Tg. Neofiti* has "they have heard that you are he, the Glory of whose Shekinah is in the midst of this people; that appearance to appearance, you have been revealed in your Memra, O Lord, and the cloud of the Glory of your Shekinah was upon them."

directness of the biblical text — "I saw the LORD sitting upon a throne" — but again with the somewhat indirect assertion — "I saw the glory of the LORD resting upon a throne" (Isa. 6:1).

In spite, then, of the biblical assertions that various individuals "saw God," both within the OT itself and in later Jewish tradition, those assertions are qualified so as to deny that anyone actually sees God directly, or face to face. At this point, then, John's Gospel stands apart, for it portrays the Son as one who has "seen God." In its explicit denial that anyone else has ever seen God, John reflects the sorts of traditions lodged in the Targums, but evident already earlier in the OT itself, where a direct vision of God, "seeing God," is not possible for human beings.[15] It is not that God is "invisible," making sight physically impossible. Rather, God's holiness and majesty cannot be seen in their fullness by human beings. God may be seen in part, or indirectly. By contrast, John's assertions that the Son has seen God are never burdened with any qualifications. As C. K. Barrett puts it, "Jesus only has immediate knowledge of God."[16] The distinctive and immediate character of Jesus' knowledge is explained by his origins: only the one who is "from God" has seen God (6:46). He has been with God (cf. 1:1).

Jesus is distinguished not only from ancient worthies who were denied a vision of God face to face, but also from his disciples, for they also fall under the rubric initially of those who have not "seen God." Although they have seen Jesus, the Son, they do not see the Father as Jesus does. That is, their vision of the Father is of a different sort than that which the Son has, for only the Son sees the Father directly. The unique character of the Son's vision is underscored rather than undercut by a passage that might at first glance indicate that the disciples have indeed seen God. Philip requests that Jesus show them the Father. This request rests on the assumption that God can be seen, even if such a vision is not frequently granted to human beings. Philip assumes that Jesus could fulfill the request. Philip's request is not a ludicrous entreaty to see an *invisible* God but rather a request that Jesus somehow grant to them a vision of the unseen God. Jesus' response to

---

15. Herman Ridderbos (*The Gospel of John: A Theological Commentary* [Grand Rapids: Eerdmans, 1997], pp. 58-59) comments: "Although the Old Testament speaks in different ways concerning the vision of God . . . the persistent view is that for no one, not even for Moses, can God be an object of direct observation and that the human person cannot even exist in God's unveiled presence."

16. C. K. Barrett, *The Gospel According to St. John*, 2nd ed. (Philadelphia: Westminster, 1978), p. 298. See also Ridderbos, *Gospel of John*, p. 234.

Philip, "If you have seen me, you have seen the Father," means not that the Father and Jesus are identical but that the Son so fully embodies the Word, glory, and life of the Father that to see the Son is to see the Father. There need be no journeys to heaven, no practice of mystical techniques, in order to gain a vision of the Father, for the Son incarnates the Father's glory and hence makes the Father known.

The Father-Son relationship is crucial to "seeing" the Father, for it is a relationship in which the very identity of the one depends upon the relationship to the other. Inasmuch as the Father and Son cannot simply be collapsed into each other and always maintain their distinct identities, the vision that the disciples have of the Father is not identical to the vision that Jesus has. Jesus sees God; but all others see Jesus, or God as manifested in and through Jesus. Only the Son has seen the Father. In this sense, the Jews and the disciples are on equal footing. As we shall discover, however, it is the perception of the Son's relationship to and unity with the Father that allows the disciples to see the Father in the Son. Hence, their seeing will also be distinguished from that of "the Jews." Even so, the Son's vision of the Father remains unique.

Philip's request also underscores a distinction between "hearing" and "seeing" in the Gospel of John. Whereas hearing is typically a means to an end, such as faith or obedience, "seeing" can be portrayed both as a means to an end *and* as an end in itself. On the one hand, then, seeing can lead to believing (2:11); on the other hand, seeing, or at least seeing God, is an end in itself. Philip's request, "Show us the Father," suggests a request for a revelation or vision of God not in order to achieve some other end or goal but simply for its own sake: Philip asks to see God. The request echoes Moses' request of God in Exodus, "Show me your glory" (33:18). Barrett writes that Philip's request expresses the "universal longing" not only of biblical figures, but of religious persons of antiquity.[17]

Other passages in John indicate that "seeing" is presented as an end in itself. As a result of the incarnation of the Word one may *see* his glory (1:14). Jesus promises his disciples that they will "see heaven opened, and the angels of God ascending and descending upon the Son of man" (1:51). He tells Nicodemus that he must be born again to "see the Kingdom of God" (3:3). Of particular interest is the repeated framing of the

---

17. Barrett, *John*, p. 459. See Barrett's comments on 1:18; 6:46; and 14:8 for references to "seeing God" in both Greek and Jewish literature.

witness to the resurrected Lord in terms of "seeing." Jesus' words to his disciples in the Farewell Discourses are full of promises that they will see him (14:7-9, 19-22). This is a seeing that comes to an end in some way (16:10, 16-22). They will see the risen Lord, but only for a limited time, an indication that these promises of seeing refer to the resurrection appearances of Jesus that will cease after a certain period. Thus Mary Magdalene reports, "I have seen the Lord" (20:18). The Beloved Disciple looks into the empty tomb, and he "saw and believed." When the risen Jesus appears to the disciples gathered in the upper room, John writes that "they were glad when they saw the Lord" (20:20). The ten in turn report to Thomas, "We have seen the Lord" (20:24). This is the form of the resurrection witness in the Gospel of John. Luke, for example, records the familiar form, "The Lord has risen indeed!" adding, "and has appeared to Simon." The element of seeing the risen Lord still plays a role, but in John the Easter witness takes the form of an explicit confession of *seeing* the risen Lord. Thomas's statement "unless I see . . . I will not believe" is not an expression of doubt and unbelief but a request for a resurrection appearance of the Lord such as the other disciples had. Jesus' subsequent benediction — "Blessed are those who have not seen and yet believe" — blesses those who will not see the risen Jesus as his first disciples did. Jesus thus addresses the question whether there is some disadvantage for those who do not see the risen Lord, a query that arises because of the value assigned to seeing the risen One.

The high value placed on seeing the risen Lord arises above all from the connection of *presence* and *seeing*. Seeing, because it refers first of all to actual physical sight, implies or necessitates the presence of the one who is seen. Jesus' promise to his disciples that they will see him after a period of absence is fulfilled in his return to and presence with them (14:7-9, 19-22). However, it is a seeing limited in both duration and scope. Disciples other than the eyewitnesses do not see him (20:29), and the world does not see him (14:19-22). Although seeing thus refers to an experience of the risen Lord that can be described in terms of literal or physical sight, it is nevertheless not exactly comparable to "seeing" Jesus during his own lifetime. What is important is the continuity between the presence of Jesus with his own prior to and after his death and resurrection. As his glory was seen by his disciples (1:14; 2:11), so it will be seen by his disciples after his resurrection. Hence the emphasis on seeing the risen Lord stands in continuity with the emphasis on "seeing" the glory of the Word made flesh (1:14, 51;

2:11). Precisely because others cannot see the glory of Jesus in the same way as his disciples did, they must be assured of his presence with them in other ways. Jesus thus assures them that their prayers will be heard and answered, a promise of his faithfulness to his own in spite of his absence, the specter of which causes fear and anxiety. Jesus seeks to quell these fears and anxieties throughout the Farewell Discourses.

First, the Gospel seeks to assure those who have the written word rather than the Incarnate Word present among them that their faith is in no way second best or inferior to that of the eyewitnesses. The written word, by recounting the signs and words that Jesus did and said, puts one in the position of "seeing" the signs and "hearing" the words of Jesus, and so of coming to faith (20:30-31). Second, a primary function of the Spirit-Paraclete is to make real the ongoing presence of the Father and the Son. The Spirit calls the past to mind (14:26; 16:14), reveals the future and teaches the disciples (14:26; 16:13), and bears witness to Jesus (15:26-27). The written word and the Spirit are necessary precisely because the Son is now absent from the sight of his followers. Since the Son can no longer be seen in the same way, neither can God be "seen" in exactly the same way. Third, the promise of continued hearing spans, at least in part, the "distance" between Jesus and his own created by Jesus' departure from them. Their prayers will be heard, in spite of Jesus' absence.

There remains in Johannine theology the hope and promise that believers will again be granted a vision of God, and it will be the same vision of God that the Son has. In anticipating this reality, those who never saw Jesus are in precisely the same situation as those who did. Although the hope of seeing God is asserted most explicitly in 1 John, it is nevertheless implied in the Gospel as well, as in Jesus' promise that he will take the disciples to be with him, that is, in the presence of the Father (14:3). The relevant passage in 1 John 3:1-2 reads as follows: "See what love the Father has given us, that we should be called children of God; and so we are. The reason why the world does not know us is that it did not know him. Beloved, we are God's children now; it does not yet appear what we shall be, but we know that when he appears we shall be like him, for we shall see him as he is." Although it is disputed whether the author refers to God or Jesus when he speaks of knowing him, his appearing, and being like him, a strong argument can be made that the intended referent is God. The author writes of the love of the *Father;* and twice of being called children of *God,* but the Son is not mentioned in the immediate context. This verse describes the future hope of the child of God in terms of *seeing* God.

Visions of God as recorded in those OT texts (Isaiah 6, Ezekiel 1, Daniel 7), central to later apocalyptic visions of God, issue properly in worship, awe, and reverence. When the prophetic voices of the OT rebuke the people for failing to hear and see what God has done for them, the implication is that they have not responded to and obeyed God. Seeing, then, is an end in itself, but only because it implies that one is in the presence of God and so has entered finally and fully into that relationship of faith and worship begun in this life.

To some extent the promise of being in God's presence is reinterpreted as the abiding presence of the Father and Son with the disciples during their earthly existence. Yet the promise of the presence of God with the disciples does not entirely exhaust the premise of "seeing God." Rather, the promise of God's presence with the disciples for the period of their earthly life ensures the continuity between the periods of seeing the glory of God in Jesus and beholding the glory of God in his presence. This "in-between" period is, in John, a time of "not seeing" the glory of God in Jesus in the way that his disciples did. The signs of Jesus, through which his glory as the Son of the Father was revealed, are no longer manifested among his own. Nevertheless, his work and words are still made known to them, and this brings us directly to a consideration of the function of the signs, which Jesus refers to as "the works of the Father" (5:36; 9:3-4; 10:24-25, 32, 37; 14:10-12) in mediating knowledge of God.

The Work of the Father in the Work of the Son

The signs of Jesus are the works of God first and foremost because they are life-giving. Through Jesus' works, God grants life, and it is the character and work of God — and of God alone — to give life. Because through the signs Jesus confers life, Jesus' works are the works of God. Because the signs embody God's life-giving character, one should "believe the works" (10:38; 14:11), that is, see in them God's own works of healing and restoration (5:19-21, 36; 6:32; 9:3, 33; 10:25, 32, 37-38; 14:8-11; 15:24). Through the work of the Son, the Father's life-giving power becomes embodied, rather than remaining merely a cipher or idea, and thus God's identity as Father is concretely realized through the work of the Son. To put it most sharply, "I am working, and my Father is working" are not two parallel statements, but rather one and the same statement.[18]

The paired accounts of the healing of the official's son (4:46-54) and the healing of the man at the pool of Bethesda underscore the life-giving character of the signs. We note, first, that each story illustrates the truth of the statement, "The hour is coming, and now is, when the dead will hear the voice of the Son of God, and those who hear will live" (5:25). Jesus gives life when death threatens. His promise, "Go; your son will live" (4:50, 53; cf. 51), becomes a word of life that is concretely effected in the healing that it accomplishes. Although death does not threaten the invalid at the pool, Jesus restores him to fullness of physical life in granting him health and strength.[19] Second, the healing of the man at the pool takes place on the Sabbath. Together these two factors — the kind of work Jesus does and the day on which he does it — lay the basis for the discourse that follows (5:17-47). Here Jesus argues the point that he works even as his Father works. With this statement Jesus defends his Sabbath healing, but he also characterizes the kind of work that he does, for he performs the kind of work reserved for God alone: he gives life (5:21, 26), as has been twice demonstrated.[20] The discourse of chapter 5 also speaks of Jesus' power to judge, which is simply another way of speaking of his power to grant eternal life (5:22, 27-29, 30), as the following statement makes clear: "he who hears my word and believes him who sent me has eternal life; he does not come into judgment, but has passed from death to life" (5:24).

Jesus argues that he works even as God works. He does the kind of work reserved for God: he gives life. Furthermore, he performs that work on a day reserved for God alone to work: the Sabbath day. These assertions probably allude to the argument — found, for example, in Philo and rabbinic writings — that although God ceased creative work on the Sabbath, God did not cease from work that sustained the creation.[21] Even on the

18. David A. Fennema, "Jesus and God According to John: An Analysis of the Fourth Gospel's Father/Son Christology," Ph.D. diss., Duke University, 1979, p. 142.

19. See the discussion in C. F. D. Moule, "The Meaning of 'Life' in the Gospels and Epistles of St. John: A Study in the Story of Lazarus, John 11:1-44," *Theology* 78 (1975): 122.

20. There is a stimulating discussion of these passages and their parallels in Philo in Jerome Neyrey, *An Ideology of Revolt: John's Christology in Social-Science Perspective* (Philadelphia: Fortress, 1988), pp. 25-29.

21. See the discussion and references in Dodd, *Interpretation*, pp. 320-23; Barrett, *John*, p. 256.

Sabbath, God gives life to the world. It is the character and prerogative of God alone to give life, but Jesus exercises those powers as he bestows life on the day reserved for God to work rather than to rest. In the assertion, "My Father is working, and I am working still," Jesus claims for himself divine prerogatives and functions, thereby implying his identification and equality with God. The equality and unity of the Son with the Father are of course precisely the point of John 5, and it is later explained in the theological statement, "Even as the Father has life in himself, so he has granted it to the Son to have life in himself."

In the discourse of chapter 5, Jesus also speaks of his power to judge. This is simply the negative corollary of his power to grant life (5:22, 27-29, 30), as the following statement makes clear: "he who hears my word and believes him who sent me has eternal life; he does not come into judgment, but has passed from death to life." Of particular relevance here is Jewish speculation on the names of God, especially as that speculation is connected with the "two powers" or "two measures" of God.[22] These two powers are judgment and mercy, and each is understood to be expressed by one of the Hebrew words for God. The rabbis understood *elohim* to denote the judgment of God, and YHWH to point to God's mercy. Philo, however, took *theos (elohim)* to signify mercy and the Tetragrammaton (read as *adonai*, and rendered in the LXX as *kyrios*, Lord) to connote judgment. Yet the point remains that the totality of God's work was understood to be expressed by these two "measures" of his providence, that of judgment and that of mercy or goodness. Thus when the Gospel of John asserts that Jesus brings both life and judgment, it is calling on the current Jewish view that God's work is merciful and just.

Thus two stories where someone has "heard Jesus' word" and been granted life are used to introduce the claim that Jesus grants eternal life.[23]

---

22. On the "two powers" of God, see the discussions in George Foot Moore, *Judaism in the First Centuries of the Christian Era*, 3 vols. (Cambridge, Mass.: Harvard University Press, 1927-30), 1:386-400; A. Marmorstein, "Philo and the Names of God," *JQR* 22 (1931-32): 295-306; Dodd, *Interpretation*, pp. 320-23; N. A. Dahl and Alan F. Segal, "Philo and the Rabbis on the Names of God," *JSJ* 9 (1978): 1-28; Alan F. Segal, *Two Powers in Heaven: Early Rabbinic Reports about Christianity and Gnosticism* (Leiden: Brill, 1977); Ephraim Urbach, *The Sages: Their Concepts and Beliefs*, ET (Cambridge, Mass.: Harvard University Press, 1987), pp. 448-61.

23. On the significance of "hearing Jesus' word," see Craig R. Koester, "Hearing, Seeing, and Believing in the Gospel of John," *Bib* 70 (1989): 327-48. Koester argues that authentic

However, what is the relationship between the gift of physical life and the granting of eternal life? A common interpretation of the Johannine signs is that they point to something that is symbolized by them but is not actually embodied in them. The "real meaning" of the signs lies in their "spiritual" significance. So, the feeding of the 5,000 points primarily to the fact that God feeds people spiritually with the bread of life. This "spiritualization" of the miracles reads them in precisely the opposite way than that intended by John. John intends the miracles to signify the *presence of God,* but when they are read as pointing to realities separable from and not actually embodied in the signs, they point not to the *presence of God* but to the *absence of God.*

For John the signs are the works of God and embody God's presence because God is the creator of all that is and, as the giver of all life, continues to sustain the world. The Gospel asserts that the world was created by God through the Logos (1:3, 10) and that there is "life in him" (1:4). The Word is the agent or instrument of bringing the world to life. Subsequently, Jesus' healing of the official's son and of the man at the pool confers physical life. Thus the Word is the agent of bringing life to the world. The Son works for the life of the world even on the Sabbath, as does his Father. The Son also has the authority to pass judgment and raise people in the resurrection to eternal life. From beginning to end, his work is characterized as bestowing life from God. John portrays the Word as both the agent of creation and, as incarnate in Jesus, the mediator of life.[24]

The signs, then, are not simply illustrations or figures of another kind of life-giving power Jesus has; the power to give life is singular and all-encompassing. Jesus' deeds are ultimately wrought by the one God (5:19, 21, 26; 10:38; 14:11) who is the source of all life. The signs of Jesus are the visible manifestation and embodiment of the life-giving work of God.[25]

---

faith in the Gospel of John is based on hearing, but never on seeing; signs confirm faith that is engendered through hearing (p. 332). The emphasis on Jesus' word is not unlike that found in Bultmann, *Theology of the New Testament,* 1:59-69. Koester's interpretation, rightly, does not play off Jesus' word against the signs. Yet one wonders whether it does not dismiss too quickly (1) the problem of those who will not see (20:30-31) and (2) the summary statements in 12:37-38 and 20:30-31, which draw a direct link between signs and believing. John 12:37-38 especially asserts the guilt of those who see but do not believe. This is hard to understand unless the signs were to serve as the occasion for faith, and not merely to confirm faith they had received another way.

24. Moule, "Meaning of 'Life,'" p. 122.

25. Gerd Theissen (*The Miracle Stories of the Early Christian Tradition,* ed. John Riches,

Those who perceive the works of Jesus as the works of God do so because they see them as life-giving and therefore discern the unity of the work of the Father and Son. Hence, it is not the power to work miracles but the power to give life that is at issue in discerning the work of God in the signs of Jesus. Inasmuch as the power to bestow life is a divine prerogative, Jesus' signs manifest his glory. Glory refers to the visible manifestation of the divine presence. The repeated affirmations that Jesus manifests glory, or will be glorified by God, or has glory from the Father, echo OT passages in which individuals are permitted to see the glory of God even when they cannot see God face to face.

"He Manifested His Glory"

The OT traditions of the manifestation of God's glory, and especially traditions in Exodus, are particularly promising for interpreting the Gospel's references to the manifestation of God in the person of Jesus.[26] Thus when Moses ascended Sinai, the text reads, "The glory of the LORD settled on Mount Sinai, and the cloud covered it six days; and on the seventh day he called to Moses out of the midst of the cloud. Now the appearance of the glory of the LORD was like a devouring fire on the top of the mountain in the sight of the people of Israel" (Exod. 24:16-17). Here "glory" refers to a visible demonstration or manifestation of God's presence. Later in Exodus, Moses can request of God, "Show me thy glory," again referring to "glory" as that which can be shown or seen. That "glory" refers explicitly to the manifest presence of God is evident in the answer "you cannot see my face, for no one shall see me and live" (Exod. 33:18-23). God's glory passes by and can be glimpsed but fleetingly (33:23); it is only the "appearance of the glory of the LORD," which is "like devouring fire," that is seen by the people.[27]

---

trans. Francis McDonagh [Edinburgh: T. & T. Clark, 1983]. pp. 226-27) writes, "There is no relativisation of miracles in John; on the contrary, they are a continuation of God's work of creation (5.17), and indeed surpass it (5.20). They are unique. No one else can perform them (15.24; 3.2)."

26. For a full discussion see Carey C. Newman, *Paul's Glory-Christology: Tradition and Rhetoric*, NovTSup 69 (Leiden: Brill, 1992); Alan F. Segal, *Paul the Convert: The Apostolate and Apostasy of Saul the Pharisee* (New Haven: Yale University Press, 1990), pp. 41-52.

27. In contrast, Paul writes that "we all, with unveiled face, [are] beholding the glory of the Lord. . . . For it is the God who said, 'Let light shine out of darkness,' who has shone in

John creatively adapts such passages to identify Jesus with the manifestation of God's glory. Early on in the Gospel, the incarnation of the Word is explicated in these terms: "And the Word became flesh and dwelt among us, full of grace and truth; we have beheld his glory, glory as of the only Son from the Father" (RSV). Furthermore, the glory to be beheld in Jesus stands in contrast with the law received through Moses: "For the law was given through Moses, but grace and truth came through Jesus Christ" (1:17). Then, following Jesus' first "sign," the narrator comments, "This, the first of his signs, Jesus did at Cana in Galilee, and manifested his glory; and his disciples believed in him" (2:11). Martha is promised that she will see the glory of God in the raising of her brother, Lazarus (11:40). Isaiah the prophet had seen the glory of Jesus (12:41). This was a glory that the Son possessed with the Father before the creation of the world (17:5, 22, 24). Moreover, the Gospel speaks frequently of Jesus' being glorified by God, a glorification that apparently takes place during his lifetime and yet will be consummated in the events of the cross, resurrection, and ascension. In short, Jesus manifests the glory of God, "the heavenly splendour which is the appearance of God, the manifestation of God's being."[28]

Not only are the verbal links suggestive of ties to the traditions of Exodus, but recent studies of these visions of God's glory have pointed out that other OT passages, and particularly Ezekiel 1:27-28, identify God's *kabod*, God's glory, with God's sometimes human appearance in the visions.[29] John does not directly equate Jesus with God's glory but speaks rather of Jesus, the incarnate Word, as embodying or revealing God's glory. Yet it is in Jesus that God's glory takes on human form, visible and tangible.

This personification of God's glory coexisted with speculation upon other figures and passages in the OT. Alan Segal sums up the situation in this fashion:

A human figure on the divine throne is described in Ezekiel 1, Daniel 7, and Exodus 24, among other places, and was blended into a consistent picture of a principal mediator figure who, like the angel of the Lord in

our hearts to give the light of the knowledge of the glory of God in the face of Christ" (2 Cor. 3:18; 4:6). It is hard to miss Paul's point here: whereas Moses and the children of Israel saw only glimpses of God's glory as it passed by, one may see the glory of God in Jesus Christ, face to face.

28. Bauckham, *God Crucified*, p. 66.
29. Segal, *Paul the Convert*, p. 11; Newman, *Paul's Glory-Christology*.

Exodus 23, embodied, personified, or carried the name of God, YHWH, the tetragrammaton. This figure, elaborated on by Jewish tradition, would become a central metaphor for Christ in Christianity.[30]

Most of these elements can be found, in some form, in Johannine Christology: Jesus is identified early on as the Son of Man (1:51; cf. Daniel 7); he bears the name of God (e.g., John 17:6, 11, 12, 26); he is God's unique mediator or agent or even "interpreting" angel (cf. 1:18); and he is a king whose kingdom is "not of this world." If then, Jesus embodies God's glory, it would be appropriate to refer to the manifestation or presence of *God* in him. On this reading, "glory" does not refer to some thing or property that God has but is rather a manifestation of the presence of God.[31] D. Moody Smith puts it this way, "[God's glory] is God's reality, his real presence, as it is manifest to humankind."[32] When God is present, it is the glory of God that is seen. Hence, Jesus' question to Martha at the raising of Lazarus, "Did I not tell you that if you believed, you would see the glory of God?" (11:40), signals that one ought to discern in Jesus' raising of Lazarus the work and presence of God. One sees God's glory, but one sees it in Jesus' sign. The glory of God is thus reflected in the life and work of Jesus. Therefore, seeing the glory of God implies indirect rather than direct observation of God's radiance or splendor, inasmuch as God's glory is seen in the person and work of Jesus.

Because God's glory is thus embodied in Jesus, it becomes Jesus' own glory but, even so, always remains the "glory as of the only Son of the Father." When Jesus manifests "his glory," it is always the glory that the Father has granted to him, even as the Father grants him life. The emphasis falls not on some attribute that Jesus has as "divine," or that elevates him to the status of divinity, but rather on the unity of Father and Son so that the Father's glory is embodied and visible in the incarnate Son. The assumption of and emphasis on the *unity* of the Father and Son and the glory as the *visible* manifestation of God lead John to reread certain passages in the OT that speak of the manifestation of God's glory; most notably Isaiah's vision of God in the temple, which John interprets as a vision of the glory of the preincarnate Son or the Word (12:41). As Herman Ridderbos puts it, "The

30. Segal, *Paul the Convert*, p. 41.
31. Newman (*Paul's Glory-Christology*, p. 137) defines the biblical sense of glory as "revealed, visual, divine presence."
32. Smith, *The Theology of John*, p. 122.

Evangelist does not mean that Isaiah already foresaw Jesus' (later) glory, but that the glory of God as the prophet foresaw it in his vision was no other than that which the Son of God had with the Father before the world was and that was to be manifested before the eyes of all in the incarnation of the Word (17:4; 1:14, 18)."[33] The Isaiah passages stress the prophet's *vision* of God — "I saw the Lord" (6:1); "my eyes have seen the king" (6:5) — as a vision of God's glory (6:3). Not unexpectedly, the *Targum of Isaiah* speaks of the vision of God as a vision of the *glory* of God. Thus, at 6:1, *Tg. Isa.* reads, "I saw the glory of the Lord."[34] John asserts that Isaiah saw "the glory of the Lord," namely, Christ. In light of the emphasis on seeing the glory of the Lord, John's emphasis in quoting the passage regarding Isaiah's commission to preach judgment to his people falls on blinding their eyes, rather than on hardening their ears. The obduracy of which Jesus' contemporaries are guilty in John is a failure to perceive the glory of God in and as the incarnate Word.[35]

The foregoing discussion leads briefly to a consideration of the various categories of "agents" that have been understood to give definition to Johannine Christology. Various designations for Jesus, including *prophet* (4:19, 44; 6:14; 7:40, 52); *king* (1:49; 6:15; 12:13, 15; 18:33, 37, 39; 19:3, 12, 14, 15, 19, 21); *Son of Man* (1:51; 3:13, 14; 5:27; 6:27, 53, 62; 8:28; 9:35; 12:23, 34; 13:31); *Messiah* (1:20, 25, 41; 3:28; 4:25, 29; 7:26-27, 31, 41; 9:22; 10:24; 11:27; 12:34; 20:31) and *Word* (1:1, 14), all fall within the broad category of "agent of God." These mediating figures have all been taken as essential for John's presentation of the significance of Jesus and his relationship to God. There is neither space nor need to offer here an exhaustive or fresh survey of all agency figures and the discussion pertaining to them as it relates to the Gospel of John. Rather, I wish simply to underscore once more the point that the agency figures that prove most illuminating in interpreting the Gospel's Christology, particularly with respect to how God is made known, are those figures that unite agent (Jesus) and sender (God) most closely. The more a term or figure presses towards the unity of the

33. Ridderbos, *Gospel of John*, p. 445.
34. At 6:5, the Targum has "My eyes have seen the glory of the Shekinah of the eternal King, the Lord of hosts."
35. For a discussion of this passage, see also Craig A. Evans, "Obduracy and the Lord's Servant: Some Observations on the Use of the Old Testament in the Fourth Gospel," in *Early Jewish and Christian Exegesis: Studies in Memory of William Hugh Brownlee*, ed. Craig A. Evans and William F. Stinespring (Atlanta: Scholars Press, 1987), pp. 221-36.

Son with the Father, and the more it allows for the exercise of divine functions, the more it elucidates how John understands knowledge of God to be available or appropriated through Jesus.

So, for example, while the oft-discussed *shaliach* figure does much to explain the character of Jesus' "agency," in the end it does not always explain enough. Jesus is hailed as a prophet, a title that is ultimately inadequate for him.[36] For although "prophet" connotes divine choice and commissioning, it does not point to heavenly origins as does the Johannine "Son of Man." The Son of Man executes judgment and bestows life at the last day, and yet the Son of Man is not the agent of creation, as is the wisdom or word of God. In order, therefore, to account for what is left unexplained, various figures or entities, such as Wisdom and Word, which permit a different sort of unity between God and Jesus, prove essential.

Put differently, the portrait of Jesus is sketched in the Gospel of John in keeping with the dual emphasis on hearing and seeing noted earlier, and in keeping with the Gospel's particular emphasis on the significance of seeing and the connection between seeing and presence. Jesus is depicted as an agent of God who hears and carries out God's will. Categories such as prophet and agent *(shaliach)* present themselves naturally for discussion under this rubric.[37] For that matter, so does the portrayal of Jesus as the Son, for an obedient Son hears and obeys his Father. However, as I have argued, John also lays great emphasis on *seeing*, on seeing the work of the Father in the work of Jesus, on seeing the Father's glory, and even on seeing the Father himself in the Son. Here categories such as prophet and *shaliach* fall short of capturing the nature of Jesus' role in making God known, and categories such as glory, Word, and Wisdom figure more prominently. We

36. Not all the titles assigned to Jesus in the Gospel are equally and ultimately adequate to express Jesus' identity and being. On this point, see Marinus de Jonge, "Jewish Expectations about 'Messiah' in the Fourth Gospel," in his *Jesus. Stranger from Heaven and Son of God: Jesus Christ and the Christians in Johannine Perspective*, SBLMS 11 (Missoula, Mont.: Scholars Press, 1977), p. 83; Ashton, *Understanding the Fourth Gospel*, pp. 238-79; Craig R. Koester, *Symbolism in the Fourth Gospel: Meaning, Mystery, Community* (Minneapolis: Fortress, 1995), pp. 39-45. On the inadequacy of using titles for delineating NT Christology as a whole, see the critical remarks of Leander E. Keck, "Toward the Renewal of New Testament Christology," *NTS* 32 (1986): 362-77.

37. "Agent" will be used as a broad and open-ended designation to refer to any figure who represents another, who is commissioned, authorized, or sent by another, or who carries on the work of another in their absence. For the more technical usage familiar from Jewish sources, I shall use *shaliach*.

turn, then, to a brief discussion of some of the agent figures that have been deemed most significant in shaping Johannine Christology.

The *Shaliach* and Johannine Christology

Various texts in rabbinic sources — none, unfortunately, contemporaneous with the Gospel of John — tell us that "a man's *shaliach* is like the one who sent him."[38] Because the *shaliach* represents "the one who sent him" not just informally but in a legally binding relationship, he is to be received and respected as the one who sent him. So striking are the parallels between Johannine Christology and halakic principles of agency that A. E. Harvey has concluded that "much of the language used of Jesus in the Fourth Gospel [is] drawn from juridical practice." According to Harvey, the Jewish conception of "agency" explains even the designation "Son of God," when it is recognized that a principal's son could be considered his supreme and natural agent.[39] The fourth evangelist's use of the *shaliach* figure as a type for explaining the relationship of Jesus to the Father would go a long way towards explaining the following features of Johannine Christology: the unity of the work of the Father and Son (5:17-18; 10:29-30); the obedience, and even "subordination," of the agent to the sender, or of the Son to the Father; the call to honor the Son as one would the Father (5:23); and the language of sending (6:29, 38, 44, 57). The presence of these themes serves to overcome objections to giving the *shaliach* figure too prominent a role in Johannine Christology in light of the absence of any sort of translation or transliteration of *shaliach* itself. John the Baptist is "one who is sent" (1:6; 3:28), and Jesus frequently refers to God either as

---

38. A common saying in the rabbis was "the one who is sent like the one who sent him" (*m. Ber.* 5:5; *b. B. Meṣ'ia* 96a; *b. Ḥag.* 10b; *b. Menaḥ.* 93b; *b. Naz.* 12b; *b. Qidd.* 42b; 43a; *Mek. Exod.* on Exod. 12:3, 6).

39. A. E. Harvey, "Christ as Agent," in *The Glory of Christ in the New Testament: Studies in Christology,* ed. L. D. Hurst and N. T. Wright (Oxford: Clarendon, 1987), p. 241. For discussion of non-Jewish Graeco-Roman practices of agency, see Margaret M. Mitchell, "New Testament Envoys in the Context of Greco-Roman Diplomatic and Epistolary Conventions: The Example of Timothy and Titus," *JBL* 111 (1992): 641-62; and for a reply to her analysis of the Gospel of John, see Peder Borgen, "The Gospel of John and Hellenism," in *Exploring the Gospel of John: In Honor of D. Moody Smith,* ed. R. Alan Culpepper and C. Clifton Black (Louisville: Westminster/John Knox, 1996), pp. 101-2, 120 nn. 21, 22.

"the One who sent me" or "the Father who sent me." Yet no term for Jesus has solidified into a designation for him as "the One who is sent."

Harvey's point that *shaliach* imagery accounts for "much of the language" in John is telling. While the category of agency helps to account for much of the specific idiom of the Gospel's Christology, it does not explain fully such themes as the heavenly descent and ascent of the Son of Man, the use of "Logos," Jesus' functions of teaching and illumination, or the Gospel's emphasis on *seeing* the Father in the Son. Furthermore, the limited duration of the commission of the *shaliach* is a chief deficiency of its application to Jesus, for upon completion of a specific task, the *shaliach* does not continue to function as the representative or agent of the one who had sent him on the assigned mission. The relationship is not permanent. This would not in and of itself be an insuperable objection to viewing the *shaliach* figure as illuminating and helpful in explaining features of the relationship of Jesus and God, but it does suggest the limited usefulness and final inadequacy of the term, especially in light of assertions such as those found in 1:1 and 1:18 regarding the Word who was with God and the Son who is "ever at the Father's side." Indeed, precisely because of the limited usefulness of *shaliach*, one must turn to other categories and figures to help illumine the presentation of Jesus in the Fourth Gospel.

In trying to establish the *shaliach* as the primary agent figure behind John's Christology, Harvey is arguing against the views of Peder Borgen and others that a combination of halakic and mystical thought, such as one finds in the early stages of *merkabah* mysticism, provides the necessary and missing link to explain Johannine Christology. Borgen contends that the *shaliach* figure does not explain "the fact that Jesus according to John is not just a human and earthly agent but a divine and heavenly agent" who has come down among human beings.[40] Similarly, J.-A. Bühner proposed that John's distinctive Christology is to be located in the fusion of prophet and angel or, more specifically, the apocalyptic-prophetic seer and the Son of Man understood as a divine angelic being.[41]

40. Peder Borgen, "God's Agent in the Fourth Gospel," reprinted in *The Interpretation of John*, ed. John Ashton (Philadelphia: Fortress; London: SPCK, 1986), p. 72.

41. J.-A. Bühner, *Der Gesandte und sein Weg im 4. Evangelium*, WUNT 2/2. Reihe (Tübingen: Mohr-Siebeck, 1977). More recently John Ashton has suggested that John's Christology is "an angel christology *tout court*" *Studying John: Approaches to the Fourth Gospel* [Oxford: Clarendon, 1994], p. 75).

In other words, both Borgen and Bühner deem it imperative to appeal to some heavenly figure to clarify the total shape of John's "agency" Christology. James D. G. Dunn agrees with the assessment that the *shaliach* figure, on its own, cannot provide an adequate hold on the distinctive and central features of Johannine Christology, such as preexistence and the intimate union between Father and Son. Indeed, these are precisely the points that John desires to underscore: "The Fourth Evangelist wants to persuade his readers of a *heavenly origin* for Jesus the Messiah which goes back to the beginning of time, and of a relationship between Father and Son which is more than simply identity of will or function."[42] The *shaliach* figure serves poorly to account for the heavenly origins assumed in the assertions of the prologue regarding the preexistence and incarnation of the Word. Therefore, the figure of Wisdom and the imagery and speculation associated with it provide a more satisfactory explanatory model. By depicting Jesus as the incarnation of divine Wisdom, the evangelist drew upon an agent figure to whom he could ascribe heavenly origin and cosmic preexistence, unity with God, and embodiment of divine presence. Wisdom serves better to portray "a divine envoy who does not merely bring information but who mediates a fully authentic and genuine encounter with the God who 'sent' him, and nothing less than that."[43]

It is doubtful whether the role of the *shaliach* could be thought to make the absent sender present through his own person. The *shaliach* is indeed fully authorized to carry out transactions on behalf of the sender and so serves as the legitimate representative of the sender. Yet the language of "seeing" Jesus and the Father evokes OT language of theophany and of visions of God, such as one finds in accounts of the visions of Mo-

---

42. James D. G. Dunn, "Let John Be John: A Gospel for Its Time," in *Das Evangelium und die Evangelien*, ed. Peter Stuhlmacher, WUNT 28 (Tübingen: Mohr, 1983), p. 330. See also Mark Appold (*The Oneness Motif in the Fourth Gospel: Motif Analysis and Exegetical Probe into the Theology of John*, WUNT 2/1 [Tübingen: Mohr, 1976], pp. 20-22, 282-83), who argues that the motif of "sending" and the "sent one" cannot be construed as the central theme of the Gospel's Christology precisely because the Jewish *shaliach* assumes a secondary and deputy-like role that the Johannine Jesus, one with the Father in love, does not take on.

43. Paul Meyer, "'The Father': The Presentation of God in the Fourth Gospel," in *Exploring the Gospel of John: In Honor of D. Moody Smith*, ed. R. Alan Culpepper and C. Clifton Black (Louisville: Westminster/John Knox, 1996), p. 261. See here also Fennema, "Jesus and God," who comments that heavenly agents, such as wisdom, who find their origins in heaven with God, can represent God with a directness and perfection denied the prophets (pp. 29, 33, 84).

ses and Isaiah. "Seeing" is the language of revelation and hence of encounter with the divine, and the *shaliach* figure cannot adequately account for the emphasis on seeing the Father in the Son. According to the Gospel of John, what the Son *hears* from the Father he in turn makes known to others, and that picture fits well with the *shaliach* as a commissioned agent. It is less clear how Jesus reports what he has *seen*, or that the emphasis on seeing can be derived from the application or adaptation of the *shaliach* figure. A typical feature of apocalyptic journeys to heaven is the recounting of at least some aspect of what was beheld. Even when there is reticence to describe God, nevertheless details of the heavenly entourage or heavenly scenery can be recounted. Yet in John Jesus never gives a report of what he has seen. Instead, what he has "seen" becomes embodied in his works, which in turn become "signs" to those who see them.

Borgen, Dunn, and others have turned to the figure of Wisdom to account for certain features of Johannine Christology not fully captured in the application of the *shaliach* to Jesus. Wisdom has a divine origin, an origin from within the very being of God, is an agent of God in creation, and also has the function of bringing illumination (light) that leads to life. The cognitive or pedagogical aspect of Wisdom thus serves to account not only for the Gospel's emphasis on Jesus' teaching but also for the fact that Jesus teaches the very words of God. Wisdom is heard and understood. Nevertheless the imagery of illumination borrows from the visual realm by stressing the light that comes through Wisdom, the illumination that enables genuine seeing. It is the combination of the figures of the *shaliach*, *Wisdom*, and the Father/Son relationship, which coalesce so as to provide a lens through which to view the figure of Jesus in John.[44]

Agent figures of first-century Judaism will not account completely for the origins or shape of Johannine Christology, but it is very clear that the Fourth Gospel presents an argument for a certain understanding of Jesus through comparison and contrast to specific figures, institutions, or entities important in first-century Judaism, such as Moses, the temple, and the law. It will not be surprising, then, to find that John has used figures such as the *shaliach* or Wisdom and applied them to Jesus in selective and creative ways. Yet if Wisdom speculation plays an important role in John in delineating the significance of the Word made flesh, then how does the de-

---

44. Ashton (*Understanding the Fourth Gospel*, p. 539) rightly comments that wisdom, mission (language of sending), and agency are linked in John.

piction of Jesus in those categories address the related problems of the manifestation and knowledge of God?

Wisdom Speculation and the Gospel of John

While the influence of wisdom speculation on the Gospel's prologue has long been acknowledged, the degree to which such speculation has colored other facets or narratives of the Gospel remains open to discussion.[45] In a recent detailed discussion of wisdom and the Gospel of John, Martin Scott suggests that to speak of "wisdom influence" on the Gospel comes up short, for "John presents a thoroughgoing sophia christology."[46] He then argues that nearly every important feature of the Gospel has significant parallels in wisdom speculation. By contrast, D. A. Carson writes in reference to John 6: "The so-called sapiential interpretation of John 6 is not so much wrong as peripheral."[47] Although Carson allows possible allusions to Proverbs 8:5 and 9:5, he suggests that the more likely intertextual links are to be found with Isaiah 55, which has both an invitation to all who are thirsty to come eat and drink (vv. 1-2) and an affirmation of the efficacy of God's word (vv. 10-11) — and both of these, moreover, in the context of eschatological salvation and the new covenant.[48]

Yet one does not need to choose between the influence on the Gospel of John of "wisdom" and "word" (or Torah) theologies, for these are al-

45. For discussion of wisdom in the Gospel of John, see J. Rendel Harris, *The Origin of the Prologue to St. John's Gospel* (Cambridge: Cambridge University Press, 1917); Raymond E. Brown, *The Gospel according to John*, 2 vols., Anchor Bible (Garden City, N.Y.: Doubleday, 1966, 1970), passim; James D. G. Dunn, "Let John Be John"; Dunn, *Christology in the Making: An Inquiry into the Origins of the Doctrine of the Incarnation*, 2d ed. (London: SCM, 1989 [1980]), pp. 163-212; Martin A. Scott, *Sophia and the Johannine Jesus*, JSNTSup 71 (Sheffield: JSOT Press, 1992); Craig A. Evans, *Word and Glory: On the Exegetical and Theological Background of John's Prologue*, JSNTSup 89 (Sheffield: JSOT Press, 1993); Ben Witherington, *Jesus the Sage: The Pilgrimage of Wisdom* (Minneapolis: Fortress, 1994); and Borgen, "The Gospel of John and Hellenism," pp. 107-9.

46. Scott, *Sophia*, p. 29.

47. D. A. Carson, *The Gospel According to John* (Grand Rapids: Eerdmans; Leicester: InterVarsity, 1991), p. 289.

48. That Isaiah 55 formed the background for John's bread of life discourse was earlier suggested by Brown, *John*, 1:521, who nevertheless also acknowledged the influence of wisdom terminology and thought on the chapter.

ready inextricably joined in Jewish thought prior to John's day.[49] The beginning of speculation on personified wisdom can be found in Proverbs 1–9. In this context one finds multiple admonitions to hear and learn from wisdom, and wisdom invites people to eat her bread (9:5), a metaphor for learning to "walk in the way of insight." In the wisdom tradition, instruction and learning are dominant themes, making an eventual identification of law with wisdom an easy and natural step. So it is that in Sirach 24 God commands wisdom to dwell in Israel (vv. 8, 12) and designates this wisdom as "the law which Moses commanded us" (v. 23; cf. 15:1, "whoever holds to the law will obtain wisdom"). Similarly, in Baruch 4:1 wisdom is called "the book of the commandments of God, and the law that endures forever." The Wisdom of Solomon equates God's word and God's wisdom (Wis. 18:15). Philo assumed this equation in speculating about the Logos, a concept in which he is arguably far more interested than in wisdom.[50]

John's preference for the term *logos* (word) rather than *sophia* (wisdom) raises the question whether it is proper to speak of a Johannine "Wisdom Christology" at all. While it is true that John uses *logos*, not *sophia*, the term *logos* does not appear outside the prologue (1:1, 14), and both in the prologue and the rest of the Gospel the imagery and language used to portray Jesus have at least as many affinities with the biblical wisdom tradition as with speculation about the Word. A typical suggestion for John's preference for *logos* to *sophia* is that *logos*, like Jesus, is male. Yet Paul had no hesitation in calling Jesus "the wisdom of God" (1 Cor. 1:24). A more likely explanation is to be found in some combination of the following factors: First, wisdom and word had already coalesced and overlapped in the tradition, making their interchange natural. Second, John's interest is particularly in the relationship of Jesus and Torah, which, however much it embodies wisdom, is nevertheless better described by "word."

49. See especially the parallels adduced by Eldon Jay Epp, "Wisdom, Torah, Word: The Johannine Prologue and the Purpose of the Fourth Gospel," in *Current Issues in Biblical and Patristic Interpretation*, ed. G. F. Hawthorne (Grand Rapids: Eerdmans, 1975), pp. 128-46; Severino Pancaro, *The Law in the Fourth Gospel: The Torah and the Gospel, Moses and Jesus, Judaism and Christianity according to John*, NovTSup 42 (Leiden: Brill, 1975), pp. 455-58.

50. A striking passage in *Fug.* 18 urges those who are able to press forward "to the highest word of God, which is the fountain of wisdom, in order that by drinking of that stream he may find everlasting life instead of death."

It is telling that in two instances where Jesus is contrasted with the law or argues from the Scriptures (chs. 1 and 6), "wisdom" imagery comes into play, suggesting that John always has in the mind wisdom as embodied in the law. As Torah became even more dominant in the self-definition of the Jewish people, particularly in conflict with Christians, it became more important to identify Jesus as "Word." Finally, John may be located historically along a trajectory in which *logos* becomes a more important concept in interpreting the faith. Philo, for example, identifies wisdom with word, but greatly prefers the concept *logos* when speculating about the manner of God's manifestation to the world. *Logos* would certainly allow a better point of contact with the Hellenistic world.

Of further interest for the Gospel of John is the fact that the law was sometimes symbolized by manna.[51] Bread itself was already a standing symbol for the nourishment provided by the law, and therefore the bread sent from heaven, the manna, served aptly as a symbol for the law. It is then but a short step to conceiving of wisdom, sometimes equated with Torah or viewed as embodied in it, as providing nourishment or inviting people to her feast (Deut. 8:3; Isa. 55:10-11; Sir. 15:3; Wis. 16:20, 26; *Gen. Rab.* 70:5 [on Gen. 28:20], which quotes Prov. 9:5). The Midrash on Exodus 16:4 combines God's promise of the "bread from heaven" with the invitation of wisdom to "Come, eat of my bread," found in Proverbs 9:5, thus at least insinuating the identification of manna and wisdom. In more than one place, Philo allegorizes the manna as the divine gift of wisdom.[52] The Gos-

51. *Mek. Exod.* on Exod. 13:17; see especially Bruce J. Malina, *The Palestinian Manna Tradition: The Manna Tradition in the Palestinian Targums and Its Relationship to the New Testament Writings* (Leiden: Brill, 1968).

52. In commenting on Exod. 16:4, Philo (*Mut.* 258-260), simply replaces the word for manna with the word for wisdom *(sophia)*, yielding the following comment: "Can you find any more trustworthy than Moses, who says that while other men receive their food from earth, the nation of vision alone has it from heaven? The earthly food is produced with the co-operation of husbandmen, but the heavenly is sent like the snow by God the solely self-acting, with none to share his work. And indeed it says, 'Behold I rain upon you bread from heaven' (Ex. xvi.4). Of what food can he rightly say that it is rained from heaven, save of heavenly wisdom which is sent from above on souls which yearn for virtue by Him who sheds the gift of prudence in rich abundance, whose grace waters the universe, and chiefly so in the holy seventh (year) which he calls the Sabbath?" See the discussion of Peder Borgen, *Bread from Heaven: An Exegetical Study in the Concept of Manna in the Gospel of John and the Writings of Philo,* NovTSup 10 (Leiden: Brill, 1965), pp. 111-12. See also *Her.* 191, where Philo, again commenting on the distribution of manna in Exodus 16, notes:

pel of John reflects the traditions that identify Torah and wisdom not only with bread, but also with the heavenly manna. These traditions are then put to use to argue for the surpassing wisdom and revelation to be embodied in the true bread of life, which came not through the mediation of Moses, but directly from God.[53]

The invitations to "eat" and "drink" (6:5, 31, 50, 52, 53, 54, 55, 56; cf. 7:37-38) echo those of wisdom in Proverbs 9:5 ("Come, eat of my bread and drink of the wine I have mixed") and Sirach 24:19 ("Come to me, you who desire me, and eat your fill of my fruits. . . . Those who eat of me will hunger for more, and those who drink of me will thirst for more"). These invitations to eat and drink are metaphorical ways of speaking of hearing, learning, and obeying. Just as eating and drinking sustain life, so too hearing, learning, and obeying lead one on the paths of life (Prov. 8:35; Wis. 8:13). One could well imagine a contrast between the words of Moses and the words of Jesus, or the teaching of the law and the teaching of Jesus, but Jesus is not pictured so much as the one who offers words of wisdom as the one who embodies wisdom, who is wisdom embodied. Hence the invitations to eat and drink are glossed by the call to believe in the one sent from heaven (6:36, 38). Eating of the bread of life that has come down from heaven leads to eternal life (6:27, 33, 35, 39-40, 44, 47-48, 50-51, 53-58).

It may well be the complexity of wisdom that served John well. Wisdom is a figure that combines in itself a heavenly origin and dwelling (Proverbs 8; Sir. 24:1-4; Wis. 18:15); a role in the creation of the world; subsequent descent to earth (Wisdom 9; Sir. 24:3-17); emphasis on learning and hearing the instruction of God; a unique embodiment in the shape of the Torah, given exclusively to Israel (Sir. 24:7-12; Bar. 3:36-37; Wis. 9:10; 4Q185 2:4, 10); and the promise of life. Wisdom plays a role in the creation of the world and the instruction of God's people, and so in medi-

---

"The heavenly food of the soul, wisdom, which Moses calls 'manna,' is distributed to all who will use it in equal portions by the divine Word, careful above all things to maintain equality."

53. See Dodd, *Interpretation*, pp. 336-37; Epp, "Wisdom, Torah, Word," pp. 135-37; Brevard S. Childs, *The New Testament as Canon: An Introduction* (Philadelphia: Fortress, 1984), p. 137: "In a conscious polemic against the synagogue the claim is being made by the evangelist that the hermeneutical key to the divine will is not to be found merely in an identity of wisdom and torah, but in the incarnation of Jesus Christ in whom both the wisdom and the law of God are united."

ating both physical life and life understood as salvation. Wisdom, in short, is the mediator of God's life-giving work.

While Wisdom preexists the created order and comes to earth at God's command, it is not clear that the Wisdom narrative can account fully for the descent-ascent schema of the Gospel. Martin Scott acknowledges this fact and argues that John presents not so much a descent-ascent schema as he does a descent-going away schema, which fits with the theme of Wisdom's hiddenness or withdrawal in judgment (Prov. 1:18; Sir. 4:19; 4 Ezra 5:9-10).[54] Similarly, Ben Witherington argues that the V-shaped plot of the Gospel (descent-ascent) is modeled after the sapiential path as found particularly in *1 Enoch* 42, where Wisdom descends to earth but is rejected and returns to heaven.[55] In other words, both Scott and Witherington argue that John appropriates the wisdom traditions in part because of the elements of judgment and rejection inherent within them. However, John Ashton contends that John "takes a stand against the pessimistic view of *1 Enoch* 42 that it was only iniquity that found a dwelling-place on earth."[56] The Gospel, like Sirach, testifies that God's wisdom did indeed find a dwelling place on earth (John 1:14; Sir. 24:8, 12; contrast *1 Enoch* 42:1-2). The whole tenor of John's depiction of Jesus as incarnate Wisdom is to stress the manifestation of God's presence which, though hidden, nevertheless remains accessible to those who have eyes to see and ears to hear. There is a striking parallel between Wisdom of Solomon 7:29-30 ("Compared with the light she is found to be superior, for it is succeeded by the night, but against wisdom evil does not prevail") and John 1:5 ("The light shines in the darkness, and the darkness did not overcome it"). In other words, the descent of the Word has positive revelatory effects.

Although one may speak of the positive revelatory effects of Wisdom, and characterize Wisdom as the mediator or agent of God's life-giving purposes in the world, Wisdom is not an "agent" of God in the same way that prophets or angels are. For while one may speak of the "relationship" between the other agent figures and God, Wisdom is not a separable being or entity that must be "related" to God but is in fact the expression of God's mind, will, or ways. In fact both Wisdom and Word refer to some-

54. Scott, *Sophia*, pp. 137-39. The lack of a parallel to this key element of Johannine Christology leads Bühner to reject the influence of wisdom tradition on the Fourth Gospel (*Der Gesandte und sein Weg*, pp. 87-103).

55. Witherington, *Jesus the Sage*, pp. 371-73, 379.

56. Ashton, *Studying John*, pp. 16-17.

thing that belongs to and comes from God, something inward or peculiar to God that is externally expressed.[57] To speak of Jesus as God's Wisdom incarnate is to say that he is God's self-expression, God's thought or mind, God's interior word spoken aloud.[58] Because and insofar as these are externally expressed, they can be known by human beings. Although Wisdom can be personified as having independent reality and existence apart from God, and depicted as inviting people to eat, offering them life, and searching for a place to dwell in Israel, this Wisdom is not, in the end, separable from God, but rather expresses God's own ways with and in the world. Wisdom's unique status can be thrown into relief when compared with God's other agents, whether heavenly or human, in the world. Whereas a prophet or angel has a separate existence and even a will distinct from God, and could be said to obey or disobey God, such predications are not possible of Wisdom. Wisdom is a category of agency that allows for the closest possible unity between the "agent" — if that is even the best word — and God. Thus Wisdom is not a force immanent and operative in the world apart from God but the power or activity of God manifest in order to bring life.[59] It is this "activity" of God that is manifested or concretized through the true Wisdom of God, the "true bread that gives life to the world," in and as Jesus of Nazareth.

Because Wisdom is not only *from* God but is also *of* God, to speak of Jesus as the embodied Wisdom of God is to speak of the embodiment of God's own presence. To know God through Jesus is not merely to know things about or from God but is rather to know God. Wisdom speculation thus provides an avenue to talk about the presence of God in the person of Jesus. In the biblical and apocryphal wisdom literature, wisdom also functions as the agent or means of God's creation of the world. This raises the

57. This is perhaps most explicit in the refined wisdom speculation in the Wisdom of Solomon 7, where wisdom is said to be "a breath of the power of God, a pure emanation of the glory of the Almighty . . . a reflection of eternal light, a spotless mirror of the working of God, and an image of his goodness" (7:25-26).

58. A point made repeatedly by Dunn of both wisdom and the word. In *Christology in the Making,* Dunn writes that Spirit, wisdom, and word "are simply alternative ways of speaking about the effective power of God in his active relationship with his world and its inhabitants" (p. 219); cf. "Let John Be John," pp. 322-23.

59. Dodd speaks of wisdom as "the hypostatized thought of God projected into creation, and remaining as an immanent power within the world and in man" (*Interpretation,* p. 275). See also John Painter, "Theology, Eschatology and the Prologue of John," *SJT* 46 (1993): 27-42.

question to what extent "wisdom theology" is used in the Gospel to argue that God is made known in or through the natural or created order.

Is God Known through Creation?

That God created the world is assumed, rather than argued, in the Gospel of John. However, John's contention that God created the world through the agency of the Logos and continues to exercise such creative life-giving power in the world through the incarnate Word reflects the influence of the wisdom traditions, for in them, Wisdom is a "master worker" alongside God in creation (Prov. 8:27-30; 3:19; Wis. 7:21; 8:4-6; 9:1-2, 9). Wisdom is not simply a blueprint that God uses as a plan to create the world but is personified as an agent or helper in creation (cf. Jer. 10:12; 1QH 9:7, 14, 19; 11QPs^a 26:14). Elsewhere, God is said to have created the world by his word (Ps. 33:6) or by the Torah (*Gen. Rab.* 1:1; *m. 'Abot* 3:15). Not only is God the creator of the world and source of its life, but God created the world through an agent — usually Wisdom or Torah. As noted, Wisdom's role as God's agent in creation likely influences the statement of the prologue that "all things were made through him, and without him was not anything made that was made. In him was life, and the life was the light of all people" (1:3; reflecting the RSV's translation and punctuation). Although there are no further references in John to God's creation of the world through the Logos, the emphasis on God's gift of life through the agency of Jesus — the Word incarnate, Wisdom incarnate — shows the unity of the life-giving work of God and Jesus, Creator and creating Word. The conception of Jesus as the incarnate Wisdom of God further facilitates the testimony to the unity of the life-giving work of Jesus and God inasmuch as both God's Wisdom and Word were understood to lead to life, or to confer life.

The use of the figure of Wisdom, consistently portrayed as God's agent in creation, as background for the Johannine Logos raises the question whether one may perhaps perceive in John a "creation theology" or a theology of the created or natural order. Craig Koester, for example, writes of Johannine symbolism:

> Earthly images could be used to bear witness to divine realities because the earth is God's creation. This is one of the main theological underpinnings of Johannine symbolism. . . . Once in the world, Jesus called

upon things that could be seen, touched, and tasted to bear witness to the unseen God who sent him, so that the commonplace — bread made from barley meal, streams of cool water, and a glimmer of light — became vehicles of revelation.[60]

John Painter similarly contends that John's incarnational Christology, fashioned as it is on the wisdom tradition, so envisions creation as the expression of God's logos that creation is

> the material expression of the language of God in which God is present in the mystery of grace. The creation has the potential to speak of God because it manifests the graciousness of God. There is bounty for all. Not only is there food to sustain life, there is food to delight the palate. Not only is there sight, there is beauty of art in nature and human creativity. . . .[61]

Whereas Painter lodges the grace of God peculiarly in the creation that "manifests the graciousness of God," it would perhaps be better to speak of the creation as manifesting God's continued providence and sovereignty over the created order. Neither in Judaism nor in the NT can one find the concept of a created order that on its own, apart from God's constant superintendence, graces human beings with its blessings. Creation points to God not because the world was once created but because God is sovereign over it. Painter acknowledges this when he speaks of the "eschatological fulfillment towards which the whole creation moves."[62] Creation is never statically conceived but is everywhere the living witness to God's sovereignty because it does God's bidding. In its obedience, creation serves as a model for human response to the Maker of all. By personifying creation as responsive to God, various biblical and later sources highlight God's dominion as well as the appropriate response to God. What is created answers to the Creator. Even in the Wisdom of Solomon and the works of Philo, both reflecting the philosophy of middle Platonism,

> "nature" is understood in the light of the OT tradition, namely as "creation," which is made and governed by God's word and wisdom. Nature

60. Koester *Symbolism in the Fourth Gospel,* p. 2.
61. Painter, "Theology, Eschatology and John," p. 34.
62. Painter, "Theology, Eschatology and John," p. 42.

is not a self-contained reality that operates according to its own inherent and inviolable laws, not a reality ultimately identifiable with God himself.[63]

In other words, God's creation of the world and God's continued sovereignty over it are inseparable themes in both the OT and later Jewish literature. Sirach, for example, stresses God's sovereignty over the earth through the regular use of the epithets "Creator" and "Maker." Not only do the events of history testify to God's execution of justice, but the obedience of the natural phenomena to God's commands also testifies to the divine sovereignty over all the earth (39:16, 28-31; 42:21). Hence Sirach draws parallels between God's creation of the heavenly bodies, living beings, and human beings (16:26–17:32). God created, ordered, and determined the boundaries of the heavenly bodies, whose perfection is shown in their orderly movements, which are due not to innate qualities but rather to God's enduring rule: "They never disobey his word" (16:28). Or, again, Sirach speaks of the natural phenomena of wind, fire, hail, famine, and pestilence as serving the purposes of God: "They take delight in doing his bidding, always ready for his service on earth; and when their time comes they never disobey his command" (39:31; 43:5, 10). The magnificence of creation is due to the fact that what we call "nature" actually lives, moves, and has its being from God. Similarly, God created human beings and gave them a fixed number of days, and yet their ways are characterized by iniquity and sin (17:20). In spite of the glories of creation, it must never be forgotten that it is God, the Maker, who gives good gifts to human beings (32:13; 34:20; 35:12). So also the Egyptian romance *Joseph and Aseneth* speaks of God's commandments to the heavenly luminaries who "never transgress your ordinances, but are doing your will to the end," inasmuch as God created them (12:2; cf. *L.A.B.* 30:5; 31:2).

The correlation between God's creation of the world and God's providential ordering of events and the destinies of human beings can be found also in the writings of the community at Qumran. So we read:

From the God of knowledge stems all there is and all there shall be. Before they existed he made all their plans, and when they came into being

63. John P. Meier, *A Marginal Jew: Rethinking the Historical Jesus*, vol. 2: *Mentor, Message, and Miracles*, Anchor Bible Reference Library (New York: Doubleday, 1994), p. 513.

they will execute all their works in compliance with his instructions. (1QS 3:15-16; cf. CD 2:7-10)

Indeed, the belief in God's creation and sovereignty is carried through with rigorous consistency in 1QS, which testifies that "God created the spirits of light and darkness" (1QS 3:25), a belief that other Jewish authors are somewhat less sanguine about.[64] The hymns of the community of Qumran apply numerous descriptive epithets to God, many of them testifying to the inextricable link between God's creation and sovereign rule over the world. God is called "my justice," "foundation of my well-being," "source of knowing," "spring of holiness," "peak of glory," and "all-powerful one of eternal majesty" (1QS 10:11-13). God's creation of the world inevitably implies God's continued governance of it. The providential ordering of events is simply a corollary of a belief in God's creation of all that is.

One could document in other literature the emphasis on the orderliness of creation as reflecting divine providence, described in terms of obedience or response to God's commands. Even in apocalyptic literature that sets its sights on God's eschatological judgment within and on history, we can find that the orderliness of creation reflects divine providence. The so-called "Book of the Heavenly Luminaries" of *1 Enoch* (chs. 72–82) contains elaborate mathematical descriptions of the movement of heavenly bodies. These movements, regular and predictable, are not the result of the inherent powers of these bodies but are rather responses to God's commands (72:36; 75:3; 81:3; 82:7-10), even as the eschatological disruption of order is due to God's governance of the world (80:2-3). In the *Testaments of the Twelve Patriarchs* the regularity and order of the movements of the heavenly bodies invite the observer "to discern the Lord who made all things" (*T. Naph.* 3:4).

In narrating the conflicts between pious Jews and the persecutions of Antiochus Epiphanes, 2 Maccabees extends the scope of God's creation by speaking of the resurrection of the righteous martyrs in terms of *creatio ex nihilo* (7:28).[65] God not only created the world and all humankind but

64. Philo, for example, argues that God created the world without intermediaries, except in the case of human beings. Because they are both evil and good, and God could not have created the evil, then there must be mediaries involved in their creation (*Opif.* 76-77).

65. Although many scholars argue that this is the first explicit instance of *creatio ex nihilo* in Jewish literature, Peter Hayman counters that the doctrine is not native to Judaism but arose in Christianity in its debates with Gnosticism in the second century ("Monotheism — a Misused Word in Jewish Studies?" *JJS* 42 [1991]: 1-15).

mercifully gives life and breath back to those who become martyrs for re-
sisting the command to disobey the law (7:9, 14, 23, 28-29). The parallel
between creation and resurrection points not only to God's unequaled
life-giving power but also to God's authority to execute justice, even if that
includes discipline of the faithful.

This leads us back, then, to the Gospel of John, and to the depiction of
the Son as the mediator of God's life and, hence, also of God's sovereign
authority over the world. As the agent of creation, the Logos mediates
God's life-giving power. As the incarnate Logos, Jesus commands the created order, and it responds to him. He changes water into wine, multiplies
bread and fish to feed multitudes, walks on the sea, creates new eyes for a
blind man, raises the dead, and bestows the life-giving spirit. The various
ways that Jesus commands and employs the physical elements to accomplish God's purposes unquestionably identify him as one who has divine
power that has been granted to him by God. The divine source and character of Jesus' miraculous works are further confirmed in the kinds of work
Jesus accomplishes. Not only does he grant life, but he works on the day reserved for God alone. This is not so much a creation ethic or theology as it
is a theology of God's far-reaching dominion and authority, exercised
through the work of Jesus. Indeed, there is no sharp demarcation between
the so-called "natural" and "supernatural" realms, and to speak of the natural world as bearing witness to God misleads somewhat. "Wisdom theology" gives expression to God's life-giving work in the world, with a dual
focus on creation and sovereignty. That Wisdom is embodied in Jesus implies the inseparability of the work of God and the work of Jesus, particularly at the point of the life-giving power of God.

Knowledge of God in the Fourth Gospel

While it is difficult to arrive at a simple and precise definition of "the
knowledge of God" in the Gospel of John, we can nevertheless draw some
conclusions in light of the previous discussion about the ways in which
God is manifested and the means by which God may be known.
Bultmann's famous dictum that in John Jesus reveals nothing but that he is
the Revealer has often been challenged, but his formulation does capture
an important dimension of the knowledge of God in John. Precisely because Jesus is the Revealer of God, knowledge of God is mediated and at-

tained through him. Knowing Jesus, therefore, is the means and even condition of knowing God. Knowing Jesus will entail an understanding of his relationship to God as the one who reveals and embodies the life-giving power, glory, and presence of God. Thus, knowing Jesus is knowing God. John does not collapse Jesus into God, or vice versa, but there is no separate and distinct knowledge of one without knowledge of the other. That this is so reflects John's theological and Christological commitments: the Word of God has become incarnate in Jesus of Nazareth. This embodied Word is the visible and even tangible manifestation of God's glory; and the only such full embodiment of God's glory.

Bultmann's dictum called attention to the fact that Jesus does not disclose new content, or even reiterate known convictions, about the God of whom he speaks. If he is indeed the Revealer of God, what then does he reveal? The answer, of course, is that he reveals quite a lot about the saving purposes of God, although not always in the form of propositional statements about God. One of the reasons that such statements are routinely absent from the Gospel is that John simply assumes that the God who is to be known in Jesus of Nazareth is the God of Israel, to whom the Scriptures bear witness. In this assumption John does not differ markedly from other NT authors, for whom the primary task was not to explain, describe, or defend God but to explicate the relationship of the God of Israel to Jesus of Nazareth and how God's purposes are worked out through his life, death, and resurrection. John speaks in a variety of ways of the relationship of Jesus to God, and how God's purposes are expressed in and through the shape of Jesus' ministry and presence on earth. Foundational to all such explanations is the affirmation of the unity of God with Jesus, whether that be expressed in terms of the relationship of Father and Son; God and the divine Wisdom or Word; or the manifestation of glory in Jesus' deeds. As C. K. Barrett aptly put it, the complete unity of the Father and Son is stated in moral terms; terms of worship; metaphysical terms; and as revelation.[66] This "complete unity" of Father and Son underlies John's understanding of knowing God. Knowledge of the Father is inseparable from knowledge of the Son, and vice versa, not just because Jesus functions as the spokesman for God, but because of the thoroughgoing character of their unity.

---

66. C. K. Barrett, "The Old Testament in the Fourth Gospel," *JTS* 48 (1947): 161-62; quoted above in full on pp. 53-54.

As indicated above, it is this "complete unity" that also implies the superiority of "agency" figures to describe the relationship of Jesus to God that bind them together most closely. Entities such as wisdom, word, and glory depict Jesus not merely as an intermediary figure, but further allow for the embodiment of these divine attributes or characteristics in the person of Jesus. That in turn underscores the importance of *seeing* in the Gospel of John, for to see the wisdom of God, the word of God, or the glory of God is to see them in and as the person of Jesus, in his deeds, but also in his very person. Moreover, because seeing in the first instance refers to physical sight, it demands the presence of the one who is seen. To see the Father in the Son is to *see* the Son and so to come to perceive or understand their relationship and their unity. The signs, as life-giving works, bear witness to that unity. Even so, they are properly speaking witnesses to, and not proofs of, the union of Father and Son. They flow out of and express that unity and hence can bear witness to it.

Seeing demands the presence of the one who is seen in a way that hearing does not. One may hear from another and pass the knowledge or message on down to others so that eventually one hears at second, or third, or fourth hand what the original speaker uttered. Truly "seeing" someone, however, requires the presence of the one who is seen. So it is that John asserts that only the Son has seen the Father, since only the Son has been in God's presence. Because of the unity of Father and Son, those who are in the presence of the Son may see God in him. When seeing is taken either as the condition of knowing God, or as virtually synonymous with knowing God, the knowledge of God is equivalent with proper perception and understanding of the work of the Father in the Son and the nature of their unity.

John also limits direct hearing from God to the Son, who speaks "only what he has heard from the Father." Hearing Jesus, understanding Jesus, yields knowledge of God. When hearing is emphasized, knowledge of God takes on a definite moral quality that is not simply the result of knowing God but part of its warp and woof. "Hearing" indicates the response of obedience, of doing God's will, of keeping the word that is heard from God. While Jesus is never said to "obey" God, he does what he has heard; he expresses perfectly the will of God and hence may be said to truly "know the Father." His doing the will of the Father thus comes from and testifies to his knowledge of God. Human beings who desire to do the will of God will know the truth of Jesus' teaching. They will understand it and believe it to be true. Similarly, human beings who know God will express that knowledge in conduct. They will do "as Abraham did," honoring Jesus, rather than seeking to persecute and kill the one who speaks the truth (8:37-39, 40 15:21; 16:3).

Because knowledge of God is described in terms not only of seeing but also of hearing God, "seeing" cannot be understood simply as contemplation of God, of a beatific vision simply for its own sake. The emphasis on response and obedience introduced by hearing forbids the reduction of "seeing" to contemplating an object. Even as seeing implies and needs the presence of the other, so knowledge of God is not contemplation of but communion with God. Knowledge of God must therefore be interpreted as experience of God, appropriate honor of God, and acknowledgment of God in his works and response to his commands and claims.

Because in this world the Son makes the Father known, one truly "sees" God: but only indirectly, and in hidden ways. The *hiddenness* of the glory of the Father in the Son informs every scene of the Gospel. One cannot simply read the glory of God off the surface of Jesus' life or from his miracles, as though it comprised a revelatory halo around his words and deeds. Even the signs of Jesus are manifestations of the hidden glory of God in Jesus. After Jesus' first sign, the changing of the water to wine, the evangelist comments: "This, the first of his signs, Jesus did at Cana in Galilee, and manifested his glory; and his disciples believed in him." They saw and believed. Yet just as often in John, people see and do not believe. A number of people witnessed the raising of Lazarus from the dead and knew a miracle had been done. Whereas some believed in him, others plotted his death. Seeing the miracles of Jesus is no guarantee of understanding what they are all about. Not all seeing leads to faith. Signs lead to faith when grasped as indicators or pointers to a greater reality, and only when they are grasped as such do they fulfill their purpose. For John the signs are the works of God and embody God's presence because God is the creator of all that is and, as the giver of all life, continues to sustain the world. Ultimately, the confession that God is the God of all life stands at the head of any list of things to be known about God and to be received and experienced in communion with God as embodied through and in the work and person of Jesus.

FOUR

The Spirit of God

At first glance it might appear to be obvious that statements about the "spirit of God" have implications for understanding God and the character of God's activity and presence, especially since John gives the most explicit attention of all the Gospels to the role of the Spirit. Yet while a good deal of scholarly ink has been spilled over the questions of the historical origins of the figure of the Spirit and the peculiarly Johannine designation "Paraclete," the Spirit-Paraclete's relationship to Jesus, and the experience of the Spirit-Paraclete in the Johannine community, actually very little space has been given over to consideration of the implications for understanding God in the Fourth Gospel.[1] To some extent, this neglect is the product of the recent tendency to interpret the Spirit-Paraclete as thoroughly "Christological." As one author puts it, "The single most important feature of the Johannine Paraclete is its christological concentration."[2] Yet inas-

---

1. Only the Gospel of John refers to the Spirit as "the Paraclete." The origins of the term and the genesis of the portrayal of the Spirit in this manner have occasioned much discussion, but the various solutions proposed have commanded no scholarly consensus. Although the term "Paraclete" occurs in the Gospel only in the Farewell Discourses (14:16, 26; 15:26; 16:7), I judge that the "Spirit" and "Paraclete" are different references to the same figure, also designated in John as the Holy Spirit (1:33; 14:26; 20:22) and the Spirit of Truth (14:17; 15:26; 16:13).

2. Gary Burge, *The Anointed Community: The Holy Spirit in the Johannine Tradition* (Grand Rapids: Eerdmans, 1987), p. 41.

much as the "holy spirit" of the OT and Judaism is always in some way related to God, the question regarding the relationship of the Spirit-Paraclete to God must be pressed more closely.

Many of the same questions regarding the nature of "wisdom" can be raised with relation to the Spirit. For although wisdom, or word, can be personified as having an independent reality and existence apart from God, in the final analysis to speak of what Wisdom does, or the Word does, is to speak of what God does. If the same is true of the Spirit, and the Spirit is the personification or hypostatization of a divine activity or attribute, then there are clearly implications for construing the character of the nature and mode of God's presence in the world. If the Spirit refers to God's own activity and presence, then what are the implications if Jesus "breathes" the Spirit upon his disciples after his resurrection?

The role and function of the Spirit, particularly in relationship to Father and Son, are dealt with in careful and nuanced ways in the Fourth Gospel. A brief survey of some of the major issues that have been raised in an attempt to discern the contours of the Gospel's portrait of the Spirit of God will set the stage for discussion of key texts from the Gospel. We begin, then, with a look at some crucial questions raised by the Fourth Gospel.

Crucial Questions in Understanding the Spirit in John

The Nature of the Spirit

Descriptions of the Spirit-Paraclete in John have raised the question of the nature or reality of the Spirit itself. Two primary conceptions of the Spirit, representing nearly opposite ends on the spectrum of opinion, have been suggested by interpreters of the Fourth Gospel. On the one hand, the Spirit has been understood, along with "wisdom" and "word," as a way of speaking of God's activity or as the manifestation of a particular divine activity or power. Exploiting the play on the words "spirit" and "breath" (*ruach* in the Hebrew, *pneuma* in the Greek), this model conceives of the Spirit on analogy with God's power, wisdom, or breath. To speak of the presence of the Spirit is to speak of the presence of God, since "spirit" connotes the means of God's power or activity in the world.[3] One might then be able to

---

3. M. E. Isaacs, in a study of word, spirit, and wisdom, argued that the Paraclete is pat-

draw some conclusions about how God worked, or in what ways God's presence was manifested and experienced, or perhaps to point to a specific aspect of God's work. In a summary of this view, George Johnston writes:

> The figurative speech in all these passages should be noted: spirit like water is a cleansing agent (1:33); spirit like breath is a vital element (20:22); spirit as teaching, guiding, defending, is a divine power (chs. 14–16). Unifying them all is surely the concept of a *Christlike power* that is finally in the control of God, the heavenly Father. . . . The Gospel material is more readily aligned with ideas of supernatural powers than with the Christian doctrine of the Third Person of the Blessed Trinity.[4]

On the other hand, the Spirit has also been conceived of as a "personal divine being distinct from and in some degree independent of God."[5] For example, Stephen Smalley asserts that 'the Spirit-Paraclete . . . in John's Gospel *is* understood as personal, indeed, as a person."[6] A substantial impetus for such an understanding of the Spirit has been provided by analysis of various figures proposed as patterns for the portrayal of the Johannine Paraclete, including particularly prophetic figures, such as Elijah and Elisha, and angelic figures, such as the archangel Michael or the interpreting angel of apocalyptic. On this model the Spirit-Paraclete can be conceived of something like an angel, a quasi-independent figure summoned by God to carry out particular divine purposes or to complete a

---

terned after the figure of Wisdom in Hellenistic Judaism (*The Concept of Spirit: A Study of Pneuma in Hellenistic Judaism and Its Bearing on the New Testament*, Heythrop Monographs 1 [London: Heythrop, 1976]). Isaacs notes the following parallels: both Wisdom and Spirit are personified and sent from God (Wis. 7:7; John 14:26); Wisdom makes its home with God's people (Sir. 24:8-12; John 14:26); Wisdom makes known the future (Sir. 24:33; John 16:13); and Wisdom is rejected by humankind (*1 Enoch* 42:2; John 14:17). Yet since the very status of "wisdom" is itself debated, the suggestion to see it as a possible model for the Spirit only exacerbates the problem of how to understand the work and identity of the Spirit.

4. George Johnston, *The Spirit-Paraclete in the Gospel of John*, SNTSMS 12 (Cambridge; Cambridge University Press, 1970), pp. 31-32.

5. The phrasing comes from James D. G. Dunn, *Christology in the Making: An Inquiry into the Origins of the Doctrine of the Incarnation*, 2nd ed. (London: SCM, 1989 [1980]), p. 131, who does not espouse this particular understanding of the Spirit, either in Judaism or in John.

6. Stephen Smalley, "Pneumatology in the Johannine Gospel and Apocalypse," in *Exploring the Gospel of John: In Honor of D. Moody Smith*, ed. R. Alan Culpepper and C. Clifton Black (Louisville: Westminster/John Knox, 1996), p. 293.

certain mission in the world. One can still draw conclusions about God's work in the world, but the nature of God's presence within the world, and especially the reality of the Spirit itself and ultimately the identity of God, become more complex since "the Spirit" cannot simply be equated with God's power or God's own presence.

Most intriguing is the way in which these two different ways of conceiving the role or identity of the Spirit find their support in different portions of the Gospel. The terms Paraclete, Spirit of Truth, and Holy Spirit appear almost exclusively in the so-called Farewell Discourses (chs. 14–17). In the narrative portions of the Gospel (chs. 1–12, 18–21), only the simple "Spirit" appears.[7] Moreover, the differences in terminology correspond to differences in the primary functions allotted to the "spirit" and the "Paraclete." As W. G. Kümmel comments, "The effects of the Spirit and of the Paraclete are not altogether described as the same; cf., on the one hand, 'to be born of water and Spirit' and the Spirit as the source of life in the believer, and on the other hand, teaching, recalling, testifying, and convicting as functions of the Paraclete."[8] Thus in the narrative portions of the Gospel, Jesus is said to be the one who will baptize "with" or "by" the Holy Spirit, where the Spirit, described on analogy with "water," is conceived of virtually as a substance poured out upon believers.[9] One must be

7. The one exception is John 1:33, where the Baptist promises that Jesus will baptize with "the Holy Spirit." Interestingly enough, the one passage outside the Farewell Discourses that uses terminology other than "Spirit" refers to something that Jesus will do at a future (unspecified) time.

8. W. G. Kümmel, *The Theology of the New Testament* (Nashville: Abingdon, 1973), p. 315. Whereas Kümmel speaks in terms of differing effects, Hans Windisch argues that the Spirit and Paraclete were originally two very different figures: "The Spirit is, according to his nature, power, an incomprehensible being that suddenly enters into man and imparts to him impulses and insights which lift him above his human existence. The Paraclete is a concrete heavenly person, a kind of angel, and when he appears on earth, it is as an emissary from God, as an angel in human form or as a prophet, as a teacher sent from God (3:2) and subordinated to the incarnate Logos but yet comparable to him" (*The Spirit-Paraclete in the Fourth Gospel* [Philadelphia: Fortress, 1968], p. 20).

9. The Stoics, for example, thought of the Spirit as a rarified sort of "substance." The description of Wisdom in Wisdom of Solomon 7 includes many elements that suggest its conception as divine "substance." The Spirit in wisdom is "mobile" (7:22); it penetrates "through all spirits" (7:23); Wisdom itself is "more mobile than any motion," which because of its purity "pervades and penetrates all things." Paul Volz argues that in certain strands of the OT, spirit is conceived of as a fluid or substance that can be distributed without diminishing the spirit in the possession of the one who gives it (*Der Geist Gottes und die ver-*

"born of the Spirit" (3:5-6), equivalent to being born "from above," through the activity of God. God brings life through the power of the Spirit, a thought certainly in keeping both with the biblical tradition of the life-giving Spirit, such as Ezekiel's prophecy of the "dry bones" brought to life by the Spirit (Ezek. 37:14), and with the Johannine conception of the Spirit as a life-giving force (3:6; 6:63). These and other passages in John have suggested that the Holy Spirit is God's power, particularly manifested as God's life-giving power.

The passages that provide the strongest evidence for conceiving of the Spirit as a distinct figure, an independent agent or actor, are all found in the Farewell Discourses, chapters 14–17 of the Gospel (14:16-17, 26; 15:26; 16:7, 13). What is peculiar to this group of passages is not only their location in those discourses, but that here, and here alone, is the spirit called the "Paraclete." The functions attributed to the Paraclete differ markedly from those attributed to the Spirit elsewhere in John. The dominant description of the Spirit-Paraclete is as a teacher and guide who will be with believers. Thus the Spirit teaches (14:26; cf. 1 John 2:27); reminds disciples of Jesus' words (14:26); testifies on Jesus' behalf (15:26); accuses or convicts the world (16:8-11); and speaks, declares, and glorifies Jesus (16:13). The Spirit is also described as "another paraclete," who in some way can be set alongside Jesus. Moreover, the Spirit is "sent" by God (14:26; 15:26; 16:7), language that calls to mind the sending of prophets and of course of Jesus himself. The Spirit "comes from" God (15:26; 16:7, 13). The Spirit can be "received" or "welcomed," as Jesus was received; believers are said to "know" and, most peculiarly, to "see" the Spirit (14:16-17).

All in all, the descriptions of the Spirit and the Spirit's activities in the Farewell Discourses comport well with a picture of the Spirit as a distinct figure who is sent, like the prophets or angels, to human beings as a divine messenger, and so who can be said to "come" in the name of the Lord, and to be welcomed or rejected by them. The Spirit is not so much the agency or manifestation of God's presence but God's present agent. Hence, God would not be present *as* Spirit but perhaps *in* or even *with* the Spirit, in much the same way that God is present in a prophetic or angelic messenger.

---

wandten Erscheinungen im Alten Testament und im anschließenden Judentum [Tübingen: J. C. B. Mohr (Paul Siebeck), 1910], pp. 23-24).

Antecedents of the Johannine Paraclete

Almost all the antecedents proposed for the Johannine Paraclete provide evidence for seeing the Johannine Spirit as cast in the second mold, that of a quasi-independent figure sent by God on a particular mission or embassy in the world. Günther Bornkamm, Raymond Brown, and others have suggested that the relationship between Jesus and the Paraclete can be derived from pairs of successor figures, such as Moses and Joshua or Elijah and Elisha, a suggestion that takes seriously the Johannine theme that the Paraclete comes only after Jesus departs.[10] Earlier Sigmund Mowinckel and others suggested that prophetic and angelic intercessor figures in the OT and Judaism provide the conceptual background for the Johannine Paraclete.[11] Otto Betz ingeniously argued that the figure of the Paraclete weaves together strands from personal figures (Michael), various powers (such as the "Spirit of Truth" of Qumran), and the metaphorical application of the term "paraclete," in the sense of "advocate," to good works, religious piety, and repentance, such as are found in rabbinic writings (m. 'Abot 4:11). In particular, the figure of Michael at Qumran explains why there are so many personal traits attached to the Johannine figure of the Paraclete. It was the archangel Michael who sat for the portrait.[12] By conflating "Michael" with the impersonal "spirit of Truth," John con-

---

10. Yet, for Günther Bornkamm, "the Paraclete is none other than the glorified Christ." See Günther Bornkamm, "Der Paraklet im Johannes-Evangelium," in *Geschichte und Glaube. Gesammelte Aufsätze,* Erster Teil, Band III (Münich: Kaiser, 1968), pp. 84, 88; Raymond E. Brown, *The Gospel According to John,* 2 vols., Anchor Bible (Garden City, N.Y.: Doubleday, 1968, 1970), 2:1137-38.

11. See Sigmund Mowinckel, "Die Vorstellung des Spätjudentums vom heiligen Geist als Fürsprecher und der johanneische Paraklet," *ZNW* 32 (1933): 97-130; N. Johansson, *Parakletoi. Vorstellung von Fürsprechern für die Menschen vor Gott in der alttestamentlichen Religion, im Spätjudentum, und Urchristentum* (Lund: Gleerup, 1940), pp. 3-62; and the examples in Johannes Behm, "παράκλητος," in *TDNT* 5:809-10. Mowinckel pointed particularly to the two "guardian" spirits of *T. Jud.* 20, and surely would have argued that the doctrine of the two spirits in the literature of Qumran supported his thesis as well.

12. The implication, of course, is that it is not Jesus; see Otto Betz, *Der Paraklet: Fürsprecher im häretischen Spätjudentum, im Johannes-Evangelium und im neugefundenen gnostischen Schriften* (Leiden: Brill, 1963). By way of contrast, see the comments of Max Turner, *The Holy Spirit and Spiritual Gifts* (Peabody, Mass.: Hendrickson, 1998), p. 79: "Whereas John's picture of the Spirit-Advocate has little substantial background in the history of ideas, it is clearly modeled on Jesus." Turner is close to Burge, who criticizes Betz's description of the Paraclete as inadequately Christological; see Burge, *The Anointed Community,* p. 30.

structed the Paraclete figure.[13] In *Understanding the Fourth Gospel,* John
Ashton argues that the Paraclete is portrayed as an interpreting angel.[14] In
apocalyptic texts, when the seer ascends to heaven, the angel who stands in
close proximity to God usually appears to help in the unfolding of the divine secrets to the seer and guides him on his heavenly journey (cf. Rev.
1:1; 22:16).[15] There is something of a parallel here to the Paraclete's function to teach the Johannine community "what is to come" and to show
them "all things." Whereas evil angels manifest their disobedience by ex-
posing heavenly mysteries without God's permission, Jesus and the Spirit
not only have the permission, but even the command, to make known
what has been shown them. And just as the Paraclete is assigned a judging
function, so in 11QMelchizedek, Melchizedek is the *elohim* who sits in
judgment over other angelic beings.

Christological Interpretations of the Spirit

The reference to the Spirit as "another Paraclete," as well as the overlap between the functions of the Paraclete and the ministry of Jesus, have led to
the Christological readings of the Spirit that so dominate interpretations
of the Fourth Gospel today. So, for example, Raymond Brown writes that
the Spirit is "the presence of Jesus when Jesus is absent."[16] In his comprehensive study of the Spirit in the Johannine community, Gary Burge argues that "the single most important feature of the Johannine Paraclete is

13. Johnston *(Spirit-Paraclete)* argued that John's identification with the Spirit as the
Paraclete serves the purpose of combating the identification of Michael with the Spirit of
Truth.

14. John Ashton, *Understanding the Fourth Gospel* (Oxford: Clarendon, 1991), pp. 423-
24. In *Studying John: Approaches to the Fourth Gospel* (Oxford: Clarendon, 1994), pp. 71-89,
Ashton contends that the Gospel manifests an "angel christology," arguing that this "angelic
christology" provides the bridge between Judaism and John's high Christology. The ambiguity of this angel Christology accounts for the vacillation between the high, "equal to God"
Christology and the Gospel's subordinationism.

15. So, for example, the guiding functions of Iaoel in *Ap. Abraham* could provide a parallel for the Johannine conception of the Spirit as one who "leads into all truth"; cf. Christopher Rowland, *The Open Heaven: A Study of Apocalyptic in Judaism and Early Christianity*
(New York: Crossroad, 1982), p. 103.

16. Brown, *John,* 2:1139. Echoed by John Wijngaards (*The Spirit in John,* Zacchaeus
Studies [Wilmington, Del.: Michael Glazier, 1988], pp. 67-63) and many others.

THE GOD OF THE GOSPEL OF JOHN

its christological concentration. Christ is the template within the Fourth Evangelist's thinking that has given shape and meaning to the Spirit in the Farewell Discourses."[17] Max Turner writes that the "Paraclete is Jesus' *replacement,* and the *substitute* for his presence. . . . The Spirit comes to replace Jesus and to mediate his presence."[18] It is not an overstatement to assert that the decidedly Christological character of the Paraclete is taken for granted by many scholars today. The evidence for this reading comes chiefly from the Farewell Discourses, precisely those passages unique to the Fourth Gospel. It is primarily from them that the picture of the Spirit in John has been constructed.

Ecclesiastical Interpretations of the Spirit

Finally, both the distinctive placement and unique content of the Paraclete passages have given rise to *ecclesiastical interpretations* of the Paraclete. M. E. Boring, for example, noted how well the description of the Paraclete's functions corresponded to those of the ideal Christian prophet, and he argued that the depictions of both Jesus and the Paraclete had been modeled to some extent after the prophets of the Johannine community.[19] These correspondences would serve to validate the role of the prophet for the later Christian community. Not incidentally, such a portrait locates the work of the Spirit in particular leaders of the Church rather than in the community as a whole or in individual believers. Boring argues that the presence of the Paraclete should not be construed primarily "in the mystical sense to refer individually to every believer," and that the promises of the Paraclete are realized "by an identifiable group endowed with the Spirit in a particular manner and exercising its gifts on behalf of and for the benefit of the community as a whole, but not a gift possessed indiscriminately by all its members."[20] In his study *The Spirit-Paraclete in the Gospel of John,* George Johnston spoke of the Spirit as a "christlike power that is finally in the control of God,"[21] but he argued that John locates the

17. Burge, *The Anointed Community,* p. 41.

18. Turner, *The Holy Spirit and Spiritual Gifts,* p. 96.

19. M. E. Boring, "The Influence of Christian Prophecy on the Johannine Portrayal of the Paraclete and Jesus," *NTS* 25 (1978): 113-23.

20. Boring, "Influence of Christian Prophecy," pp. 113, 114.

21. Johnston, *Spirit-Paraclete,* p. 32.

activity of the Spirit entirely within the Church, remaining either unconcerned with or uninterested in the activity of the Spirit of God outside its confines.[22] The active divine power is "embodied in certain outstanding leaders within the catholic Church: the exegete, the teacher and evangelist, the prophet, the consoler out of sorrow, and the witness for the defence in times of persecution."[23]

Summary Observations

There is little question that these various studies of the Spirit in John have identified important exegetical and historical issues. Studies that have focused on a Christological reading of the Spirit have done so because of the distinctive material in John, particularly Jesus' promises that he would send "another Paraclete" after his departure. Jesus is the one who sends the Spirit, and in some way the Spirit is like him. Similarly, ecclesiastical interpretations of the Spirit in John have noted the importance of the prophet and prophetic-inspired utterance in the Johannine community. Although this is more explicit in 1 John, where the issue of discerning the spirits comes to the fore, than in John, nevertheless the role of the Spirit as one who "leads into all truth" has rightly raised the question whether the Gospel's characteristic and distinctive understanding of Jesus is not just such an instance of truth given by the leading of the Spirit. Finally, the terminology itself — Paraclete, Spirit of Truth — cannot but help send investigators to historical sources for illumination. They will not be disappointed to discover parallels to these terms, albeit perhaps not to the entire conception of the Spirit in the Fourth Gospel. In short, these various ways of understanding the Spirit in John have rightly identified important questions and significant issues that must be dealt with in order to properly delineate John's view of the Spirit.

By way of taking advantage of the best of what these studies have offered, and building on what they have done, we can briefly catalog some further items that stand out from this brief survey. First, the Gospel's use of the term "Paraclete," and the distinctive features attributed to it, have dominated scholarly investigation of the Spirit in John. On the whole,

22. Johnston, *Spirit-Paraclete*, p. 38.
23. Johnston, *Spirit-Paraclete*, p. 119.

scholars have focused on that which is unique in John to fashion a portrait of the Spirit in John. Less effort and interest have been devoted to developing a synthetic and unified portrait of the Spirit in the Gospel of John.[24] In other words, scholars have attended far less to chapters 1–12 than to chapters 13–17. In the following study, both parts of the Gospel and the somewhat different angles of presentation of the Spirit will be considered. Here we should hasten to add that a unified portrait need not be one in which all surface differences are either ignored or smoothed out. Rather, a "unified portrait" ought to reckon with the different aspects of the figure of the Spirit in the Gospel of John. It may well turn out that what is perceived as a problem attributable to the use of various sources and backgrounds can better be explained in terms of John's deliberate theological presentation of the Spirit.

Still — and this is the second conclusion to be drawn from the brief survey of issues — historical considerations have dominated the scene. Scholarly treatment of the Spirit-Paraclete in John has assumed that the question of John's view of the Spirit ought to be raised and answered on historical grounds, whether the "history" in question is that of the general religious milieu of the Fourth Gospel, the Early Church, other NT traditions or communities, or the Johannine community itself. So, for example, "explanations" for the view of the Spirit have been sought in the religious milieu of first-century Judaism, and particularly of so-called "sectarian" Judaism, or in the religious experience or organization of the early Johannine community. Similarly, in searching for possible models for understanding the Spirit, it has apparently been assumed that the two poles of interpretation specified earlier are mutually exclusive options. Either the Spirit is a "distinct figure," or the Spirit is the personification of God's activity. The resultant "tension" must therefore be accounted for either by a multiplicity of sources or redactional efforts to meld disparate figures or conceptions of the Spirit into a unified whole. In other words, as with so much study of the Fourth Gospel, explanations of the Spirit-Paraclete in John have been sought first outside the Gospel, and along historical paths. Such an approach falls short of its goal of attaining an adequate explanation of the Spirit in John because it often fails to approach the question also along *theological* paths.

I will argue in this chapter that the evidence of the Fourth Gospel sug-

24. As Burge points out in *The Anointed Community,* p. 4.

gests that the evangelist has shaped his material first of all as a reflective theologian who saw the question of the identity of the Spirit as a profoundly *theological* issue, in the sense that it implicated the very identity of God. John's portrait of the Spirit emerges not only as cogent and unified but also as theologically focused. This is not to dismiss the role of historical investigation; quite the opposite. It is precisely historical study that demands that we attend to the *theological* dimension of the Spirit in John, for inasmuch as the Spirit is always God's spirit, the question that naturally arises is what it can mean to talk about *Christological* interpretations of the Spirit in John. There is no question that John's view of the Spirit-Paraclete can be greatly illumined by the light of historical study; but unless the investigation is pressed to its logical end, to a consideration of the very identity of God, historical study will not account for John's view of the Spirit — precisely the point of the following analysis.

This leads us to a third observation that arises from an overview of studies on the Spirit in John, as well as to a need to make more precise what is meant by a "theological" approach to the Spirit in John. On the whole, the various passages on the Spirit have not been treated within the flow of the narrative but have rather been extracted from the narrative to see if a synthetic "theology" of the Spirit could be fashioned from them. This enterprise, quite common to all manner of topics in the NT, should not without further ado be eschewed. It ought to follow, rather than precede or substitute for, a close reading of the narrative itself, for it is the logic of the Gospel narrative, as well as the theological reflection that shaped that narrative, that in the final analysis provides the framework that accounts for the Gospel's distinctive representation of the Spirit. Explanations for the different functions predicated of the Spirit, and even for the different conceptions of the Spirit operative at various junctures in John, must also be sought within the narrative progression of the Gospel and in light of the functions of the Spirit that arise from each passage. That is to say, the Gospel ought not to be construed as a sort of hodgepodge of mismatched statements about the Spirit-Paraclete that John never quite finished sorting through. There are genuine differences between statements about the "spirit" in the narrative portions of the Gospel (chs. 1–12, 20) and statements about the "Paraclete" found in the Farewell Discourses. These can, and indeed must, be accounted for by the narrative movement of the Gospel itself, as well as by John's theological reflection upon the identity of the Spirit.

155

We next turn our attention to the Gospel itself. We shall focus our discussion in two different ways. First, we shall pay careful attention to what the Gospel does *not* say about the Spirit. The need to point out at some length what the Gospel does not say about the Spirit, and particularly about Jesus' relationship to the Spirit, is due to the fact that too often the gaps in John's portrait of the Spirit are filled in with material from other Gospels, or from Paul, rather than taken on their own as constructive indicators of the understanding of the Spirit found in the Gospel of John. Second, we shall turn to a reading of specific passages that pertain to the Spirit in order to develop a positive statement about the Spirit in the Fourth Gospel. This will allow us, at the close of the chapter, to offer some theological reflections on the activity and reality of the Spirit in John. Thus, the following analysis will endeavor to pay due attention both to the Gospel as a whole and to the Paraclete passages, to the spirit as a distinct figure and as a personification of divine activity, and to the narrative and theological dimensions of the Gospel.

The Spirit in John: The Silences of the Text

We note, first, the difference in terminology between the Fourth Gospel and other documents of the NT. Here there is no language of filling or being filled with the Spirit, such as is common to Luke-Acts (e.g., Luke 1:15, 41, 67; Acts 2:4; 4:8, 31; 9:17; 13:9, 52). The Spirit is not said to be "poured out" upon or in a person (Acts 2:33; 10:45; Titus 3:5-6; Rom. 5:5). In John, Jesus is not driven by the Spirit (Mark 1:12). Neither is he said to do anything "in the Spirit" or "in the power of the Spirit." In fact, the Spirit is not explicitly linked with power, a clear attribute of the Spirit and of God both in the OT and the NT. While in other documents of the NT the Spirit is the "power from on high" (Luke 24:49; Acts 1:8); the power that raised Jesus from the dead (Rom. 1:4); a power working within Christians (Rom. 15:13, 19); and a power explicitly associated with miracles or some sort of deeds of power (Acts 8:19; 10:38; Rom. 15:19; 1 Cor. 2:4; 1 Thess. 1:5), terms for power or strength are not a feature of the descriptions of the Johannine Spirit-Paraclete.

This is further borne out in the omission of all demon exorcisms from John. John does not portray Jesus as an exorcist who does battle in order to destroy the demons (Mark 1:23-27), or who casts out demons by the Spirit (or finger) of God (Matt. 11:28; Mark 3:26-31; Luke 11:20), a feature characteristic of Jesus' ministry in the Synoptic Gospels.[25] Jesus himself is charged with demon possession not, as in the Synoptic Gospels, because of his exorcisms, but rather because of his teaching (7:20; 8:48; 10:19). Since therefore the charge is linked in John with teaching, Jesus refutes the charge by appeal not to the Spirit of God at work in his own deeds but to the origin in and authorization of his words by God. Contrast the Q account, where Jesus dismisses the charge that he is possessed by Beelzebul and casts out demons by the power of Beelzebul with the assertion that he rather does so "by the spirit of God." In John we do not have a clear case of opposing "spirits," for there is no corresponding "evil Spirit." Jesus appeals not to his empowering by the Spirit but rather to his relationship to God in order to refute the charges of his adversaries.[26] John 16:7-8 does speak of the Paraclete with respect to overcoming the "ruler of this world," but the activity of the Paraclete is described as that of "reproving" or "convicting" in terminology reminiscent of a lawsuit.

Similarly, Jesus' signs are never explicitly attributed to the power of the Spirit on, in, or through him. Here the most notable contrast comes with Luke 4:17-19, where Jesus is shown to quote from the book of Isaiah, explaining the course of his ministry as a fulfillment of Isaiah's prophetic vision of a Spirit-endowed preacher and healer. Later, Jesus is described as a "prophet mighty in word and deed" (Luke 24:19), and as one who, "anointed with the Holy Spirit and with power . . . went about doing good and healing all that were oppressed" (Acts 10:38). The familiar picture of Jesus as a healer and teacher with the power of the Spirit of God upon him finds its home explicitly in the pages of Luke-Acts, not in the Gospel of John.

There is no explicit link in the Fourth Gospel between the Spirit and Jesus as a prophet, a connection found only in the NT in Paul, Luke-Acts, and Revelation. As just noted, not only is the portrait of Jesus in Luke-Acts colored in vividly prophetic shades, but the parallelism between the empowering presence of the Spirit upon Jesus and subsequently upon the

---

25. Betz (*Der Paraklet*, pp. 113-14) argued that the dualism of Qumran is "demythologized," in that the battle between the forces of good and evil is embodied in the "sons of light" and the "sons of darkness," rather than in a multiplicity of spirit beings.

26. Kümmel (*Theology of the New Testament*, p. 313) comments similarly that the bestowal of the Spirit on the disciples does not endow them with supernatural abilities, but rather authorizes them to forgive or retain sin.

157

apostles is programmatic in the overall structure and thematic concerns of that two-volume work. Paul speaks at length about the gifts of the Spirit. Among them he not only includes the gift of prophecy but names it first (Rom. 12:5; 1 Cor. 12:10). The importance of the Spirit, and its link to prophecy, are attested also in the Revelation of John (e.g., 19:10). The connection between the Spirit and prophecy, and the high status assigned to the Spirit-inspired prophet, figure prominently in Luke, Paul, and the Apocalypse.

While the link between the Spirit and prophecy is absent from John, it is explicitly found in the epistles. 1 John 4:1-6 speaks of "many prophets" having gone out into the world, and of various spirits inspiring true and false confessions about Jesus. In line with the promises in the Farewell Discourses that the Spirit of truth will guide into all truth (16:13), the Spirit inspires true confession of Jesus. Here the Spirit of God — curiously not referred to as the Paraclete in 1 John — is active primarily as "the spirit of prophecy."[27] Just this description of the Spirit is found in the book of Revelation, where we read that "the testimony of Jesus is the spirit of prophecy" (19:10).[28] The Spirit's function to guide the disciples into all truth that they may in turn speak the truth echoes the role assigned to the Spirit in Luke 12:12, where Jesus promises his disciples that the Spirit will teach them what they are to say when they are called upon to bear witness in court. The Spirit-Paraclete enables the disciples to recall Jesus' words,

27. "Paraclete" is used in 1 John for Jesus, but not the Spirit (2:1). In light of the fact that Jesus is portrayed in the Gospel as promising "another Paraclete," the absence of this designation for the Spirit in the epistles is quite surprising. In light of the close connection in 1 John between the Spirit and prophets, it is not surprising that some scholars have argued that the Paraclete is "an active divine power that becomes embodied in certain outstanding leaders within the catholic church" (Johnston, *Spirit-Paraclete*, p. 119). Similarly, Boring advances the hypothesis that "paraclete" was a designation of the Johannine community for its own prophets ("Influence of Christian Prophecy," pp. 113-23).

28. On the Spirit as the Spirit of prophecy in Judaism, see Max Turner, *Power from on High: The Spirit in Israel's Restoration and Witness in Luke-Acts* (Sheffield: Sheffield Academic Press, 1996), and *The Holy Spirit and Spiritual Gifts*; Craig Keener, *The Spirit in the Gospels and Acts: Divine Purity and Power* (Peabody, Mass.: Hendrickson, 1997). Keener devotes a chapter in the book to "The Spirit and Purification in the Fourth Gospel." It is telling, however, than when he wants to discuss a "more prominent characterization of the Spirit of God in early Judaism, namely, the Spirit of prophecy," he turns away from John to Luke, where the evidence is more at hand. For some caveats against too reductionistic a reading of the Spirit as the spirit of prophecy, see John R. Levison, *The Spirit in First Century Judaism* (Leiden: Brill, 1997), esp. pp. 244-54.

bears witness to the disciples and to the world, and will guide Jesus' disciples into all truth.

Yet the Spirit does not exercise analogous functions with respect to Jesus. In other words, there is a difference in the relationship of the Spirit to Jesus and of the Spirit to Jesus' disciples, a difference between what the Spirit is said to do to or for the disciples and what it does to or for Jesus. If we begin with passages in which the "Spirit" is named as actor or agent, we find that the Spirit engenders new birth from above (3:5-8), makes true worship possible (4:23-24), and gives life (6:63; 7:37-39). The Spirit exercises these functions with respect to the disciples, and never with respect to Jesus. By contrast, while Jesus speaks of the need to be "born from above," Jesus himself is the one who *is* or *comes* from above. Jesus is the bread that gives life, the one whose words are life, the resurrection and the life, the one in whom there is life because he has it "as the Father has life in himself" (1:4; 5:26; 6:35, 63; 11:25). Clearly the mode of the Spirit's presence in, with, or on Jesus differs from the mode of the Spirit's presence with the believer.[29] To the extent that the Spirit is the means or agent of life, Jesus is not its recipient but its dispenser.

In the Farewell Discourses, the Paraclete carries out a specific cluster of functions associated with teaching and guiding with respect to the disciples, but not with respect to Jesus. The Spirit is not the source or means of Jesus' extraordinary knowledge, for what Jesus speaks he hears from God, whose voice he has heard, and whose face he has seen (1:18; 3:32-34; 5:30, 37). Furthermore, although Jesus promises that the Spirit-Paraclete will guide the disciples into all truth, bear witness on behalf of Jesus, and recall to memory the words that Jesus had spoken, the Spirit does not recall to Jesus' memory what he has seen or heard or provide the witness to him that he then speaks to the world. In short, the central functions of the Spirit with respect to the disciples have no parallel with respect to Jesus. It is time, then, to develop the Gospel's portrait of the Spirit on a more positive note, and we shall do this under the rubrics, first, of Jesus and the Spirit, and second, of the Father and the Spirit.

---

29. In *The Spirit-Paraclete in the Fourth Gospel*, Windisch argued that the Paraclete's role was superfluous with respect to the disciples as well, and that the Paraclete sayings were not original to the Farewell Discourses.

Jesus and the Spirit

As has been briefly noted already, John lacks much of the data, found in
the Synoptic Gospels, that give rise to the portrait of Jesus as a Spirit-
inspired prophet, charismatic man of the Spirit, or one infused with the
power of the spirit of God. The relationship of Jesus and the Spirit seems
to be conceptualized along somewhat different lines. John stresses the role
of Jesus as the one who bestows or gives the Spirit to others. To be sure,
Jesus is the "bearer" of the Spirit, but the term must be carefully qualified
in John. Jesus bears and gives the Spirit, not because the Father pours it
out upon him as upon the disciples and others, but because the Father
gives it to him in unique fashion, even as the Father grants the Son to
"have life in himself" (5:26). In probing the distinctive contours of the
Johannine conception of the Spirit, and the relationship of Jesus and the
Spirit, we again come upon the Johannine portrait of Jesus as one who
has and exercises divine prerogatives. That Jesus "has" the Spirit and
"gives" it to others is a divine prerogative granted to him by his Father.
Thus the reason for John's lack of emphasis on the Spirit as the empowering agent of Jesus' life and ministry is profoundly theological and directly
connected to his Logos theology.[30] Although this view has been criticized,
there is nevertheless much to commend it.[31] The one who was with God,
and who was God, does not need the filling of the Spirit to accomplish his
mission; rather, part of his mission is to grant the Spirit of life to those
who believe. Put differently, Jesus is not the passive recipient of the Spirit
but rather the active agent in giving God's Spirit to others.[32] The Spirit
does not make Jesus who or what he is — rather, it is because of *who* Jesus
is, the incarnate Word of God, who is with God and is God, that he has
the Spirit and gives it to others. In order to support this argument, we

30. Ernst Käsemann, *The Testament of Jesus: A Study of the Gospel of John in the Light of
Chapter 17*, ET (Philadelphia: Fortress, 1968), pp. 20-26; Eduard Schweizer, "πνεῦμα," in
TDNT 6:438. Rudolf Bultmann went so far as to assert that the evangelist had not "clearly
thought out the relation between the Spirit which Jesus receives in his baptism and his character as the Logos" (*The Gospel of John* [Philadelphia: Westminster, 1971], p. 92 n. 4).

31. For criticisms, see Burge, *The Anointed Community,* pp. 71-72, 81-110; Turner, *The
Holy Spirit and Spiritual Gifts,* pp. 58-59.

32. This is not to claim that this picture is unique to John. Acts 2:33 speaks of the risen
Jesus as having received the promise of the Father, the Holy Spirit, that he then pours out on
his followers.

shall turn next to the various passages that present the relationship of Jesus and the Spirit.

Jesus and the Descent of the Spirit

The narrative of the descent of the Spirit at Jesus' baptism adumbrates the role and identity of the Spirit in the Gospel of John. Three items are of particular note. First, while John's baptism serves to *reveal Jesus to Israel* (1:32), the descent of the Spirit upon Jesus *reveals Jesus to John himself.* The Baptist asserts that he "did not know him," but that the descent of the Spirit upon Jesus was to mark him out as the one who "baptized with the Holy Spirit" (1:33). John not only proclaims Jesus to be the one who baptizes with the Holy Spirit, but he also declares him to be "the one who is before me," the Lamb of God who takes away the sin of the world, and the Son of God. Already from the beginning, then, the Spirit testifies to Jesus, in order to make him known.[33] Thus the descent of the Spirit upon Jesus can also be said to mark him as God's chosen one.[34]

Second, the Fourth Gospel does not speak of a heavenly voice at Jesus' baptism that identifies Jesus as the "beloved Son," as do the Synoptic Gospels. Instead, it is the Spirit who reveals to the Baptist that Jesus is "the Son of God," and it is the Baptist who in turn confesses this to others. The Baptist's primary function is to witness to the truth of God's testimony to Jesus, and the truth of this testimony is sealed to John by the descent of the Spirit on Jesus.

Third, the Baptist testified that he was told that he would *see* the Spirit "coming down and *remaining*" (καταβαῖνον καὶ μένον) upon the one who was to baptize with the Spirit. Whereas the Synoptic Gospels note that the Spirit descended upon Jesus like a dove (cf. Matt. 3:16; Mark 1:10; Luke 3:22), the Fourth Gospel alone adds the twin comments that (1) John would *see* the Spirit (1:32, 33, 34) and (2) that he would see the Spirit *re-*

33. Lesslie Newbigin, *The Light Has Come: An Exposition of the Fourth Gospel* (Grand Rapids: Eerdmans, 1982), p. 16: "Only the action of the Spirit can reveal who Jesus is. In the most fundamental sense it is the Spirit who is the witness."

34. Craig R. Koester, *Symbolism in the Fourth Gospel: Meaning, Mystery, Community* (Minneapolis: Fortress, 1995), p. 159. Koester contends that the descent of the Spirit marks Jesus as God's anointed and so confirms him as the messianic heir of David's throne, as the title "Son of God" suggests.

maining upon Jesus. Here the Spirit provides witness first of all to the Baptist, rather than to Jesus, for it is John who "sees the Spirit." The Spirit who remains on Jesus, then, testifies to Jesus by making him known, first to John and through him to others. The Spirit is the spirit of witness and illumination.[35]

An important part of the Baptist's testimony is lodged in the word that the Spirit would "remain" on Jesus. John's assertion may reflect the view that the Messiah was the bearer of the Spirit, such as is found in Isaiah 11:2, "And the Spirit of the LORD shall rest upon him. . . ." John understands Jesus as the messianic bearer of the Spirit, underscoring the permanence of the Spirit's "resting upon" Jesus with the theologically significant word "abide."[36] That word is further taken to contrast the permanence of the Spirit's resting on Jesus with the sporadic inspiration by the Spirit of the prophets and teachers of Israel, such as one encounters in narratives of the inspiration of Saul and the prophets in the OT. In those texts, the Spirit is said to "come upon" Saul and to cause him to prophesy. The NRSV translates "to prophesy" as to fall into "prophetic frenzy," apparently taking its cue from the words that Saul will be "changed into another person," or so overcome by the power and inspiration of the Spirit that he comports himself in completely atypical and ecstatic ways (compare 1 Samuel 10 with 1 Samuel 19). Hence, the presence of this Spirit on Saul is also temporary since the ecstatic or prophetic state does not continue, given its intense and frenzied nature (see 1 Samuel 19).[37] Later, the author of 1 Samuel also notes that "the spirit of the LORD departed from Saul" and "came mightily upon David from that day forward." Such charism leads not to continued or even intermittent prophecy but rather to military success and leadership in Israel (1 Sam. 16:13-16).[38]

---

35. Particularly emphasized by Felix Porsch, *Pneuma und Wort. Ein exegetischer Beitrag zur Pneumatologie des Johannesevangeliums* (Frankfurt am Main: Josef Knecht, 1974).

36. Burge (*The Anointed Community*, pp. 54-55) argues that the Johannine μένειν ἐν τινι denotes an inward and enduring personal communion and is used elsewhere to depict the mutual indwelling of Father and Son. With respect to the statement that the Spirit "remained on" Jesus, Burge thus concludes, "The unity of Spirit and Son was as permanent and comprehensive as the unity between Father and Son (10:30)." However, since the idiom here is μένιν ἐπι, and not μένειν ἐν, the argument loses its cogency.

37. This is not the only conception found in 1 Samuel of the Spirit — or, perhaps better, *a* spirit — operative in the life of Saul. In 1 Sam. 11:6, for example, the Spirit is said to "come upon Saul" with the result that he becomes very angry.

38. On the varieties of ways in which various Jewish authors thought "spirit" could in-

The description of the Spirit's *remaining* upon Jesus stands in sharp contrast, then, to these descriptions of the Spirit's possession of Saul and the Spirit's departure from him, and it is easy to think that the evangelist intended to contrast the duration of the Spirit's presence on Jesus with that of the Spirit on Saul or other prophets. However, since, as was noted earlier, Jesus' "prophetic" status in the Fourth Gospel is never explicitly attributed to the presence or empowering of the Spirit, the contrast between the intermittent or sporadic presence of the Spirit on someone like Saul and the "abiding" of the Spirit on Jesus cannot simply be reduced to an explanation of differences in the duration of their prophetic endowments. The relationship of Jesus to the Spirit cannot be described as similar to that of other Spirit-inspired figures; it is at its core a different kind of relationship.

Philo also distinguishes different durations of the Spirit's presence with individuals, coupling them with the piety and merit of specific individuals. Commenting on Genesis 6:3, "The LORD said, 'My spirit shall not abide for ever among mortals, because they are flesh,'" Philo writes, "Among such as these then it is impossible that the spirit of God should dwell and make for ever its habitation. . . . The spirit sometimes stays awhile (μένει), but it does not abide for ever (καταμένει δ' οὐκ εἰσάπαν) among us, the mass of mortals." However, proper reverence, obedience, abstention from evil-doing, and contemplation of the one true God help to insure that "the divine spirit of wisdom not lightly shift His dwelling and be gone, but long, long abide with us, since He did thus abide with Moses the wise" (*Gig.* 47-48, 52, 54). Moses, in other words, is the exception that proves the rule, since the spirit of God remained with him as it did not with the mass of ordinary mortals or even as it would not with the most devout and dedicated of the wise. Following his entrance into the darkness of Sinai, where he learned the "secrets of the most holy mysteries," Moses "has *ever the divine spirit at his side, taking the lead in every journey of righteousness* [or, "leading him in every right way"]" (*Gig.* 55).

While Moses' piety and devotion merit a vision of God and the presence of God's spirit, nothing in the Gospel of John suggests that Jesus has somehow *achieved* a vision of God; quite the opposite. From the beginning, the Word was with God; the Son has seen the Father. The Spirit's presence on Jesus in John is evidence of the (prior) relation of the Son to

---

fluence and transform human beings, see particularly, Levison, *The Spirit in First Century Judaism*, pp. 84-98.

the Father. The Spirit descends in order that Jesus "might be revealed" as the Son of God to Israel. The emphasis falls on making Jesus known to others, and not on making of him something that he was not before.

The significance of John's *seeing* the Spirit "remaining on" Jesus lies not in what the Spirit does *to Jesus* but rather in what the Spirit does *for the Baptist.* With respect to Jesus, the result of the Spirit's "descending" ought not to be classified under the rubric of inward illumination, filling,[39] endowment,[40] equipping,[41] or any of a number of other terms redolent of Pauline or Synoptic descriptions of the Spirit's work. Rather, the descent of the Spirit leads the Baptist to recognize Jesus as the One who would baptize with the Spirit, the Lamb of God who takes away the sin of the world, and the Son of God. Such a portrayal of the Spirit in relationship to Jesus stands in continuity with the Spirit's role throughout the Gospel as bearing testimony to Jesus. From the earliest days of Jesus' public ministry, the Spirit bears this witness — and bears it continually. The Spirit is permanently his and not a temporary possession. "Jesus would eventually give the Spirit to believers, but that did not mean he would give it away."[42] Jesus would give *of* the Spirit that was in him, graphically depicted in the scene where he "breathes" it out from within.

This passage summarizing the Baptist's witness thus both assumes and adumbrates the essential configuration of the work and identity of the Spirit that come to expression in the rest of the Gospel: the Spirit bears witness to Jesus precisely in his role as the one who baptizes or cleanses with the spirit of life. The role of the Spirit in bearing witness to Jesus is introduced first in the testimony of the Baptist, a role that is picked up and emphasized in descriptions of the Paraclete in the Farewell Discourses. There the Paraclete, the Holy Spirit, the Spirit of Truth, is described as bearing witness to and glorifying Jesus, guiding the disciples into all truth,

---

39. Rudolf Schnackenburg, *The Gospel According to St. John,* 3 vols. (vol. 1: New York: Seabury, 1968; vol. 2: New York: Seabury, 1980; vol. 3: New York: Crossroad, 1982), 1:304. Similarly, on John 3:34, Schnackenburg comments, "God himself makes the words of his envoy inspired and divine words through the fullness of the Spirit bestowed upon him" (1:387).

40. Burge, *The Anointed Community,* p. 55.

41. Herman Ridderbos, *The Gospel of John: A Theological Commentary* (Grand Rapids: Eerdmans, 1997), p. 76; D. A. Carson, *The Gospel According to John* (Grand Rapids: Eerdmans; Leicester: Inter-Varsity, 1991), p. 152.

42. Koester, *Symbolism in the Fourth Gospel,* p. 161.

and calling to mind Jesus' teaching. Elsewhere the narrative portions of the Gospel that bracket the Farewell Discourses underscore the creative and life-giving role of the Spirit. In both the Farewell Discourses and the narrative sections of John, Jesus "has" and "gives" the divine Spirit, thus exercising a divine prerogative in bestowing the life-giving Spirit. Each of these aspects of the identity and work of the Spirit requires some further exploration, and we turn first to the life-giving role of the Spirit.

The Life-giving Role of the Spirit

The first reference to the work or activity of the Spirit following the encounter with John comes in the conversation with Nicodemus. Jesus tells Nicodemus that he must be "born anew," further explicating that in terms of being "born of water and the Spirit." Because of the narrative thread that connects "baptism by the Spirit" to birth "of *water* and the *Spirit*," it is natural to expect that these two passages are mutually illuminating. What unites these passages is not only the common term "Spirit" but the role of the Spirit as life-giving that is central to each. Several passages from the OT and texts of Second Temple Judaism testify to the Spirit as the agent of renewal that leads to new life.

In Ezekiel 36, God promises his people cleansing through the Spirit that will lead to their obedience and the renewal of the relationship between God and the people of God:

> I will sanctify my great name, which has been profaned among the nations, and which you have profaned among them; and the nations shall know that I am the LORD, says the Lord GOD, when through you I display my holiness before their eyes. I will take you from the nations, and gather you from all the countries, and bring you into your own land. I will sprinkle clean water upon you, and you shall be clean from all your uncleannesses, and from all your idols I will cleanse you. A new heart I will give you, and a new spirit I will put within you; and I will remove from your body the heart of stone and give you a heart of flesh. And I will put my spirit within you, and cause you to walk in my statutes and be careful to observe my ordinances. You shall dwell in the land which I gave to your fathers; and you shall be my people, and I will be your God. (36:23-28)

Not only does this passage link water and the Spirit, but in the context in which this passage appears God also promises that he will sanctify his name (36:23), gather his people together (36:24, 28), cause them to obey his commandments (36:27), and renew his relationship with them (36:28). Each of these themes plays an important role in the Fourth Gospel in describing the work of Jesus.

In the very next chapter of Ezekiel, the work of the Spirit is pictured in terms of life-giving power (37:5-6):

> Thus says the Lord God to these bones: "Behold, I will cause
>   breath to enter you, and you shall live.
> And I will lay sinews upon you, and will cause flesh
>   to come upon you, and cover you with skin, and put breath in
>   you, and you shall live; and you shall know that I am the Lord."

In this passage, the Spirit gives life so that the dead live and know the Lord. Similar is the passage in Isaiah 44:3-6, where the Spirit also creates a people who are obedient to and acknowledge the Lord.

> For I will pour water on the thirsty land,
>   and streams on the dry ground;
> I will pour my spirit upon your descendants,
>   and my blessing on your offspring.
> They shall spring up like a green tamarisk,
>   like willows by flowing streams.
> This one will say, "I am the Lord's,"
>   another will be called by the name of Jacob,
> yet another will write on the hand, "The Lord's,"
> and adopt the name of Israel.
> Thus says the Lord, the King of Israel
>   and his Redeemer, the Lord of hosts:
> "I am the first and I am the last;
> besides me there is no god."

Here again the water serves as an image for the Spirit, which God promises to pour out. The result, much as in Ezekiel, is the creation of a renewed people who belong to the Lord. Moreover, both Ezekiel and Isaiah speak of the expulsion of idolatry. Ezekiel, however, pictures this in terms of the water of cleansing or purification, whereas Isaiah depicts the Spirit as a life-giving spirit, analogous to life-giving water. The promise of God in Isaiah to give the Spirit is grounded in and by the declaration of God's ultimate sovereignty. Both passages testify to the ultimate point of the Spirit's work as the creation of a people who acknowledge that "there is no god" besides the Lord (Isa. 44:6; cf. Ezekiel 36).

The association of a new Spirit with the obedience of a renewed people is attested by various texts of Second Temple Judaism. In *Jubilees*, for example, Moses prays that God's mercy will be demonstrated to his people through the creation for them of 'an upright Spirit." Moses' prayer continues:

> And do not let the spirit of Beliar rule over them to accuse them before you and ensnare them from every path of righteousness so that they might be destroyed from before your face. But they are your people and your inheritance. . . . Create a pure heart and a holy spirit for them. And do not let them be ensnared by their sin henceforth and forever. (1:20-21)

The Lord grants Moses' request:

> I shall create for them a holy spirit, and I shall purify them so that they will not turn away from following me from that day and forever. And their souls will cleave to me and to all my commandments. And they will do my commandments. And I shall be a father to them, and they will be sons to me. And they will all be called "sons of the living God." And every angel and spirit will know and acknowledge that they are my sons and I am their father in uprightness and righteousness. And I shall love them. (*Jub.* 1:23-25)

Once again God's gift of a holy spirit purifies people for obedience, who will live uprightly, following God in righteousness. God's spirit creates a restored and renewed Israel, children of the living God, their father who loves them.

Strikingly similar views of the Spirit's cleansing role are found in the Dead Sea Scrolls. In 1QS 4:20-22, we read this promise:

> God will refine, with his truth, all human deeds, and will purify for himself the configuration of humankind, ripping out all spirit of deceit from the innermost part of his flesh, and cleansing him with the spirit

of holiness from every irreverent deed. He will sprinkle over him the spirit of truth like lustral water (in order to cleanse him) from all the abhorrences of deceit and from the defilement of the unclean spirit. In this way the upright will understand knowledge of the Most High, and the wisdom of the sons of heaven will teach those of perfect behavior. For these are those selected by God for an everlasting covenant.

The Spirit cleanses people so that they will have knowledge of God and live in obedience, as those who are the "sons of heaven" chosen for the everlasting covenant.

The prayer of Joseph for Aseneth in *Joseph and Aseneth* 8:9-11 points in much the same direction. Joseph prays:

Lord God of my father Israel
the Most High, the Powerful One of Jacob,
who gave life to all (things)
and called (them) from the darkness to light,
and from the error to the truth,
and from the death to the life,
you, Lord, bless this virgin,
and renew her by your spirit,
and form her anew by your hidden hand,
and make her alive again by your life,
and let her eat your bread of life,
and drink your cup of blessing,
and number her among your people
that you have chosen before all (things) came into being,
and let her enter your rest
which you have prepared for your chosen ones
and live in your eternal life for ever (and) ever.

Here the function of God's spirit is depicted in terms of giving new life and of renewal, so that Aseneth may be numbered among the chosen people of God and thus pass from darkness to light, error to truth, death to life. There are striking similarities to the depiction of the Spirit's life-giving work with that of the Spirit in the Gospel of John.

Two dominant portrayals of the work of the Spirit emerge from these texts of Scripture and Second Temple Judaism. In Ezekiel 36, *Jubilees*, and 1QS, the Spirit cleanses or purifies. In the texts from Ezekiel 37, Isaiah, and

Joseph and Aseneth, the Spirit is described as life-giving. Whether the work of the Spirit is described primarily as cleansing or purification, or primarily as life-giving, the purposes and goals of the Spirit's work are depicted in much the same manner. Obedience to God, knowledge of God, and the covenant with God are renewed in such a way that the people become the people that God has willed for them to be all along.

In turning to Jesus' discussion with Nicodemus in John, we encounter the Spirit as the power or means of effecting the "new birth" or "birth from above." Various clues in this passage alert the reader that the discussion between Nicodemus and Jesus is more than a discussion between two individuals, and that both speak on behalf of or represent a group.[43] Although Jesus speaks directly to Nicodemus, the pronouns and verbs that are used throughout the conversation are plural. Nicodemus's opening statement, "We know that you are a teacher come from God," implies that he speaks on behalf of others, perhaps the other rabbis gathered with him. Jesus similarly speaks on behalf of his disciples, using the plural "we," and speaks to "you," a plural envisioning Nicodemus and his fellow rabbis.[44]

Still, the plural verbs and pronouns make it evident that the challenge to Nicodemus is not merely or primarily a personal, individualistic challenge ("You, Nicodemus") but a challenge to those on whose behalf he speaks and whom he represents. Jesus' challenge goes out to all those who are contemporaries of and taught by Nicodemus. They must, in order to enter the kingdom of God, be "reborn," that is, receive a new identity, family, and set of allegiances and loyalties.[45] They must receive new life, life that is effected by the Spirit, resulting in being born anew. Jesus' words are thus a challenge to consider what it means to be "Israel," the people of

43. See David Rensberger, *Johannine Faith and Liberating Community* (Philadelphia: Westminster, 1988), pp. 52-53; J. L. Martyn, "Glimpses into the History of the Johannine Community," in *L'Évangile de Jean: sources, rédaction, théologie*, ed. M. de Jonge (Gembloux: Duculot, 1977), p. 112.

44. Rensberger writes, 'It is Nicodemus' group that is challenged by Jesus' group to be 'born from above'" (*Johannine Faith*, p. 56). This may represent the perception of the Johannine church and the Jewish synagogue, but the evangelist first of all presents Jesus as the one who challenges a leading Jewish teacher and, through that challenge, all those who adhere to his ways. It is Jesus who issues this challenge, and this is the primary thrust of the narrative itself.

45. See here Wayne A. Meeks, "The Ethics of the Fourth Evangelist," in *Exploring the Gospel of John: In Honor of D. Moody Smith*, ed. R. Alan Culpepper and C. Clifton Black (Louisville: Westminster/John Knox, 1996), p. 323.

God, and to invite identification with the people of God who are renewed through the life-giving Spirit of God that Jesus confers.

In the Gospel of John, then, as in those five texts examined briefly, the work of the Spirit has a corporate manifestation, in that the Spirit effects the life-giving transformation that makes people "children of God" (1:12) who are "born from above" to eternal life (3:3, 5-6). That transformation is described, in keeping with the life-giving function of the Spirit, in terms of "new birth," a graphic description of the life given by the Spirit. Similarly, the water that flows from Jesus' pierced side represents the release of the life-giving Spirit. When, following his resurrection, Jesus "breathes" the Spirit upon his disciples, he breathes upon them the power to forgive sins, the concrete manifestation of the Spirit's life-giving power through them. Sin brings death, but the removal of sin brings life (cf. 16:7-8; 7:37-39; 8:24, 31-36). The Spirit gives life to a renewed people of God. This is the Spirit "breathed out" from Jesus upon the disciples. Jesus is the one who "has" and so "gives" the Spirit.

Jesus as the Giver of the Spirit of Life

The previous assertion needs a bit more unpacking, especially in light of the persistent interpretation of Jesus as a Spirit-endowed prophet along the lines of the Lukan portrait of Jesus. Alongside the narrative of the "descent" of the Spirit, the one passage in John that seems most amenable to interpretation along prophetic lines reads as follows: "He whom God has sent speaks the words of God, for he gives the Spirit without measure. The Father loves the Son and has placed all things in his hands" (3:34-35).[46] There is some ambiguity in the Greek concerning the subject of the clause "he gives the Spirit without measure." Although Origen and Cyril, along with some modern commentators, take the subject of "he gives" to be Je-

---

46. W. C. van Unnik ("A Greek Characteristic of Prophecy in the Fourth Gospel," in *Text and Interpretation: Studies in the New Testament presented to Matthew Black,* ed. Ernest Best and R. McL. Wilson [Cambridge: Cambridge University Press, 1979], pp. 211-29) argues that knowledge of "all things" was widespread as a characterization of prophets in relation to prophetic insight in the Greek-Hellenistic world, and that it can be found in a few texts of Greek-speaking Judaism. On this point see Christopher Forbes, *Prophecy and Inspired Speech in Early Christianity and Its Hellenistic Environment,* WUNT 2/75 (Tübingen: J. C. B. Mohr [Paul Siebeck], 1995), p. 313.

sus, this reading makes it difficult to understand how the clause "for he gives the Spirit without measure" provides the reason or explanation of the previous clause, "he speaks the words of God."[47] How would Jesus' capacity to give the Spirit without measure explain why or how he speaks the words of God? Similarly, if the subject of the statement "he gives the Spirit without measure" is Jesus, then it is difficult to understand how the assertion there leads logically to the following verse: "The Father loves the Son, and has given all things into his hands." Indeed, the statement that the Father "has placed all things in his hands" presumably explains and includes the previous statement, "he gives the Spirit without measure." God has "placed all things" into the Son's hands; God has given him the Spirit "without measure." God is the subject of "has sent," "gives the Spirit," "loves the Son," and "has placed all things."

If God is understood to be the subject of "he gives," then the passage makes three predications as follows:

- The One whom God has sent (the Son) speaks the words of God.
- God has given to the Son the Spirit "without measure."
- The Father loves the Son and has placed all things into his hands.

These three statements are virtually parallel to each other and refer to three powers or capacities that the Father has given to the Son: the capacity to speak the very words of God; the unlimited possession of the Spirit; and the power over "all things." Jesus therefore speaks the words of life because he has the life-giving Spirit of God (6:63-64).

This is the same spirit of God described in the creation accounts of Genesis as the breath of God. Genesis 2:7 reads, "Then the LORD God formed man from the dust of the ground, and breathed into his nostrils the breath of life; and the man became a living being." It is God's own breath that brings human beings to life. Thus the phrase "breath of life," frequently used throughout the OT to refer to the life of an individual, carries ambiguous overtones (Gen. 1:30; 2:7; 6:17; 7:15, 22; Job 12:10; 33:4; Isa. 57:16; 2 Esdr. 3:5; 16:61; Wis. 15:11). On the one hand, human beings breathe, and the cessation of breathing signifies death; the "breath of life" is their own breath. On the other hand, the account of creation in Genesis

---

47. Origen commented as follows: "The redeemer who is sent to speak the words of God does not give the Spirit only in part"; quoted in Schnackenburg, *St. John*, 1:387.

intimates that God's "breath" creates and sustains life. The image of God's life-giving breath clearly underlies Ezekiel's vision of the valley of the dry bones, where the "breath" that animates the bones is eventually identified as the Spirit of God:

> Thus says the Lord GOD to these bones: "I will cause breath to enter you, and you shall live. . . ." Thus says the Lord GOD: "I am going to open your graves, and bring you up from your graves, O my people; and I will bring you back to the land of Israel. . . . I will put my spirit within you, and you shall live, and I will place you on your own soil; then you shall know that I, the LORD, have spoken and will act," says the LORD. (Ezek. 37:5, 12, 14)

A few other passages equate the "spirit of God" and the "breath of God." Job 33:4 reads, "The spirit of God has made me, and the breath of the Almighty gives me life." Likewise, in Isaiah 57:16 we find these words:

> For I will not contend for ever,
>   nor will I always be angry;
> for from me proceeds the spirit,
>   and I have made the breath of life. (cf. Mal. 2:15)

It is difficult to doubt that this conception lies behind John 20, where Jesus "breathes" the Spirit into his disciples. Herman Ridderbos comments, "If the reference to these texts were direct, then the meaning would be that just as in the beginning God breathed a living spirit into humankind, so in this moment of the new creation Jesus breathes the Holy Spirit into the disciples and so grants them eternal life."[48] Ridderbos actually favors instead the view that in giving the Spirit Jesus equips the disciples for the work assigned to them. Yet the parallel between Jesus' "breathing" the Spirit on the disciples and God "breathing" the breath of life into humankind can scarcely be judged accidental, particularly in light of John's portrayal of the Spirit as the Spirit of life. Exercising his God-given prerogative, Jesus breathes the life-giving Spirit into his disciples. This view is

---

48. Ridderbos, *Gospel of John*, p. 643. See C. K. Barrett, *The Gospel According to St. John*, 2nd ed. (Philadelphia: Westminster, 1978), p. 570; Brown, *John*, 1:1023, 1035, 1037; Koester, *Symbolism in the Fourth Gospel*, p. 161. George R. Beasley-Murray (*John*, 2nd ed., Word Biblical Commentary [Nashville: Nelson, 1999], pp. 380-81) argues for a close link to Ezekiel 37, interpreting the breath of life as the power of the resurrection.

confirmed by the command given to the disciples, which entails the forgiveness of sin, which brings life and is emphasized elsewhere in John. The Lamb of God, who takes away the sin of the world, is the one who "baptizes with the Spirit" (1:29-33), who "convicts the world in respect of sin, of righteousness, and of judgment" (16 7-8). Jesus thus breathes new life into his disciples by bestowing the Spirit of life.[49]

Elsewhere in the OT the Spirit is the life-giving power of God. In Genesis 6:3, for example, we read these words of the Lord, "My spirit shall not abide in mortals forever, for they are flesh; their days shall be one hundred twenty years." Two items are of interest. First, God's spirit is that which gives them life; second, God's spirit does not "abide in mortals" forever; that is to say, mortals die, for they are "flesh," and enlivened only by God's spirit. The statement at John 3:6 echoes the contrast between the mortal "flesh" and life-giving "Spirit": "What is born of the flesh is flesh, and what is born of the Spirit is spirit." It is God's spirit that gives life; only birth by the Spirit leads to the kingdom of God, to eternal life.[50]

The Son speaks the words of God because he has been entrusted with all things, including the very words of God, as well as the Spirit, who quickens those words to the understanding of listeners and hence brings them life (6:63). Jesus speaks words that are life because he *has* the Spirit as he has "all things" from the Father.[51] Illuminating parallels can be found in links between the spirit of God and understanding and speaking the truth in wisdom literature.[52] In Job, for example, there is a link between the presence of the spirit of God and the ability to understand the truth (32:6-9) and to speak the truth (27:2-24; 32:15-20). At Job 33:4, where the NRSV translates the MT "The spirit of God has made me, and the breath of the Almighty gives me life," the LXX renders. "The spirit of God has made me,

49. Schnackenburg, *St. John*, 3:325; Koester, *Symbolism in the Fourth Gospel*, pp. 158-59.

50. Levison. (*The Spirit in First Century Judaism*, p. 60) shows how Pseudo-Philo repeatedly cites Gen. 6:3 in envisioning the Spirit not as "the special endowment of the so-called prophetic spirit but instead as the life-giving spirit which each human has for a limited time."

51. Wijngaards (*The Spirit in John*) argues that because John emphasizes the post-resurrection appearance of the Spirit, he "minimizes" it in the life of Jesus. I would argue rather that the theological motive lies elsewhere, namely in John's conception that Jesus has the Spirit in order to bestow it rather than to be empowered by it.

52. For detailed discussion, see Levison, *The Spirit in First Century Judaism*, pp. 62-65. For discussion of the unusual knowledge of the pneumatic, see also Volz, *Der Geist Gottes*, pp. 32-41, 103-5.

and the breath of the Almighty *teaches* me."[53] Similarly, Daniel is portrayed in the OT as a man of wisdom and understanding because of the spirit within him (5:11-14). Josephus underscores, but subtly alters, this view of Daniel in assigning his wisdom to "the divine spirit that attended him," rendering him alone "fully able to discover things that were not in the understanding of others" (*Ant.* 10.239). Josephus alters the LXX by changing a preposition, for although the LXX states several times that there was an excellent spirit "within" (*en; ἐν;* 5:11, 12, 14), Josephus speaks rather of "the divine spirit that attended him" (*symparesti;* συμπάρεστι). As John R. Levison comments, "In other words, the spirit did not inspire Daniel's wisdom by existing within, i.e., possessing him, but by accompanying him."[54]

In the Fourth Gospel, the Paraclete exercises just this function with respect to the disciples — but not with respect to Jesus. In contrast, as the one who is the truth, Jesus speaks the words of God. It is possible, of course, that John thought of the Son as speaking by the power or inspiration of the Spirit, but the dramatic absence of texts that are amenable to such an interpretation, or to an interpretation of Jesus as a Spirit-inspired prophet, suggests another route for understanding the Spirit's relationship to Jesus' work. Once again, Jesus is the one who gives the Spirit who enables others to know and understand the truth. He has, and so bestows, the life-giving, illuminating Spirit of God.

Two similar assertions in John provide striking parallels. According to the assertions found in John 5:21-27, the Father has given two other powers into the hands of the Son: First, the Father has given the Son the power to give life: "Indeed, just as the Father raises the dead and gives them life,

53. The way in which *Tg. Jonathan* retells the story of Saul is particularly suggestive for the conception of the Spirit's activity in John. In the story of Saul's prophetic frenzy in 1 Samuel 10 and19, the Targum "tames" the ecstatic spirit, with two results: While the Targum still refers to "the spirit of prophecy," this spirit does not inspire prophets, who in turn prophesy, but rather the spirit of prophecy inspires teachers who "sing praises." The familiar story, now rewritten, runs as follows, "And everyone who knew him yesterday and the day before it saw, and behold he was singing praise with the teachers. And the people said, each man to his neighbor: 'What is this that has happened to the son of Kish? Is Saul also among the teachers?' . . . Therefore it became a proverb: 'Is Saul also among the teachers?'" (*Tg. Jon.* 1 Sam. 10:11-12). Apparently the Targum recasts the role of the spirit of prophecy in light of social functions more familiar to it: the spirit of prophecy produces *teachers.*

54. Levison, *The Spirit in First Century Judaism,* p. 169. See also Forbes, *Prophecy and Inspired Speech,* pp. 18-19.

so also the Son gives life to whomever he wishes. . . . For just as the Father has life in himself, so he has granted the Son also to have life in himself" (5:21, 26). Second, the Father has granted the Son the power of judgment: "The Father judges no one but has given all judgment to the Son . . . and he has given him authority to execute judgment, because he is the Son of Man" (5:22, 27; cf. 10:29-30). Crucial to the interpretation of these texts are the twin affirmations that (1) the Son exercises certain divine preroga-tives, and (2) the Son exercises them even as God does, because God has given him those prerogatives. Jesus exercises judgment and confers life be-cause God has conferred these powers upon him, and this implies that Je-sus exercises these powers as no other figure — save God — can or does. Similarly, the way that Jesus has and confers the Spirit differs from the way that all others have the Spirit. Although Jesus confers the Spirit, he confers it *from within:* it flows from within (7:37-39; 19:34); he breathes it from within. He does not "pass on" the Spirit as Elijah passes it to Elisha; the spirit cannot depart from him as it does from Saul to David, for he has it without measure: this is how the Father has given it to him.

Who speaks the words recounted in 3:34-35 ("For he whom God has sent utters the words of God, for it is not by measure that he gives the Spirit . . .")? Although it is difficult to tell whether these words are a contin-uation of the Baptist's words of 3:27-30, or whether they are to be con-strued as an editorial comment, it is entirely possible that they are to be taken as the words of the Baptist. If so, then it is once again the Baptist who bears witness to the way in which the Spirit testifies to Jesus' unique status as God's spokesman, even as the descent of the Spirit at the Jordan revealed to John who Jesus was. In both instances, John the Baptist is the one who bears testimony to Jesus; first, that Jesus will baptize with the Spirit; then, here, that Jesus truly speaks the words of God. In both cases, the gift of the Spirit provides the witness that Jesus is God's unique spokesman. Even more, the gift of the Spirit to Jesus is the testimony that the Father has given all things into his hands. In fact, one of the gifts of God to the Son is the gift of the Spirit.[55] This, however, is not conceived of in John as occur-ring through or at the time of the descent of the Spirit. The Spirit does not

55. As Ridderbos comments, "Jesus is not merely a prophet who speaks the word of God on occasion, when called on to do so. His authority to speak as God is unlimited, or as vs. 35 has it: 'The Father loves the Son and has given all things into his hand'" (*Gospel of John,* p. 150).

create the relationship between Father and Son; it is the relationship between Father and Son that means that Jesus has and gives the Spirit.[56] The descent of the Spirit is witness of this.

Earlier in this chapter we quoted Philo's description of Moses as one who learned the secrets of the "holy mysteries" and consequently had "ever the divine spirit at his side." As has often been pointed out, there is a clear contrast between the portrayal of Moses as one who "ascended" to the mountain to hear the oracles of God and the Johannine portrayal of Jesus as the incarnation of the Logos, as the one who "came down from heaven." In fact, the emphatic statement that "No one has ascended into heaven except the one who descended from heaven, the Son of Man" (3:13) implicitly acknowledges — by explicitly denying accounts of ascents — the sort of knowledge that only the Son, who has heard and seen God, has and brings (1:17-18; 5:37-39). The Son's knowledge comes to him uniquely. He does not ascend to attain such knowledge; he descends to bring it. Similarly, he does not enter into the mysteries of God in order to be inspired or to receive illumination through the Spirit, but he himself has the Spirit and so brings the words of light and life.

The disciples will have the accompaniment of the Spirit as the one who will teach them everything, guiding them into knowledge of the truth (14:26; 16:13), but the Gospel does not say that the Spirit teaches or guides Jesus. Clearly the relationship of Jesus and the Spirit is not perfectly analogous to the relationship between the disciples and the Spirit that Jesus promises them. Jesus speaks of what he hears from the Father; so also the Spirit will speak what he hears (16:13). This is made more specific in the explanation that the Spirit will take what belongs to Jesus to declare it to the disciples (16:15). Jesus speaks the words given to him by the Father, and he speaks the words of life, thus conferring the Spirit of life (6:60-63), but he does not take "what belongs to the Spirit" and declare it to his disciples.

In the portions of the Gospel that bracket the Farewell Discourses, the Spirit is a life-giving power through which God creates, renews, and revivifies a people. Through the Spirit one is born anew (3:3, 5-6); through the Spirit one receives life (6:63; 7:37-39); and through the Spirit sins are forgiven, thus bringing one from death to life (20:22-23). These portions of

---

56. Similarly, "For just as the Father has life in himself, so he has granted the Son also to have life in himself; he has given him authority to execute judgment, *because he is the Son of Man*."

the Gospel use imagery of water and breath coming from within to show that Jesus bestows life from within, not as something alien to himself but as a power or attribute that belongs properly to him. Because the Father has given "all things" into the Son's hand, the Son also has the power to bestow the Spirit and to give life. The Son thus "has" the Spirit and gives it not as an entity foreign to himself but as that which comes from within. Jesus exercises the prerogatives that belong to God alone — because God has granted him to have this power "in himself."[57]

Yet the picture is somewhat complicated by the Gospel's clear assertions that the Spirit is not given until after Jesus' departure. In the Farewell Discourses, Jesus endeavors to ameliorate the distress caused by his absence by promising the disciples that the Father will send the Paraclete to be with them forever (14:16, 26; 15:26 16:7). Unless Jesus departs, the Paraclete will not come. This had already been spelled out earlier in the narrator's interpolation that in speaking of "living water" Jesus was speaking "about the Spirit, which believers in him were to receive; for as yet there was no Spirit, because Jesus was not yet glorified" (John 7:39; οὔπω γὰρ ἦν πνεῦμα ὅτι Ἰησοῦς οὐδέπω ἐδοξάσθη).

Some commentators argue that the verse should be punctuated as follows: "If any one thirst, let him come to me, and let him drink, whoever believes in me. As the Scripture has said. . ." This makes it more natural to read the following statement, "Out of his heart shall flow rivers of living water," as a reference to the "heart of Jesus." One comes to Jesus and drinks because rivers of living water flow out of Jesus' very being. This would clearly fit with the Gospel's repeated emphasis on Jesus as the one who gives the Spirit, and foreshadow the later scenes in which blood and water flow from the side of the crucified Jesus (19:34) and in which he breathes

57. In arguing for the divinity of the Son, the Church Fathers also included the "Spirit" among the list of "all things" that the Son has; see Anthony J. Casurella, *The Johannine Paraclete in the Church Fathers: A Study in the History of Exegesis* (Tübingen: J. C. B. Mohr [Paul Siebeck], 1983), pp. 32-35, 85-86. In his study of the Spirit in the OT and Judaism, Volz contends that passages such as Isaiah 11 and *1 Enoch* 49:3; 62:2, which speak of the messianic king's endowment with the Spirit, reflect the general trend towards the divinization of kings in the ancient eastern world. Yet Volz argues that whereas in antiquity the king was often an incarnation of divinity, in Judaism the king is bound to the spiritual world only and precisely through the spirit (*Der Geist Gottes*, p. 89). Volz thus helpfully underscores the divine identity of the Spirit, as well as the way in which Judaism reflects this understanding precisely by modifying it. The spirit remains God's power.

the Spirit upon his disciples (20:22). Together these three scenes graphically depict the way in which the Spirit is internal to Jesus and flows from within him.

The passage can also be construed so as to take the "rivers of living water" as flowing from within the "heart" (κοιλία) of the believer. Then Jesus not only promises that those who drink will have their thirst quenched, but also that they shall have within them "rivers of living water." On this reading, the passage has a clear parallel to Jesus' promise in John 4:14: "Those who drink of the water that I will give them will never be thirsty. The water that I will give will become in them a spring of water gushing up to eternal life." Both passages imply that Jesus is the one who gives the water; but the water then becomes "a spring . . . gushing up to eternal life" or "living water." The water symbolizes eternal life, Jesus' gift that is effected by the life-giving Spirit. However, this promise appears to be deferred until after Jesus' death because "the Spirit had not yet been given, for Jesus had not yet been glorified." Then, those who were "believers in him" could receive the Spirit.

If the Spirit is not given until after Jesus' death, what then are the implications for receiving life from Jesus during the time of his ministry? For elsewhere Jesus refers to his words as "spirit and life" (6:63) and speaks of the life he confers as a present reality ("Whoever believes in the Son has eternal life," 3:36; cf. 5:24; 6:47). Jesus warns that unless one is "born by the Spirit," that person will never receive life. To the extent that the Spirit and life are identified with each other, then the actual reception of life seems to be deferred until after Jesus' death. Consequently, when Jesus speaks of giving life (e.g., 3:5-8; 6:63), he speaks proleptically of a situation that will obtain only after his death. Similarly, Jesus' gift of the Spirit is subsequent to his death and glorification. Jesus' death and resurrection seal the effects of his ministry. From beginning to end, Jesus' presence and purpose are characterized as life-giving.

What also needs to be emphasized is that what happens *after* Jesus' death also happens *because of* Jesus' death, whether that be the conferring of life or the giving of the Spirit. The same tension between present and future exists in John 6. There Jesus uses a present tense to speak of himself as the "bread of life," but he goes on to assert that "the bread which I shall give for the life of the world is my flesh," a reference to his death on the cross. Jesus' promise anticipates his death; his death actualizes the promise. Those who believe in Jesus receive life after Jesus' death, but also — and here is the main point — *because of* Jesus' death. In the same manner, those who believe in Jesus receive the Spirit after Jesus' death, but also *because* of Jesus' death. It is not simply that Jesus must send a surrogate in his absence, but that the life that he brings is life that is effected through his death on the cross, and the bestowal of the Spirit is contingent upon that death. Without his death there will be no life for the world (6:51-58; 12:24).

Jesus thus promises those who hear and respond in faith that they do have life, even though its reception depends on his death, and even though they shall wait to be raised at the last day. The present tense of the Johannine promises of life does not obliterate the need for a future event that seals those promises. In the same manner, Jesus promises that one can be born again, even though Jesus' death has not yet made possible the new birth, and even though the Spirit has not yet been given. The Gospel speaks in the present tense of the need to be born again, even though the future death of Jesus and coming of the Spirit ultimately seal and make possible those realities. While Jesus *has* the Spirit, even as he has life, upon his death he gives the Spirit to his disciples so that they may receive the life that he has.

The Spirit and the Risen Christ

As noted earlier, the term "Paraclete" is applied to the Spirit only in chapters 14–16. This distinctive terminology, coupled with the specific functions of the Paraclete in these chapters, has often been taken as indicating that the Paraclete is an "independent being" or "distinct figure" rather than the power or means through which God brings life, a view more in keeping with the portrayal of the Spirit as water and breath.[58] In the Farewell Discourses, the Paraclete is not compared to wind or breath or water but is described as one who teaches, bears witness, convicts the world of judgment,

---

58. Betz *(Der Paraklet)* takes the differences to indicate that the "Paraclete" is essentially a different figure than the "Holy Spirit," and that in the present form of the Gospel the two figures have been merged into one. Numerous theories have been propounded in which the Paraclete is taken to be a human figure. Origen, for example, argues against the view that the Paraclete is the Apostle Paul! Montanus apparently identified himself as the Paraclete, but not as the Holy Spirit. For discussion, see Casurella, *The Johannine Paraclete*, pp. 4, 89. Both Boring ("Influence of Christian Prophecy") and Johnston *(Spirit-Paraclete)* have argued for the function and role of the Paraclete as lodged in a specific group of leaders within the Church.

is present with the disciples, and glorifies Jesus. In other words, the Paraclete is described not with terms that lend themselves to interpretation of the Spirit as God's activity or attribute but in terms that lean toward the portrayal of the Paraclete as a separate and distinct figure whose functions and activities are very similar, and sometimes even identical, to those of Jesus elsewhere in the Gospel. This portrait of the Paraclete in the Farewell Discourses has led to the view that the Paraclete is a "replacement for Christ." Once Jesus has departed to the Father, the Spirit essentially takes his place and carries on his ministry.

The view that the Paraclete is a "replacement" for Jesus is rather widely held among interpreters of the Gospel of John. Raymond Brown, for example, states that Jesus comes back "in and through the Paraclete."[59] Brown argues that, given the delay of the parousia, the evangelist emphasized the very real way in which Jesus had come back to his disciples: "as the Paraclete, Jesus is present within all believers." Brown's first formulation — "in and through the Paraclete" — maintains a distinction between the figures of Jesus and the Paraclete and lends itself to language of "mediation." However, Brown's second formulation — "as the Paraclete" — virtually collapses any distinction between Jesus and the Paraclete. That both formulations — "in and through the Paraclete" and "as the Paraclete" — are echoed widely and indiscriminately without much attention to the differences between them merely underscores how difficult it is to interpret the Gospel at precisely this point.

Indeed, it is possible to draw up a list of correspondences between Jesus and the Spirit that imply that Jesus' activities are carried on through or by the Spirit, or perhaps even "as the Spirit."[60] The overlapping functions are primarily those of teaching and disclosing God's word.

- Jesus teaches (7:14-15; 8:20; 18:19), as does the Spirit (14:26);
- Jesus gives testimony (5:31-32; 7:7; 8:13-14), as does the Spirit (15:26);
- Both Jesus (7:17; 8:26; 14:10) and the Spirit (14:26; 16:13-14) speak of what they have heard;
- Both Jesus (1:18; 4:25) and the Spirit (16:13) disclose and reveal.

---

59. Brown, *John*, 2:1143. Beasley-Murray is one of the few commentators to oppose this interpretation of John in recent times (*John*, pp. 257-58); for a response see Turner, *The Holy Spirit and Spiritual Gifts*, p. 81.

60. See Burge, *The Anointed Community*, p. 141.

One can see in such similarities part of the impetus for the view that the Paraclete comes as Jesus' replacement. What Jesus had once done among the disciples the Paraclete now does. Yet the Paraclete's functions are decisively and characteristically related to Jesus, and to his person and work. The Paraclete is said not only to "teach you everything," but to "remind you of all that [Jesus has] said to you" (14:26). So also the Paraclete testifies to Jesus (15:26-27). The Paraclete glorifies Jesus; the Paraclete will take what belongs to Jesus and "declare it to you" (16:14). In other words, while there are many parallel descriptions of Jesus and the Paraclete, the Paraclete exercises the specific function of making Jesus' word and presence real among the disciples. If the Spirit is taken primarily as a "replacement" for Jesus, then it is difficult to understand the Spirit's role of testifying and bearing witness to Jesus.

The view that the Paraclete is a replacement for Jesus also arises from Jesus' promise in the Farewell Discourses that, if he goes away, he will send "another Paraclete" (14:16), and that this Paraclete will *not* come *unless* Jesus departs (16:7). Thus when Jesus speaks of his imminent departure, he promises the disciples that he will not abandon them: "I will not leave you orphaned; I am coming to you" (14:18). Yet the mode of his coming will be such that the world will not be able to see him (14:19). When Judas (not Iscariot) puzzles over this obscure promise, Jesus tells him that those who love him will keep his word and "my Father will love them, and we will come to them and make our home with them" (14:23). Then Jesus promises that he will send the Paraclete to the disciples (14:26). The climactic promise of the coming of the Paraclete has suggested that Jesus will "come to" his disciples in or as the Paraclete. Such a presence explains how it is that the world cannot see the Paraclete, as well as how it is that the disciples will not be alone after Jesus' departure.

Jesus does not promise his disciples the presence of the Paraclete only; he also promises them a mutual indwelling: "you in me, and I in you" (14:20). Presumably this could be understood to happen through the Paraclete, but it is never explicitly asserted. Similarly, Jesus does not simply say that he will be with the disciples, or that the Paraclete will be with them, but that "my Father and I will come" and "make our home with them" (14:23). In other words, Jesus speaks of his presence, his Father's presence, and the Spirit's presence with the disciples. In some fashion, Jesus, the Father, and the Paraclete will all be "with" believers. Just as Jesus does not "replace" the Father but rather makes the Father known, testifies to him, and discloses him, so the Spirit does not "replace" Jesus but makes Jesus known, testifies to him, and discloses him to the disciples. In this manner, the Spirit does not *replace* Jesus, or even become the real presence of Jesus; the Spirit makes the presence of Jesus real.

Thus there are several ways of formulating the promise of presence in the Farewell Discourses: Jesus will come to the disciples; Jesus and the Father will come to them; and the Spirit will come to be with them. While it is clear that these three are distinct figures, or can be spoken of as distinct "entities" with different functions or identities, this is not to imply that the disciples experience their presence as the presence of multiple realities or powers. Indeed, the language of the Gospel rather suggests the unity of the experience of divine presence in the life of the believer. The disciples are assured that they will know and experience the ongoing presence of the Father in the Son through the agency of the Spirit.

Even the language of the Spirit's origin and mission shows that, ultimately, the Spirit comes from the Father in order to bear witness to the Son, to call to mind Jesus' teaching, and to make the presence of Jesus real precisely because of his absence. Furthermore, although the Paraclete is sent by Jesus, the Paraclete is never "the spirit of Jesus."[61] If the Spirit-Paraclete calls to mind Jesus' words, it is precisely as the Spirit of the Father, given to the Son and sent "in the name of" the Son to his disciples, that the Spirit-Paraclete does so.[62] We turn then to a closer examination of the relationship between the Spirit and the Father in the Gospel of John.

---

61. See Smalley, "Pneumatology in the Johannine Gospel and Apocalypse," p. 293: "The Evangelist distinguishes the Spirit-Paraclete from both the Father and the Son. . . . [Yet the] Fourth Evangelist is well aware of the unity that exists between the Spirit and both God and Christ. The Spirit is God's Spirit. . . . He is also the Spirit of Christ." The phrase "Spirit of Christ" or "Spirit of Jesus" is not used in John; Jesus sends the Spirit, but it is telling that he sends it "from the Father." Moreover, in 1 John, the Spirit is explicitly designated as the Spirit from God.

62. D. Moody Smith (*The Theology of the Gospel of John* [Cambridge: Cambridge University Press, 1995], p. 142) highlights the ambiguity of Johannine pneumatology when he writes, "The Spirit is *Jesus' presence* to strengthen and encourage the disciples. . . . The Spirit is *the renewed action and presence* of God by which what happened with Jesus and his disciples in the first place is made known as revelation."

The Father and the Spirit

In light of the widespread view of the Spirit as a "replacement for Christ," it is particularly arresting that many of the functions attributed to the Spirit are elsewhere predicated not of only *Jesus* but also of the *Father*.

- The Father testifies to Jesus (5:37; 8 18; 1 John 5:9), as does the Spirit (15:26-27).
- The Father glorifies Jesus (5:44; 8:54; 12:23, 28; 13:31-32; 17:1, 5), as does the Spirit (16:14).
- The Father will be with the disciples (14:23; 17:11, 15, 26), and the Spirit will be with them as well (14 17).
- The Father has the authority and right to judge but has handed judgment over to the Son (5:22, 27, 30; 8:16); so too the Paraclete convicts the world of judgment (16:8-11).
- The Paraclete teaches (14:26; 16:13), as does God (6:45; 1 John 2:26-27; Jesus teaches what God tells him to teach, 7:16-17).

The Paraclete teaches, guides, testifies, and is with the disciples; all these functions are predicated of the Father as well. In some way, then, the Paraclete carries on the same work of the Father in relationship to Jesus; both the Father and the Paraclete are said to bear witness to and glorify Jesus. The overlap between the work of the Father and that of the Paraclete is scarcely surprising, for if the Spirit and the Paraclete are one and the same entity, and the Spirit is the Spirit of God and properly to be construed as the life-giving "breath of God," one might well expect that John could speak of the work of God and the work of the Spirit as interchangeable.

Yet in the Farewell Discourses there seems to be a clear distinction drawn between the Father and the Paraclete, whom the Father will send in Jesus' name (14:26) or at his request (14:16-17; cf. 16:7). To what extent does this distinction apply, then, to the rest of the Gospel? When John speaks of being born anew by the Spirit, is this a way of talking about the activity of God's life-giving Spirit and, therefore, of the very activity of God? Or does John envision a distinct presence or figure who is "the Spirit" that is sent by God, as God might send an angel or other heavenly messenger? As pointed out earlier in this chapter, when one takes the Farewell Discourses as a starting point for interpreting the Spirit of God in the Gospel of John, one is more likely to speak of the Spirit as a distinct figure, and perhaps also to read the Spirit in Christological terms. The Spirit is a figure modeled on Jesus himself. But if one takes those portions of the Gospel outside the Farewell Discourses as a starting point, then one is more likely to speak of the Spirit as the power of God, the activity of God, or the breath of God. The Spirit is God's own life-giving Spirit, and, hence, the Spirit is drawn first not with Christological but with theological strokes.

At this point we may again call attention to some rather striking silences in the Fourth Gospel with respect to the Spirit's relationship to God. There is no explicit argument for the unity of the Spirit and God or, for that matter, for the Spirit and Jesus, whereas these are commonplace with respect to Jesus and the Father.[63] Missing are notable affirmations of and prayers for unity, such as "I and the Father are one" (10:30) and "That they may all be one; even as thou, Father, art in me, and I in thee, that they also may be in us" (17:21). In other words, there is no need to build a case that the Father and the Spirit are one, for the Spirit is the Spirit of God and, hence, by definition, nature, and character, comes from God. There are no formulas of mutual indwelling that relate the Father and the Spirit in the Gospel. Indeed, there are no explanations of the divine origins or source of the Spirit, perhaps because these are simply taken for granted. From where would the "Holy Spirit" come but from God?

If we note the extent to which the activity of God and the Spirit overlap, the frequent use of Spirit as the means through which God acts, and the consistent assumption that God is the source of the Spirit, then it seems that the Spirit is primarily the means or mode by which God acts in the world. This is the portrait that emerges from the portions of the Gospel outside the Farewell Discourses. The Spirit is depicted here as God's life-giving power granted to the Son, who in his word and work granted the Spirit of life to others. However, in the Farewell Discourses, Jesus speaks of the Spirit's work and presence in rather different terms. Because Jesus has now returned to the Father, the Spirit is portrayed in terms that show not only how the Spirit bears witness to and carries on the work of

63. Thus, for example, when Hans Weder ("The Hermeneutics of Christology in the Johannine Writings," in *Exploring the Gospel of John: In Honor of D. Moody Smith*, ed. R. Alan Culpepper and C. Clifton Black [Louisville: Westminster/John Knox, 1996], p. 337), writes, "The Christology of the Gospel is consistently characterized by the unity of the Father and the Son, and this recurs in the notion of the Paraclete," I would argue that the textual evidence supporting the second part of the statement is missing from John.

the Son but also how the Father, the source of all life, continues to give life into the world when the one who is bread of life and life itself is no longer in the world. The Spirit is portrayed in the Farewell Discourses as the Paraclete who testifies to the Son's life-giving word and work, just as the Father had done in the ministry of Jesus. Hence, the Paraclete carries on the work of the Father. The Spirit's work is necessary because of the departure of the Son from the world, which might be taken to imply his absence from the world and the disciples, and hence a concomitant absence of the Father's glory, life, word, wisdom, and presence from the world. Although the Son has now returned to the Father, he continues to be the means through which the Father gives life to the world, and the Spirit both bears witness to Jesus' life-giving work and makes the presence of Jesus real and known to his followers.

An analogy, imperfect but illuminating nevertheless, is provided by the incarnation of the Word in Jesus. The Word both dwells with and is God; the Word takes on the specific form of human flesh; the Word returns to God. This Word is both differentiated from God and yet also identified with God. The Word can be construed, on the one hand, as the spoken expression of God's thought, and, on the other hand, as virtually distinct from God, much as the Torah or Philo's Logos is described. Jesus is the man the Word becomes, and in his earthly life he is known as the Son of the Father. So also the Spirit of God can be spoken of, on the one hand, as the very life-giving breath of God, and, on the other hand, as a distinct agent of God. While the Spirit is the means through which God gives life to the world, at a particular time the Spirit takes on a specific set of functions, and even a particular "form," as the Paraclete. The Paraclete is now with Jesus' followers as the Spirit of truth, a teacher, and the witness to the one who was truth and embodied truth.[64] As the Word of God became incarnate, thus embodying

---

64. Volz (*Der Geist Gottes*, p. 139) argues that in the postexilic period, a variety of conceptions of the Spirit existed side by side in Judaism. Levison (*The Spirit in First Century Judaism*, pp. 238-43) concludes from his survey of selected authors (Josephus, Philo, Pseudo-Philo) that these ancient authors were able to embrace "multiple conceptions of the spirit which might appear to us to be inconsistent." Levison argues that these authors spoke of a wide variety of effects of the Spirit's presence and of a diversity of natures of the Spirit, and that these can often be correlated with contextual exegetical needs and background. He thus suggests that the example of these ancient authors should caution us against seeking a single conception of the Spirit in any one document, or looking behind the document to its sources for an explanation of the diversity. While these caveats are well taken, in the Gospel

God's glory, truth, and grace, so the life-giving Spirit of God becomes present as the Paraclete, bearing witness to the embodied grace of the Father in the Son and convicting those who do not believe of their unbelief, and so making the life-giving presence of the Father in the Son a concrete reality.

Summary Reflections and Observations

At the outset of this chapter, I suggested that one of the widely shared conclusions of studies of the Spirit-Paraclete in John was that one ought to construe the Spirit in Christological terms. This viewpoint is most evident in the argument that the Spirit carries on Jesus' functions and is the replacement or substitute for the risen and departed Christ. On the contrary, I have argued that the primary conception of the Spirit that runs throughout the Gospel is that of the Father's life-giving power that has been granted to and is conferred through the Son. The life-giving work of the Spirit underlies every passage concerning the Spirit in John, including even the Paraclete sayings in the Farewell Discourses that emphasize the forensic arena of the Spirit's work of bearing witness to Jesus. That is to say, the Farewell Discourses speak of the Spirit-Paraclete's work confronting the world concerning sin, righteousness, and judgment (16:7-9). The Spirit's work is to bear witness to Jesus as the one who spoke the "words of life." As the Spirit of Truth, the Paraclete leads one to the proper response to Jesus and his words, thus enabling one to pass from sin and its judgment to life. The functions of the Spirit in the Gospel of John are directly related to the reception of new life, the forgiveness of sins, and testimony to Jesus.

The currency of the "Christological" reading of the Spirit-Paraclete in John has unfortunately often been purchased at the expense of a "theological" understanding of the Spirit. However, the "theological" coloring of the Spirit both precedes and undergirds the "Christological" shaping. As one writer put it, "It can hardly be denied that πνεῦμα is a 'God' word."[65]

---

of John we need to reckon not only with diverse conceptions of the Spirit but also with the way in which these fall out along the trajectory of the narrative and the course of Jesus' own life. What distinguishes John from some of the ancient documents that Levison studied is that the different conceptions of the Spirit correspond precisely not only to different literary portions of the Gospel, but also to distinct parts of the ministry and life of Jesus.

65. Neil Richardson, *Paul's Language about God,* JSNTSup 99 (Sheffield: Sheffield Academic Press, 1994), pp. 154-55.

Clearly the Fourth Evangelist assumed that Spirit (πνεῦμα) is a "God" word. For this reason the Gospel contains no arguments for the unity of the Spirit and God, no arguments for the derivation of the Spirit from God, and no arguments for the mutual indwelling of God and the Spirit. By definition, Spirit refers to the mode of God's presence, power, and action. Hence, the Spirit in John is the Spirit of God, who comes from the Father (15:26). However, "just as the Father has life in himself but has given the Son to have life himself," so the Father gives the Son the power and prerogative to have the Spirit and to give the Spirit to others. The Father gives the Paraclete (14:16), who comes from the Father (15:26), but the Paraclete is sent at Jesus' request (14:16) and in Jesus' name (14:26). He will baptize with the Holy Spirit (1:33), but he also breathes the life-giving Spirit from within upon his disciples (20:22). The Spirit is God's Spirit, but the Spirit can be sent and given by Jesus because God has given him this prerogative.

If Spirit (πνεῦμα) is a "God" word, it is no less so when used of Jesus. The recent focus on the Christological coloring of the Spirit has not often enough fostered reflection on the theological implications of assigning to the Son the prerogative to send and confer the Spirit. In other words, recognition that Spirit is a "God" word ought to lead to the question how then one understands the identity of Jesus and, in turn, how one understands the very identity and character of God. For if the Spirit is intrinsic to the very identity and being of God, then to speak of the Son as having the prerogative to bestow the Spirit from within characterizes the Son in a way typical of the "unique divine identity" of God.[66]

It is always important to underscore that the power to bestow the Spirit is a divine prerogative that the Father has given to the Son. Jesus is neither a Spirit-inspired prophet, nor one on whom the Spirit of God "falls" or "comes." He speaks words of life not because he is possessed by the Spirit but because he possesses the Spirit even as he possesses life and has the power to give it. In other words, even as the Father is by definition the one who gives life to the Son, so too the Father is understood as the one who gives the Spirit of life to the Son. Because "Spirit" is a distinct way of envisioning God's activity and presence in the world, the functions that are exercised necessarily imply the very activity and presence of God. God is

---

66. The phrase "divine identity" comes from Richard Bauckham, *God Crucified: Monotheism and Christology in the New Testament* (Grand Rapids: Eerdmans, 1998), esp. pp. 7-9.

not understood as God in the Gospel of John unless the relationship of Father and Son, construed in terms of the Father's conferring upon the Son the power to give life and to send the Spirit, is taken as essential to the very identity of God.

FIVE

The Worship of God

In the second edition of his magisterial commentary, originally published in 1955 and revised in 1978, C. K. Barrett appended a short comment to his remarks on John 4:23, a verse that reads as follows; "The hour is coming and now is, when those who worship the Father must worship him in Spirit and in truth, for such the Father seeks to worship him." Focusing on the explanatory clause at the end, Barrett remarked, "This clause has perhaps as much claim as 20.30f. to be regarded as expressing the purpose of the gospel."[1] The much-debated statement in 20:30-31 gives a summary of the purpose of the Gospel in terms of leading people to believe in Jesus as the Messiah, the Son of God. Barrett's assertion that 4:23 rivals 20:31 in capturing the purpose of John may look like just a passing comment, but it actually charts a huge shift in the Fourth Gospel's center of gravity. In essence, Barrett gauges "worship" in the Gospel of John as possessing fully enough mass to counterbalance all that had hitherto been imputed to "belief" or evangelism as constituting the evangelist's purpose. Simultaneously, Barrett shifts the center from the Son to the Father. It is tempting to speculate that the gloss which Barrett added in 1978 was a response to a number of studies that, in the years between the two editions of the commentary, laid increasing stress on the Gospel as a "dogmatic" Gospel that makes *Jesus* the object

---

1. C. K. Barrett, *The Gospel According to St. John*, 2nd ed. (Philadelphia: Westminster, 1978), p. 238.

and content of belief.[2] Barrett's assertion underscores and unites two items of concern in the present chapter, namely, the centrality of God in the Fourth Gospel and the singular importance of genuine worship to its argument.

Indeed, many other scholars have called attention to the importance of the theme of worship by underscoring the large role that Jewish festivals, rituals, and places of worship play in the themes, structure, and polemic of the Gospel. In fact, the intense focus in recent decades on Christology as the heart of the Gospel fits hand in glove with an understanding of its place and polemic vis-à-vis Judaism. By contending that John intends to show how Jesus "replaces" or "supersedes" — words we shall have occasion to return to — the various festivals and rites of Judaism, they argue that Johannine theology repudiates Judaism by means of its allegedly Christocentric "replacement theology."

Typical characterizations include statements such as the following: "All previous religious institutions, customs and feasts lose meaning in [Jesus'] presence."[3] Or: "Jesus supersedes the great pilgrim festivals; he fulfills the symbolism of the feast of tabernacles. . . . Jesus fulfills and thus supersedes the purity regulations of Judaism . . . in Jesus the Messiah the old Temple and cult has been rendered redundant."[4] Or: "Jesus even replaced the Sabbath, Passover, Feast of Booths, and Feast of Dedication."[5] And: "According to the Fourth Gospel, the earthly Jesus advocates the supersession of the entire system of traditional Jewish worship."[6] These readings assume or argue that in its treatment of themes, institutions, and figures related to Jewish worship the Fourth Gospel repudiates Jewish cultic practices and religious feasts, and does so by radically reinterpreting these practices and feasts through and in the person of Jesus Christ.

On a slightly different tack, J. Louis Martyn refocused the argument

---

2. Most notably, perhaps, Ernst Käsemann, *The Testament of Jesus: A Study of the Gospel of John in the Light of Chapter 17*, ET (Philadelphia: Fortress, 1968).

3. Raymond E. Brown, *The Gospel According to John*, 2 vols., Anchor Bible (Garden City, N.Y.: Doubleday, 1968, 1970), 1:104.

4. James D. G. Dunn, *The Partings of the Ways between Christianity and Judaism and Their Significance for the Character of Christianity* (London: SCM; Philadelphia: Trinity, 1991), pp. 93, 94, 95.

5. Craig R. Koester, *The Dwelling of God: The Tabernacle in the Old Testament, Intertestamental Jewish Literature, and the New Testament*, CBQMS 22 (Washington, D.C.: Catholic Biblical Association, 1989), p. 108.

6. Charles H. Talbert, *Reading John: A Literary and Theological Commentary on the Fourth Gospel and the Johannine Epistles* (New York: Crossroad, 1992), pp. 92-93.

about the relationship of Jesus and Judaism from the text to the community behind the text and for which the Gospel was written.[7] In his influential study, *History and Theology in the Fourth Gospel,* Martyn argued that the Johannine community's gradual development of a relatively exalted view of Jesus eventually drove the wedge between it and the synagogue community from which it broke or was expelled. Yet even the high Christology of the Johannine community could not, on its own, account for the palpable tension in the Gospel between the two communities. Rather, this tension developed because a relatively exalted view of Jesus was coupled with the *practice* of *worshipping* him. This practice led to the charge of di-theism, belief in two gods, which contains an implicit charge of false worship. Having abandoned monotheism, the Johannine Christians added insult to injury by abandoning monolatry as well. Thus, if one were to ask the Jewish authorities why they wished to apprehend Christians, they would answer, "We persecute Jewish Christians because they worship Jesus as a second God!" This echoes the charge that Martyn believes was leveled against Jesus, namely, that he led the people astray because he led them into worship of a god alongside of God.[8] In short, Jews found Christians troublesome not simply because they developed a relatively exalted view of Jesus' role but because they coupled this understanding of Jesus with the practice of worshipping him.

David Aune emphasized the importance of the cultic practices of the Johannine community by suggesting that "the pneumatic experience of the presence of the exalted Jesus in the midst of the worshiping community" accounts for the dominance of realized eschatology in the Fourth Gospel.[9] Aune argued that the Gospel's distinctive theology cannot be accounted for adequately by attributing it to a lone theologian, however creative and sophisticated he may be.[10] Rather, the "essential elements of the

7. For a recent critique of Martyn's assumptions, see Richard Bauckham, "For Whom Were the Gospels Written?" in *The Gospels for All Christians: Rethinking the Gospel Audiences,* ed. Richard Bauckham (Grand Rapids: Eerdmans, 1998), pp. 22-26; and the references to other studies that have criticized Martyn's use of the *birkhat ha-minim* as an interpretative tool for understanding the Gospel (p. 23, n. 26).

8. See J. Louis Martyn, *History and Theology in the Fourth Gospel,* 2nd ed. (Nashville: Abingdon, 1979), pp. 72, 75, 78.

9. David E. Aune, *The Cultic Setting of Realized Eschatology in Early Christianity* (Leiden: Brill, 1972), p. 133.

10. Aune, *Cultic Setting,* p. 65; see in response John Ashton, *Understanding the Fourth Gospel* (Oxford: Clarendon, 1991), p. 171, n. 20, who seems to misunderstand Aune's main point here.

theology of the Fourth Gospel generally, and the eschatology of the Gospel in particular, were developed within the context of the worship, preaching and teaching of . . . the 'Johannine community.'"[11] Moreover, Aune suggests that the Christology of John expresses the religious needs, values, and ideals of the Johannine community. John's Christology is comprised of elements of tradition about the historical Jesus, a framework of various images used to conceptualize the revelatory and soteriological significance of Jesus, and, finally, the Church's own experience of the living Jesus as mediator of salvation and an object of cultic worship.[12] Not only does the theology of the Gospel, particularly with its emphasis on realized eschatology and its distinctive Christology, reflect the practices and beliefs of the Johannine community, but it finds its particular home in the concrete practices of a worshipping community.[13]

Aune's proposal removes the community's disagreements with its opponents from the theological or conceptual realm and lodges them within their differing practices. John's community was in conflict with "the Jews" not simply because of what it believed but because of the way in which its beliefs were mirrored in practices and, more specifically, in the practices of cultic worship. Martyn's thesis had already hinted at such conflict: the "test" applied to those suspected to be Christians was whether they could, without hesitation, lead the synagogue in prayers to curse the "heretics" (or Christians). Moreover, as already noted, Martyn suggested that Christians were persecuted for worshipping a second God. Whether or not one agrees with the assumptions of both Martyn and Aune that the Gospel is relatively transparent to a communal situation that gave birth to it, the argument that the conflict in John is framed not only in terms of *what* is to be *believed* but also *how* one is to *worship* seems right on target. Jewish history and literature demonstrate repeatedly that what often mattered most and caused the greatest conflicts was centered in practices and objects of worship. The causes of the Maccabean revolt, the polemics against idolatry that surface still in Philo and Josephus, and the protests to Gaius regarding his impossi-

---

11. Aune, *Cultic Setting*, p. 63.

12. Aune, *Cultic Setting*, p. 76.

13. Cf. Larry W. Hurtado, *One God, One Lord: Early Christian Devotion and Ancient Jewish Monotheism* (Philadelphia: Fortress, 1988), p. 13: "The cultic veneration of Jesus in early Christian circles is the most important context for the use of the christological titles and concepts." See also Martin Hengel, "Christological Titles in Early Christianity," in his *Studies in Early Christology* (Edinburgh: T. & T. Clark, 1995), pp. 370, 383.

ble demand for worship show the zeal not for a theoretical monotheism but for the insistence on exclusive worship of the God of Israel.

To be sure, the actual practices of the Johannine Church with respect to baptism and the Lord's Supper have been much discussed, with particular focus on the stance of the Johannine community on these matters vis-à-vis other forms of early Christian faith.[14] John's Gospel has sometimes been branded as "sacramental," and sometimes as "anti-sacramental," standing over against the developing "great Church" in its interpretation of baptism and the Lord's Supper. Obviously such deductions are drawn from material that offers little by way of intentional guidance on the meaning of the Church's sacramental practices. Nevertheless, by picking up clues from within the text, scholars deem themselves able to offer suggestions not only about the theology but also about the practices of the Johannine community with respect to the sacraments. Similarly, the conception and practices of church life have often been deduced from an analysis of imagery such as the vine and the branches, or the picture of the good shepherd gathering the flock. These extended parables are assumed to mirror the ecclesiology of the Fourth Gospel as well as of the community from or for which it was written.

In this chapter I am interested not so much in the rituals and practices of the Johannine community but rather in the overt and implicit polemic in the Gospel regarding worship, as well as the use of the imagery of Jewish rites and festivals to explain the significance of Jesus. A common assumption today is that John's Gospel essentially creates a broad, ugly ditch between itself and "the Jews," as if all common ground had been removed. A closer look at the rhetoric of the Gospel concerning worship will therefore be instructive in delineating the ways in which the Gospel explains and defends its understanding of God, thus mapping the extensive common ground between its conceptions and those of the Judaism out of which it emerges.

What I propose to do in this chapter, then, is to reexamine certain passages related to worship of God in the Gospel by setting them against a taxonomy of contemporary Jewish polemics regarding worship. The literature

---

14. For a brief summary of the issues, see D. Moody Smith, *The Theology of the Gospel of John* (Cambridge: Cambridge University Press 1995), pp. 155-60; and for a somewhat more detailed discussion, David Rensberger, *Johannine Faith and Liberating Community* (Philadelphia: Westminster, 1988).

of Second Temple Judaism testifies to a wide range of ongoing discussion and argument about the character, means, and object of true worship, ranging from sectarian debates about halakic practice, purity regulations, the temple, and issues of calendar (*Jubilees,* 11QTemple, 4QMMT); to the possibility of various visionary or mystical experiences allowing for participation in heavenly worship (e.g., *Songs of the Sabbath Sacrifice, 1 Enoch*); to the necessity of the continued defense of monotheism and monolatry (e.g., *Embassy to Gaius, Joseph and Aseneth*). By reading Johannine polemics against this backdrop, I hope to show, first, the need for greater exegetical precision in tracing the argument of the Fourth Gospel. This precision, in turn, can spur us, second, to rethink some assumptions commonly held about the Gospel, its Christology, and its stance over against Judaism and its festivals, rituals, and worship. In the end, then, reconsideration of this data will compel reflection on the Fourth Gospel's understanding of the God who ought to be worshipped "in spirit and in truth."

A Taxonomy of Polemics regarding Worship of God in Second Temple Judaism

The assumption that God is the only God and the source and creator of the life of the world functions to underscore the demand for exclusive worship of this God. Yet there is a difference how one conceives of the unity of God and the corresponding worship owed to that God, and a noticeable gap between the rhetoric regarding the unity of God and allowance for different forms of worship. A schema of positions with respect to the uniqueness of God and worship of God would include at least the following four main positions, with nuances and variations within each one: (1) assimilationists, who were willing to engage in worship of Yahweh, either alongside or under the name of another god, with a supporting rationale; (2) non-assimilationist apologists, who, while maintaining the uniqueness and particularity of Israel's God, nevertheless sought to find common ground with pagans, in shared philosophical or moral convictions; (3) separationists, who labeled all practices and beliefs of pagans either idolatrous or demonic, or perhaps both; (4) and sectarians, who found objectionable practices or beliefs even among their fellow Jews, who also worshipped the one God of Israel.

1. Assimilationist[15]

Perhaps the most notorious exemplars of this position are those Jews who were willing to follow Antiochus Epiphanes' commands to engage in pagan sacrifices and worship. According to Josephus, the high priest Onias (Menelaus) had persuaded Antiochus "to compel the Jews to abandon their fathers' religion" in order that he might secure his own position (*Ant.* 12.238-240; 2 Macc. 13:4). What sort of justification Menelaus may have suggested for such practice is not known, but one suggestion is that he and others adopted the view that religious particularism or exclusivism was an unenlightened barbarism.[16] It may well be that the philosophical or theological rationale that would have been offered would have included an argument for the unity and uniqueness of the Most High God, known in Israel as Yahweh but to the Greeks under another name. By whatever name one might know and worship God, ultimately there was only God. It is clear not only from the revolt itself but also from later writings that explain it that such syncretism was viewed by the majority of Jews as nothing other than idolatry.

2. Nonassimilationist Apologists to the Greek World

This rubric characterizes, albeit in different ways, such different authors and writings as Philo, Josephus, and the *Sibylline Oracles*. While they undeniably emphasize the superiority and uniqueness of Judaism and its God, there also exists within these writings a tendency to find common ground with pagan ethics, or philosophy although not with cultic practice.

---

15. For further discussion, see Elias Bickerman, *The God of the Maccabees: Studies on the Meaning and Origin of the Maccabean Revolt* Studies in Judaism in Late Antiquity 32 (Leiden: Brill, 1979), esp. pp. 64-65, 76-92; Martin Hengel, *Judaism and Hellenism: Studies in the Encounter in Palestine during the Early Hellenistic Period*, 2 vols. (Philadelphia: Fortress, 1974), 1:264-65 Emil Schürer, *The History of the Jewish People in the Age of Jesus Christ*, rev. and ed. Geza Vermes and Fergus Millar 3 vols. (Edinburgh: T. & T. Clark, 1973), 3:1:523. For a taxonomy related to social identity and acculturation, see Alan F. Segal, *Paul the Convert: The Apostolate and Apostasy of Saul the Pharisee* (New Haven: Yale University Press, 1990), p. 87. Segal outlines the options for Jewish relationship to pagan society as follows: leaving Judaism, downplaying its value, or reforming it to make it more acceptable to Gentiles.

16. Bickerman, *God of the Maccabees*, pp. 76-92.

In an effort to portray Judaism in a positive light, certain authors tried to win a sympathetic hearing for Judaism, particularly for its understanding of God. Both Philo and Josephus, for example, endeavor not only to maintain the uniqueness of Israel's God but also to show the commonality between the God of the Jews and the God of the philosophers, particularly by maintaining the unity of God as the single source of all existence.[17] A Christian example of such an overture is found in Paul's speech to the Athenians in Acts 17 that maintains that "the God who made the world and everything in it, being Lord of heaven and earth . . . is not far from each one of us, for 'In him we live and move and have our being'" (Acts 17:24, 28). This God does not live in handmade temples, nor ought one to represent God by handmade artifacts. The emphasis on God as living, acknowledged as the source or creator of all that is, accounts for the polemic against the worship of animals and artifacts even in writers who also endeavor to demonstrate the commonality between the conceptions of deity in Judaism and in other religions. It is noteworthy that Acts portrays Paul as in dialogue with the *philosophers* of the ancient world but critical of the cultic practice of the pagans. The same tendencies are evident in Philo, Josephus, and others.

In the writings of Josephus we encounter the desire to build bridges between the Jewish religion and pagan world while maintaining the fundamental commitments of Jewish faith in God. Of particular concern to Josephus are the conceptions of true deity as the source of all life, one in essence or nature, upholding and demanding morality, and properly laying claim to human obedience. We may look briefly at how these themes come together in Josephus, and how they serve both to build bridges and erect barriers between Judaism and certain philosophic views.

As noted in an earlier chapter, Josephus assumes that the God of Israel is "the God who made heaven and earth and sea" (*Ag. Ap.* 2.121, 190-192; see also Jdt. 9:12; *Jub.* 2:31-32; 12:19; 16:26-27; 22:5-7; 2 Macc. 1:24; 7:28), "the bountiful giver of life" (*J.W.* 2.131), "father and source of the universe, as creator of things human and divine" (*Ant.* 7.380; cf. 1.230; 2.152). Josephus's inclination to portray God consistently as the Creator and Lord of all the world thus makes a surface rhetorical appeal to non-Jews. Josephus does this as well in the language he uses for God and in his conceptions about God. Most frequently Josephus speaks of *theos* (θεός) or *ho*

---

17. See also Schürer, *History of the Jewish People,* 3:1:154.

theos (ὁ θεός) and sometimes even uses the phrase *to theion* (τὸ θεῖον), a phrase not found for divinity in the LXX.[18] Josephus's use of the neuter substantive reflects his familiarity with nonbiblical language for God. Some of Josephus's rhetoric resounds with similar echoes. So, for example, he speaks of Moses' representation of God as "One, uncreated and immutable to all eternity" (*Ag. Ap.* 2.167). Once he refers to God as ὁ ὤν, "the Eternal," or "the One who is," which parallels the LXX rendition of Exodus 3:14 as "I am the One who is" (ἐγώ εἰμι ὁ ὤν). Josephus contends that Moses taught of God's universal sovereignty and authority, the source of all blessings: "One, uncreated and immutable to all eternity . . . although the nature of his real being passes knowledge." According to Josephus, "the wisest of the Greeks," including Pythagoras, Anaxagoras, Plato, the Stoics, and "nearly all the philosophers," show that they "held similar views concerning the nature of God."[19]

In other words, Josephus employs the idea of the unity of God not to ridicule all other gods but to suggest that, insofar as the philosophic conceptions of deity approximate the Jewish idea of the one, universal God, they offer truths about God — partial truths, to be sure, but truths nonetheless. Moses attained to the purest conception of God, but others were able to speak accurately of God.[20] Josephus puts himself in the company of "the admired sages of Greece" in mocking the Greek myths that portrayed the gods as numerous, born from each other, locally limited, immoral, and cruel (*Ag. Ap.* 2.239). In contrast, one can infer from the views of deity that he championed that God is one, uncreated, universal, and beneficently disposed towards the world, demanding righteousness and justice. In thus insisting on the uniqueness and universal sovereignty of God, Josephus shows himself fundamentally in line with traditional Jewish conceptions

18. R. J. H. Shutt, "The Concept of God in the Works of Flavius Josephus," *JJS* 31 (1980): 172. Although τὸ θεῖον sometimes means something like "religion" or "the practice of religion," there are instances where it means 'divinity" or "God," as in *Ant.* 1.85, 194; 4.326; 2.13, 63, 267, 293, 300, 304, 332. In the Loeb editions, the translators render most of these instances as "the Deity." Shutt ("Concept of God," pp. 175-79) argues that τὸ θεῖον generally refers to "deity" or "God" but not "the God of Israel."

19. *Ag. Ap.* 2.168; cf. 2.255-257, 281-282; *Ant.* 12.22. Adolf von Schlatter describes Josephus's universalist view of God as a function of his own political fate (*Wie sprach Josephus von Gott?* BFCT 14/1 [Gütersloh: Bertelsmann, 1910], pp. 49-55, 68).

20. Such views are not novel to Josephus and can be found in earlier writings such as the *Letter of Aristeas* 15-16. See also Hengel, *Judaism and Hellenism*, 2:264-67.

about the nature and being of God, emphasizing God's creation of the world and continuing exercise of his sovereignty, providence, and will.[21] Once again, however, we note that Josephus appeals to the common ground of certain beliefs about God, beliefs shared between Judaism and ancient philosophical schools, rather than to the common ground of religious practices.

Like Josephus, Philo argued for the superiority of Jewish notions of God, summarizing the purity of the Mosaic conception of deity in terms of God's eternity, unity, creation, and providential care of the world (*Opif.* 170-172). David Runia sums up Philo's approach this way:

> Nowhere in Philo's writings do we find polemic against the "God of the philosophers," but rather against the "gods" of misguided thinkers, who fail to recognize the utter uniqueness of the First and only true cause.[22]

Indeed, in a striking passage Philo asserts:

> What the disciples of the most excellent philosophy gain from its teaching, the Jews gain from their customs and laws, that is to know the highest, the most ancient Cause of all things and reject the delusion of created gods. For no created being is God in reality, but only in men's fancies, bereft as it is of the essential attribute of eternality. (*Virt.* 65)

God is the sole uncreated — hence eternal — being, and so necessarily the source of the life of the world (*Her.* 206). Philo furthermore employs a wide range of titles for God as the origin of all things, including Creator and Maker (*Spec.* 1.30; *Somn.* 1.76; *Mut.* 29; *Decal.* 61); Planter of the world (*Conf.* 196); Father;[23] Parent (*Spec.* 2.198); "Cause of all things"

---

21. In spite of Josephus's concessions with respect to non-Jewish conceptions of deity, scholars have nevertheless contended that Josephus retains the "fundamental theological principles of Judaism" in his writings. See Schlatter, *Wie sprach Josephus von Gott?*; Shutt, "Concept of God," p. 185. The degree to which questions about the sovereignty of God dominated Josephus's thought can be shown by noting that his descriptions of the four "sects" of Judaism are carried through in terms of their understanding of the providence of God (as well as the immortality of the soul); cf. *Ant.* 18.11-25; *J.W.* 2.162-166.

22. David T. Runia, in "God of the Philosophers, God of the Patriarchs: Exegetical Backgrounds in Philo of Alexandria," in his *Philo and the Church Fathers: A Collection of Papers,* Supplements to *Vigiliae Christianae* 32 (Leiden: Brill, 1995), pp. 214-15.

23. "The Father," *Spec.* 2.198; *Opif.* 74, 75; *Mut.* 29; "Father of all things, for he begat them," *Cher.* 49; "Father and Maker," *Opif.* 77; "Father and Maker of all," *Decal.* 51.

(*Somn.* 1.67);[24] Fountain of life (*Fug.* 198);[25] and Light (*Somn.* 1.75). The sweeping statements of God's creation of "all things" underscore, for Philo, the inseparable affirmations of the unity and universality of the one true God.

Philo therefore criticizes the notion that there is more than one God, or that human beings may worship other created things:

> Created things, in so far as they are created, are brothers, since they have all one Father, the Maker of the universe. Let us instead in mind and speech and every faculty gird ourselves up with vigour and activity to do the service of the Uncreated, the Eternal, the Cause of all. . . . Let us, then, engrave deep in our hearts this as the first and most sacred of commandments; to acknowledge and honour one God who is above all, and let the idea that gods are many never even reach the ears of the man whose rule of life is to seek for truth in purity and guilelessness. (*Decal.* 64-65)

Here Philo joins together the affirmations that there is but one God, that this one God made all that there is and, therefore, that God is alone worthy to be worshipped by human beings. Central to such an argument is the understanding of God as the "Uncreated" and "Eternal" (*Decal.* 60), whereas human beings and all things within the world are created by God. Philo strikes the same note in *The Embassy to Gaius*, when he writes not merely in defense of the "ancestral traditions, even the smallest" but of the great evil of calling for worship of a human being:

> The created and corruptible nature of man was made to appear uncreated and incorruptible by a deification which our nation judged to be the most grievous impiety, since sooner could God change into a man than a man into God. Apart from that it included the supremely evil vices of infidelity and ingratitude to the Benefactor of the whole world who through His power bestows blessings poured in unstinted abundance on every part of the All. (*Legat.* 118; cf. 332, 347)

Here God's universal creation and beneficence to all the world are taken as

24. See *Decal.* 52: "The transcendent source of all that exists is God."
25. "God is the most ancient of all fountains. . . . God alone is the cause of animation and of that life which is in union with prudence; for the matter is dead. But God is something more than life; he is, as he himself has said, the everlasting fountain of living."

support of the Jewish practice of exclusive worship of Yahweh alone and, more to the point, as absolutely forbidding the worship of anything or anyone made by God.

The third of the *Sibylline Oracles* contains a picture of God that one writer has labeled "highly spiritualized."[26] The following description of God, appearing early in the book, typifies the conception of God found throughout: "There is one God, sole ruler, ineffable, who lives in the sky, self-begotten, invisible, who himself sees all things" (*Sib. Or.* 3:11-12). The book speaks of God as eternal or immortal (3:15, 35, 48, 56, 101, 276-278, 283, 301, 583, 593, 601, 604, 617, 628, 631, 672, 693, 698, 708, 711, 717, 742); as Creator or, sometimes, "Begetter" (3:24, 35, 296, 542, 550, 604, 726); and as one who is "heavenly" (3:174, 286) and "dwells in the sky" (3:11, 81, 757). The diatribe continues with an attack on the worship of idols, those things made by a "sculptor's hand" (3:13; cf. 3:29-39, 721-723). Moreover, this vision of the uniqueness and unity of God grounds a universal call to all humankind: the Living One (763), who alone is God (629, 760) and alone is sovereign (718), who ought to be worshipped (763) and obeyed (719). The declaration of God as immortal and living serves as the basis for the view that the affairs of the earth are ordered according to God's will and as the foundation for ethical exhortation.

The Hellenistic book of *Wisdom* argues that only the ignorant and foolish worship the heavenly luminaries, assuming them to be gods, but failing to perceive "how much more powerful is the one who formed them" (13:4). Idols, in contrast to God the Lord and Creator, "did not exist from the beginning, nor will they last forever" (14:13). They are lifeless (14:29). Indeed, the affirmation that life distinguishes the true God from the false characterizes this attack against idolatry (13:10, 17-18; 14:8, 13, 15, 29). God alone has "power over life and death" (16:13). Therefore, idolatry, itself a confusion of the created with the Creator, leads to further confusion and disorder, including sexual perversion, murder and violence, deceit, and all kinds of impurity (14:24-29). "The worship of idols . . . is the beginning and cause and end of every evil" (14:27).

---

26. See the introductory material by John J. Collins to "The Sibylline Oracles, Book 3," in *Old Testament and Pseudepigrapha*, ed. James H. Charlesworth, 2 vols. (Garden City, N.Y.: Doubleday, 1985), 1:361. Collins places the book in second-century-B.C. Egypt.

3. Separationist

The majority of Jews, including those cited in the previous section, no doubt adopted a negative and separationist stance towards the pagan gods and pagan worship of them.[27] Following the trajectory of prophetic polemic against idol worship, some Jewish writings leave no room for common ground between Jews and pagans: Jews alone worship the true God, and any other worship is offered to idols and demons (Daniel, Bel and the Dragon, Judith, *Joseph and Aseneth*, much apocalyptic), themes already attested in passages such as Deuteronomy 32:17 and Psalms 96:5; 106:37. Paul gives evidence of such polemic when he writes to the Thessalonians that they "turned from idols, to serve a living and true God" (1 Thess. 1:9). Similarly in Romans, Paul censures those who "worshipped and served the creature rather than the Creator" (1:25). In these instances, as well as other places in the writings of Paul and Hebrews, the epithet "living God" serves particularly well in missionary contexts, pointing to the way in which it contrasts the one true God with the false, "dead" gods of pagans. Here the unity of God, and the emphasis on God as alone the living one, serves not as a bridge but a barrier to accepting apparently even the philosophical convictions of those who acknowledge other gods than the God of Israel.[28] Again, God's creative power and eternity provide the foundation for the call to worship the one God.

Some texts that arise from social situations with strong assimilationist pressures draw the lines between Jews and Gentile both on the basis of obedience to the law and of worship of God. In *Joseph and Aseneth*, the Egyptian woman Aseneth turns from the worship of multiple idols to acknowledge "the Lord God of Heaven, the Most High, the Mighty One of the powerful Joseph," who is also the true, living, and merciful God (11:5-13; cf. 2:3; 3:10-11; 9; 10:3-6; 21:13-14). These are, to be sure, stock biblical phrases for distinguishing the God of Israel, used in this context to underscore God's renewing as well as creative powers. Joseph's prayer for Aseneth addresses God with the following invocation:

27. See Hengel, *Judaism and Hellenism*, 2:261-67; Schürer, *History of the Jewish People*, 3:1:138.

28. On the anti-assimilationist stance of the rabbis, see A. Marmorstein, "The Unity of God in Rabbinic Literature," *HUCA* 1 (1924): 476-99.

> Lord God of my father Israel,
> the Most High, the Powerful One of Jacob,
> who gave life to all (things)
> and called (them) from the darkness to the light. (8:9)

On Aseneth's behalf, Joseph petitions God to "renew her by your spirit, form her anew by your hidden hand; make her alive again by your life . . . number her among your people . . . and let her live in your eternal life for ever and ever."[29]

Aseneth's own prayer echoes many of the same themes, emphasizing at some length God's creative and life-giving powers (12:1-3). Although not spoken of as demons, the gods of the Egyptians, which Aseneth renounces, are regularly characterized as "dead and dumb idols" (11:8; 12:5, 12), in contrast to the living Creator (8:2, 6, 9). Aseneth's contact with them defiles her, but the denunciation of her idolatry is neither so harsh nor so sarcastic as that of the prophets, presumably because of the allowances made for Aseneth due to her ignorance and willingness to repent (6:7; 12:9-12; 17:10; 21:10-21). Conversion is described in terms of renewal, creation, and the granting of life because, as an idolater, Aseneth not only worships "dead and dumb idols" but needs to acknowledge the Creator of life.

In contrast, the plight of the wicked is rather more desperate in *1 Enoch* since their idolatry amounts to worship of "evil spirits and demons" (99:7), and those who think they are offering sacrifices to gods are in fact offering them to demons (19:1). In the book of *Jubilees* (second century B.C.), evil spirits bear responsibility for leading people into idolatry, which has moral consequences, including war, error, and various sins and transgressions (11:4; 22:16-17, 22). People should not worship idols because there is no spirit in them, they are mute, and they are made by human beings (12:3-5). Instead, they should worship "the God of heaven, who sends down rain and dew upon the earth, and who makes everything upon the earth, and created everything by his word, and all life is in his presence" (12:4, 19; 22:5-7, 27).[30] Once again, this stock imagery for God,

---

29. From Christoph Burchard's note in his translation of "Joseph and Aseneth," in *The Old Testament Pseudepigrapha*, ed. James H. Charlesworth, 2 vols., Anchor Bible Reference Library (Garden City, N.Y.: Doubleday, 1983 and 1985), 2:213, n. *u*. The citation is from *Jos. Asen.* 8:9.

30. The vehemence of the polemic in *Jubilees* against idolatry is demonstrated by the fact that in rewriting Genesis, *Jubilees* says that Jacob did not "hide" the idols Rachel had brought (Gen. 35:4), but rather burned, crushed, and destroyed them (31:2).

emphasizing God's creation and sustenance of the world, is pressed into the service of calling for single-minded devotion.

Similarly, *Pseudo-Philo* (ca. first century) brands idolatry as the major sin that further leads to all sorts of other evils (25:9-13; 44:6). In an interesting twist, the *Testament of Judah* makes love of money the fundamental sin, a sin so pernicious that it leads to idolatry (*T. Jud.* 19:1; cf. 23:1-5)! Because an inextricable link between idolatry and immorality was simply assumed and asserted, either one can be said to lead to the other, and either one can be deduced as a consequence from the other. To be sure, these characterizations and invective are the stock-in-trade of first-century polemic against either Gentiles or Jews with whom one disagreed.[31] Yet they do not completely cloak the fact that each group felt there was a right and wrong way to worship God.

A number of other works penned at approximately the same time as *Jubilees* also employ the topos of "the living God" to rebuke idolatry and counsel worship of Israel's God (Bar. 4:7). Baruch (second century B.C.?), for example, characterizes God as "everlasting" (employing both adjectival and substantival formulations; 4:8; 10, 14, 20, 22, 24, 35; 5:2). The repetition particularly of the designation "the Everlasting" not only highlights this central conception of the nature of God but explicates it in terms of God's constant presence and power to deliver. The fictional satire Bel and the Dragon (second century B.C.) ridicules the worship of Bel, an "idol made with hands," and of a great dragon that is cleverly slain by Daniel. Neither artifact nor beast is "the living God," and so neither is worthy of worship (vv. 5, 25).

The novel Judith (late second century B.C.) deals with the issue of exclusive worship of the one true God.[32] Judith reflects a scenario like that of the book of Daniel, when the pressure to syncretism and worship of kings and idols is strong. The plot of Judith concerns Nebuchadnezzar's command that Holofernes destroy all the gods of the land so that the king alone would be worshipped. In their distress, the Jews cried out to God for deliverance, but Judith warned the people that while God might rescue

31. On this point, see Luke T. Johnson, "The New Testament's Anti-Jewish Slander and the Conventions of Ancient Polemic," *JBL* 108 (1989): 419-41.

32. George W. E. Nickelsburg (*Jewish Literature between the Bible and the Mishnah: A Historical and Literary Introduction* [Philadelphia: Fortress, 1981], p. 105) summarizes the fundamental tension in the story with the questions, "Who is God? Yahweh or Nebuchadnezzar?"

them in response to their pleading, they should be careful not to presume upon the sovereign freedom of God. Judith herself appeals to God's far-reaching sovereignty in her urgent entreaty, "Please, please, God of my father, God of the heritage of Israel, Lord of heaven and earth, Creator of the waters, King of all your creation!" (9:12). This address to God subsumes God's dominion over Israel under God's sovereignty over heaven and earth as their Creator. Nevertheless, the universality of God does not, in this instance, mean that all gods other than Nebuchadnezzar are really one and the same, but rather that the God of Israel is the God of all the world. As is typical of polemical Jewish works of this time, appeals to the sovereignty and the power of God lead not to a broadening concept of God, but rather to an increased emphasis on the sweep of God's powers.

4. Sectarian

Perhaps the best-known example of sectarian polemics that contain specific arguments about worship can be found in the Dead Sea Scrolls. There the polemic against false worship takes a somewhat different shape than in other contemporary writings. On the one hand, there are attacks on the worship of false gods and idols, with the warning that "on the day of judgment God will obliterate all the worshipers of idols, and all the wicked from the earth" (1QpHab 12:10–13:4; CD 4:17; 6:11-21). Since the Scrolls, like the prophets of old, direct some of their polemic not against Gentiles but against other Jews, the more frequent reproof is voiced against those Jews who have abandoned the covenant, failed to observe the law or properly to celebrate festivals, or defiled the holy temple and city — and have manifested their wickedness in their violence or opposition to the covenanters (1QpHab 2:6-7; 8:10; 12:8-10; 4QpPsᵃ 2:14-20; CD 4:17; 6:11-21). Because the priests in Jerusalem had defiled the temple, the Community offered a number of alternatives, speaking of itself as something of a "spiritual temple," "a holy house for Israel and the foundation of the holy of holies for Aaron" (1QS 8:5-14) or hoping for the rededication of the present temple. Without access to the temple, a member of the Community was urged to "bless his Creator" with the offering of his lips (1QS 9:3-6, 26; 10:6, 14) and to "circumcise in the Community the foreskin of his tendency" (1QS 5:5). The marking of the years of Jubilee was done in terms of the day of atonement, so that the promised "release" was a release from the debt of sin (11QMelch 2:1-9).

Even as temple worship, circumcision, and Jubilee are spiritualized, so to some extent is idolatry, at least when applied to an Israelite. The *Rule of the Community*, for example, dictates that the priests and Levites shall pronounce this curse: "Cursed by the idols which his heart reveres whoever enters this covenant leaving his guilty obstacle in front of himself to fall over it" (1QS 2:11-12). Those of the lot of Belial stray "from following God on account of [their] idols" (1QS 2:16-17). Again the document speaks of the spirit within the sons of truth that "detests all unclean idols" (1QS 4:5). Surely we have here traditional polemic against idol worship applied to those who do not adhere to the ways and customs of the Community (but cf. 11QTemple 2:1-15; 62:13-16). Yet it is doubtful that it should be read literally, as though the covenanters thought of all others outside the fold as actually worshipping idols. The polemic serves to demarcate the respective communities and to shore up the truth claims of the Qumran Community. However, if they regard other Israelites as belonging to the "sons of darkness," they do not rouse them to worship "the living God," but rather summon them to the appropriate ways of worshipping that God. Whatever else they may be, the "sons of darkness" are not crass idolaters. The argument of the Scrolls becomes sharpened in later rabbinic sources, where the one who denies belief in one God — such as the Gnostic or the Christian — is *kōfēr bā-'Iqqār* ("one who denies the root"). Regardless of the differences between Gnostics and Christians, in rabbinic eyes they were both idolaters inasmuch as they denied the unity of God.[33] A saying attributed to R. Tarfon distinguishes between idolaters who disavow God out of ignorance, and the Minim (probably Christians) who "know him and yet deny him."[34]

Summary

There are, then, different perspectives within Judaism regarding pagan conceptions of deity. In some Jewish writings there is no endeavor to find common ground with pagan authors, while in others there is a concerted effort to show the commonalities. However, having said that, we should

33. Ephraim Urbach, *The Sages: Their Concepts and Beliefs* (Cambridge, Mass.: Harvard University Press, 1987), p. 26.

34. *T. Šab.* 13:5, cited in Urbach, *The Sages,* p. 26.

hasten to add that whatever apologetic strategy may be adopted, only the assimilationist position allows for any sort of actual participation in the worship and cult of other deities. Josephus, Philo, and others still carry on polemic against idolatry. It is also to be noted that each approach depends in one way or another on an affirmation of the unity and uniqueness of God. On the one hand, to say "there is one God" can be taken as an exclusive statement, categorizing all "other gods" as false gods and all worshippers of deities other than the one known as the Lord God of Israel as idolaters. On the other hand, to say that "there is one God" can be taken as inclusive, implying either that the one God is known to different people under different names, or that there is one high god above all others, or that the one high god is known through the others.[35] It can, of course, also conduce to pantheism.[36] This second approach finds little purchase in the Jewish writings of this period, not least because it severs the specific connection between God and Israel and renders these "lesser deities" as independent gods rather than created beings, either angelic or demonic. Martin Hengel speaks of the "refusal of the overwhelming majority of Jewish people to allow a transference of non-Jewish divine names — and thus conceptions of God — to the God of Israel."[37] Where there are universalist sentiments emphasizing God's creation of and sovereignty over all peoples, nevertheless, the particularism of God's special election of Israel cannot be and is not abandoned. One may perceive this as an irreconcilable tension, but in fact it runs throughout books from Isaiah on.[38]

For most of these authors, while certain conceptions of or thoughts about the deity might be deemed unworthy, they were nevertheless not idolatry. James Barr argues that while in much Christian theology the concept of idolatry was broadened to cover the realm of people's ideas about

35. See Nils A. Dahl, "The One God of Jews and Gentiles (Romans 3:29-30)," in his *Studies in Paul: Theology for the Early Christian Mission* (Minneapolis: Augsburg, 1977), p. 180. Erik Peterson (*HEIS THEOS: Epigraphische, formgeschichtliche und religionsgeschichtliche Untersuchungen* [Göttingen: Vandenhoeck & Ruprecht, 1926]) argued that in the formula "one god," the numeral "one" can refer to the uniqueness of a deity without necessarily denying the existence of other gods. Hence, what appear to be monotheistic formulations in pagan thought may be such, but are not necessarily so.

36. On these points, see Hengel, *Judaism and Hellenism*, 1:261-66; Hurtado, *One God, One Lord*, pp. 1, 129 n. 1; Paul A. Rainbow, "Monotheism and Christology in 1 Corinthians 8:4-6," D.Phil. diss., Oxford University, 1987, pp. 25-28.

37. Hengel, *Judaism and Hellenism*, 1:266.

38. See also Dahl, "One God," pp. 180-88.

God, such an extension was not made in Judaism.[39] Idolatry, which is so clearly and consistently forbidden, refers to what people do, specifically, how they worship. This does not open the floodgates to a radical revision of beliefs about God, but it does suggest that the bottom line for Israel was and remained the worship of God. All the arguments adduced above point in this direction. So Philo may endeavor to argue that the Torah was in agreement with the traditions of Greek philosophy and thus served to confirm the truth of Judaism, but he in no way moves to condone the worship of physical images of God.[40]

Israel's confession of one God initially served to distinguish its God, *YHWH*, from all other gods and to underscore the supremacy of its God. Israel, moreover, understood itself to belong to this God and to owe exclusive allegiance to the one who had faithfully preserved it. "One God," therefore, meant that this people would serve no other God. In Second Temple Judaism "one God" comes increasingly to mean not just "one God for Israel" but also "there is only one God." When one finds the confession of "one God" in various texts of Second Temple Judaism, it is naturally linked to the confession of God as Creator.[41] Such a rubric is broad enough to encompass the special election of Israel within it. Now the polemic against other gods aims to establish the sovereignty of God not just over Israel but over all peoples. God's sovereignty was manifested universally — and ought correspondingly to be recognized universally. Here we find one of the main differences between Israel's God and the gods of its neighbors. Whereas there are striking similarities between Israel's God and the anthropomorphically depicted gods of the ancient Near East, there remains the singular difference that Israel held its God to be the only God, jealously seeking undivided worship and loyalty.

In short, even when it is granted that other peoples have correct notions of deity, or proper sentiments about the nature of god, that does not imply a blanket approval of all their beliefs or of their worship of other deities. In fact, the authors of Jewish writings of the Second Temple period are more, not less, strict in their insistence on sole worship of God and on the temple as the appropriate place of worship and sacrifice. Hence, the

39. James Barr, *Biblical Faith and Natural Theology: The Gifford Lectures for 1991* (Oxford: Clarendon, 1993), pp. 64-65; see also pp. 91, 97, 100-101, 148.

40. Barr, *Biblical Faith and Natural Theology,* p. 65.

41. Ferdinand Hahn, "The Confession of the One God in the New Testament," *HBT* 2 (1980): 72.

polemic of a group like the Dead Sea covenanters takes on an all the more strident note since it is contending with the very obvious and compelling argument that in the Jerusalem temple alone must sacrifice be offered. While there are strands in the prophets that may be exploited to the benefit of the separationist stance of this group, and of a critique of the priests of the temple, even so they must deal with the plain fact that the argument for "one God, one temple" is common ground. What Luke Johnson says with respect to the vehemence of NT polemic at certain points applies equally to the polemical arguments of the Dead Sea Community: the rhetoric is defensive, since the group using it has no real power, and the symbols that it wishes to appropriate for itself are in fact in the hands of the dominant group, which does hold the power.[42]

The Johannine Polemic regarding Worship

The Gospel of John has no exact analogue to polemic against idols, although it does contain discussions about both true worship and true knowledge of God.[43] Although the Gospel vigorously defends its view of the relationship between Jesus and the Father as evidence for the unity of God, its argument about true worship of God stands somewhere between the extremes found in Jewish propaganda. On the one hand, there is no pulling of punches in the harsh criticism of the Jews' failure to believe in God through the manifestation of his Word, both in Scripture (5:39) and in Jesus. Yet John never explicitly states nor even implicitly implies that the Jews offer false worship because they worship a false God. The Gospel does give voice to criticism of Samaritan worship — and shows how the faith of the Jews is superior to theirs precisely because "we worship what we know" and "salvation is from the Jews." To be sure, there is also the charge that the Jews are "children of the devil," but they are never said to worship demons or idols. The clear assumption is that they are aware of the one whom Jesus claims to be his Father, for he is the one the Jews claim to be "their God."

In short, the argument of the Gospel depends on the fact that Jesus

---

42. Johnson, "New Testament's Anti-Jewish Slander," pp. 419-41.

43. There is obviously a close connection between monolatry and monotheism. On this point, see especially Larry Hurtado, *One God, One Lord;* and "What Do We Mean by 'First-Century Jewish Monotheism?'" in *SBLSP* (1993): 348-68.

and his adversaries are talking about the same God, but that they differ over how and where God's presence is manifested to human beings.[44] In this regard, the polemic of the Fourth Gospel comes closest to the sectarian position as found in the Dead Sea Scrolls, in suggesting that it is the worship practices of co-religionists that signal their failure to understand the truth. In the Scrolls we also find the label "sons of darkness" applied to those outside the Community and the charge that they follow Belial or have Belial's spirit within. How God is to be worshipped and honored are central issues of debate in those documents. These issues surface also in the Fourth Gospel. Because for John the supreme manifestation of God's presence occurs not through temple, Scripture, and festival, but through the Son to whom all these bear witness, then because the Son is not properly acknowledged, God is not properly acknowledged. Hence the author of John writes that Jesus' opponents have never seen God, never heard God, and never known God. For John, those who deny the presence of God in Jesus are guilty of denying God.

Throughout this argument the author of the Gospel assumes that Jesus and his adversaries in the Gospel are talking about the same God, each claiming to have the proper and sole way of knowing that God. Each side makes exclusive claims for the way in which God is known, but the Gospel does not charge "the Jews" with idolatry or blasphemy, although the latter charge is of course leveled against Jesus by the Jews (5:18; 10:32-39; 19:7). Neither of the two charges leveled against idolaters — that they worship that which is made by human hands, and that they exchange the created for the Creator — characterizes either the Jews' criticisms of Jesus and his followers or John's censure of "the Jews," for they are not infidels, or at least not in the same position as Gentiles. Indeed, Jesus speaks for them when he says, "we worship what we know, for salvation is of the Jews." Exactly what the points of disagreement are may be illuminated by closer exegetical investigation.

44. Thus I disagree with Halvor Moxnes's claim that John denies that there is a common basis for Christians and nonbelieving Jews in faith in God (*Theology in Conflict: Studies in Paul's Understanding of God in Romans*, NovTSup 53 [Leiden: Brill, 1980]).

Jesus, the Temple, and Worship of God

In his book *The Scepter and the Star,* John J. Collins writes, "Alienation from the Temple cult was one of the root causes of Jewish sectarianism in the Hellenistic era."[45] The Community at Qumran serves as a prime exemplar of such alienation, but its literature testifies to diverse remedies for the ailment, including the establishment of a new, eschatological temple; a "takeover" or rededication of the present Jerusalem temple; and an interpretation of the Community itself as an alternate temple where atonement for sin is made.[46] Not surprisingly, these views are coupled with sharp polemic against the corrupt practices of the priests in the Jerusalem temple (CD 4:16-18; 5:6-7). The Scrolls testify not only to the community's dissatisfaction with the way in which the office of the priesthood was exercised, but also to its differences with the Jerusalem priesthood in calendrical matters and halakic regulations regarding purity (4QMMT).[47] In view of the deficiencies of the current priesthood, the current temple cult was deemed ineffective. Yet atonement for sin could be made within the "holy house for Aaron," the Community itself (1QS 8:6, 10; 9:3-6, 26; 10:6, 14), perhaps a sort of interim sanctuary until the eschatological sanctuary could be built.[48]

Jewish literature written after the First Jewish War and the destruction of Jerusalem evidences a difficulty of another sort, one that has to do with accounting for the absence of the temple. Not unlike the sectarians, Josephus lays the blame for the pollution of the temple at the feet not of Gentiles but of fellow Israelites. While Josephus faults the high priesthood

---

45. John J. Collins, *The Scepter and the Star: The Messiahs of the Dead Sea Scrolls and Other Ancient Literature,* Anchor Bible Reference Library (New York: Doubleday, 1995), p. 84.

46. The relevant passages from Qumran (1QS 5:5-7; 8:4-10; 9:3-6; CD 3:18–4:10; 1QH 20:3) are discussed by Donald Juel, *Messiah and Temple: The Trial of Jesus in the Gospel of Mark,* SBLDS 31 (Missoula, Mont.: Scholars Press, 1977), pp. 159-68.

47. Josephus also criticizes the high priesthood for its corruption, greed, collaborationist tendencies, and violence (*Ant.* 20.181, 206-207).

48. Yet other documents point to the promise of a new or eschatological temple, and in these documents the equation of the temple with the Community is either lacking or ambiguous. The particular text most in discussion here is 4QFlor (4Q174); see the discussion and bibliography in Collins, *Scepter and the Star,* pp. 106-9. It is not entirely clear that 4QFlor equates the temple with the Qumran community itself; so also Juel, *Messiah and Temple,* p. 164.

for its corruption, greed, and violence (*Ant.* 20.181, 206-207), elsewhere he criticizes the revolutionaries for turning the temple into a fortress. Although he continues to refer to it as the "Holy Place" (*J.W.* 4.147-154), he also laments to the temple, "You were no longer the place of God" (*J.W.* 5.19-20). Josephus even goes so far as to argue that while the revolutionaries have polluted the temple, the Romans have endeavored to keep it pure, thus subverting the assumption that it is Gentiles who render sacred space unclean (*J.W.* 4.182-183; 5.362-363; 6.99-102; 6.124-128). Likewise, Josephus virtually exonerates Pompey for his obvious profanation of the temple by arguing that, because of his piety and virtue, he ordered it to be cleansed immediately (*J.W.* 1.152-153; *Ant.* 14.72-73). Obviously, then, one of the key attributes of the temple is purity, and its absence accounts for the destruction of the temple.

The Fourth Gospel never mentions the corrupt practices of the priesthood, the ineffectiveness of the temple cult or sacrifice, or the defilement of the temple. Jesus does excoriate the money changers and merchants for having turned his "Father's house" into a "house of trade." Interestingly, however, John does not refer to the charge, found in the Synoptic Gospels, that the temple has been turned into a "den of robbers" when it should be a "house of prayer" ("for all nations"; Mark 11:17; Matt. 21:13; Luke 19:46). Clearly, the Johannine Jesus does not approve of the practice of selling and trading in the temple, but the charge is explained in terms of Jesus' zeal for his Father's house, and the temple is understood as an image of Jesus' own body. The theme of the proper place of worship will be picked up again in John 4, in discussion with the Samaritan woman, but in the meantime it is clear that in its present configuration the temple cannot serve as the place of worship.

John's account of Jesus' action in the temple is preceded by and paired with the changing of water to wine at a wedding feast in Cana, which defines Jesus' glory in terms of the abundance and fullness of the messianic age. Jesus has already been presented in the first chapter of the Gospel as Messiah, Son of God, King of Israel, the one written of in the law and prophets. With a variety of terms and epithets, Jesus is presented as Israel's Messiah. Jesus' first sign, the changing of the water to wine at Cana, with a likely allusion to the abundance of wine promised in various OT visions of the future, signals messianic fulfillment in abundance (Amos 9:13-15; Hos. 14:7; Jer. 31:12; *1 Enoch* 10:19; *2 Bar.* 29:5).

The Johannine version of the "cleansing" of the temple follows this account, rather than the account of Jesus' triumphal and kingly entry into Jerusalem, described both in John and in the Synoptic Gospels in terms of Zechariah 9:9. John thus prefaces the scene in the temple with a catalog of titles and a sign that underscore the messianic identity of Jesus. The action in the temple serves as another witness to his messianic status. In the Fourth Gospel, the account concludes with Jesus' challenge regarding the destruction and raising of the temple in three days. An editorial comment makes it clear that Jesus is talking not about the Jerusalem temple but rather about "the temple of his body" (2:21). To be precise, then, the text does not say that if the Jerusalem temple is destroyed it will be replaced by *another* temple, but rather that if the temple of Jesus' body is destroyed, it will be raised up in three days. By referring Jesus' word regarding the destruction and rebuilding of the temple to his death and resurrection, John presents Jesus as the indestructible eschatological temple.[49] The argument is not that Jesus' followers do not need a temple, but rather that in him they have a temple that cannot be destroyed. Jesus is not only the Messiah who would come to rebuild the temple, but the one who serves most fully as the embodiment of God's glory, the dwelling place of God and, hence, his Father's "house."

The link between Messiah and temple surfaces explicitly in John 4, where the discussion about the locale for true worship leads to a discussion of messianic expectations and Jesus' acknowledgment that he is the Messiah. The passage develops the expectation that the Messiah would rebuild the temple in keeping with the account of the cleansing in chapter 2, namely, that the temple that would be rebuilt was in fact the person of Jesus himself. This argument rests primarily upon the temple conceived of as the locus of God's presence.[50] In this understanding of the temple, "the

49. For discussion and bibliography concerning the link between Messiah and temple, see N. T. Wright, *Jesus and the Victory of God*, vol. 2: *Christian Origins and the Question of God* (Minneapolis: Fortress, 1996), pp. 489-519.

50. "In the eyes of the people [the temple] constituted primarily the divine dwelling-place of the God of Israel which set them apart from other nations" (*The Jewish People in the First Century: Historical Geography, Political History, Social, Cultural and Religious Life and Institutions*, ed. S. Safrai and M. Stern, vol. 2 [Assen: Van Gorcum; Philadelphia: Fortress, 1976], p. 906). For recent discussions emphasizing the centrality and importance of the temple and its significance in first-century Judaism, see E. P. Sanders, *Judaism: Practice and Belief, 63 BCE–66 CE* (London: SCM; Philadelphia: Trinity, 1993), chs. 5-8, and *The Historical Figure of Jesus* (London: Penguin Books, 1993), p. 262; Carol Meyers, "Temple, Jerusalem," in

closer one gets to the inner sanctum, the nearer one is to the perfection of the divine presence."[51] According to the prologue of the Gospel, one is near to "the perfection of the divine presence" in Jesus: "The Word became flesh and dwelt among us, and we have beheld his glory, glory as of the only Son from the Father, full of grace and truth." This assertion recalls the account of God's dwelling with Israel in the wilderness, as well as the revelation of God to Moses in response to the demand, "Show me thy glory" (Exod. 33:18). The language of John 1:14 is that of theophany, of the revelation of the glory or presence of God.[52] So also in John 1:51 the disciples are promised revelation: heaven will be opened, and the heavenly presence will be manifested, as it was for Jacob at Bethel, the "house of God." Jesus is the "sanctuary," the house of God, in and through which God's presence, God's glory, is manifested.[53]

It is in the context of Jesus' discussion with the Samaritan woman that the most explicit conversations about worship arise in the Fourth Gospel. To the woman's challenge, "Our ancestors worshiped on this mountain, but you say that the place where people must worship is in Jerusalem," Jesus responds, "Woman, believe me, the hour is coming when you will worship the Father neither on this mountain nor in Jerusalem. You worship what you do not know; we worship what we know, for salvation is from the Jews. But the hour is coming, and is now here, when the true worshipers will worship the Father in spirit and in truth, for the Father seeks such as

ABD 6:350-69; as well as the older discussion by George Foot Moore, *Judaism in the First Centuries of the Christian Era: The Age of the Tannaim,* 3 vols. (Cambridge, Mass.: Harvard University Press, 1927-30), 1:369. Craig Koester, in his recent study on symbolism in the Fourth Gospel, comments that the pericope of the cleansing of the temple suggests that "the function of sacrifice . . . is fulfilled and replaced by Jesus" (*Symbolism in the Fourth Gospel: Meaning, Mystery, Community* [Minneapolis: Fortress, 1995], p. 83). Yet the polemic is much more pointed in a book like Hebrews than in John, where it is at best latent.

51. Meyers, *ABD* 6:360.

52. Compare Rev. 21:22-27, which speaks of the absence of the temple in the holy city, since the temple has been rendered superfluous by the very presence of God, whose glory is the light of the city.

53. The verbal parallels with the Temple Scroll from Qumran are striking. In 11QTemple 29:7-8, we read this description of the temple: "They shall be for me a people, and I will be for them for ever, and I shall establish them for ever and always. I shall sanctify my temple with my glory, for I shall make my glory reside over it until the day of creation, when I shall create my temple, establishing it for myself for ever, in accordance with the covenant which I made with Jacob at Bethel."

these to worship him. God is spirit, and those who worship him must worship in spirit and truth." This passage offers one of the few explicit statements about God in the Gospel — "God is spirit" — and with it also a rationale for why true worshippers of God must worship "in spirit and in truth."

The contrast between the "true worship" that God demands and worship in a specific temple is neither a general polemic regarding the interiorization of worship nor a criticism of the idea of "sacred space" *per se*.[54] Rather, it finds its proper context in the eschatological assertion that the "hour is coming, and is now here." That hour is, of course, the hour of Jesus' death and return to the Father, after which the Spirit will be given (7:37-39), thus making possible "worship in Spirit and truth." While the phrase "in spirit and truth" is sometimes taken as referring to the inner feelings or actions of the human worshipper, there are a number of factors that mitigate against this reading and argue instead for taking "spirit" as a reference to the Holy Spirit. The first bit of evidence is the eschatological focus of the material, which speaks of the "coming hour" as the hour that brings true worship. Both in pagan philosophy and in Jewish authors of the period, the contrast between worship in outer form and true internal worship is already well known.[55] It would scarcely take an eschatological warrant to argue for the feasibility of "true worship" in this sense.

Second, the broader literary context of the Gospel strongly suggests that "in spirit and truth" points to the truth put into effect by the Holy Spirit. Specifically, a lengthy section that weaves together the themes of the Spirit and worship begins with 2:13 (possibly already with 2:1) and continues through the end of the account of Jesus' encounter with the Samaritan woman (4:42). This section includes the narratives of (1) the "cleansing" of the temple; (2) Jesus' conversation with Nicodemus; and (3) Jesus'

---

54. Ashton (*Understanding the Fourth Gospel*, pp. 65-66) reads this passage as a formal and explicit statement of the "interiorization of worship"; see also Peder Borgen, "The Gospel of John and Hellenism," in *Exploring the Gospel of John: In Honor of D. Moody Smith*, ed. R. Alan Culpepper and C. Clifton Black (Louisville: Westminster/John Knox, 1996), pp. 111-12. Dunn (*Partings of the Ways*, pp. 93-95) interprets the passage as arguing that all arguments regarding holy places, and even the very idea of sacred space, is now rendered redundant by the person of Jesus.

55. The commentaries of Rudolf Bultmann (*The Gospel of John* [Philadelphia: Westminster, 1971]) and Ernst Haenchen (*A Commentary on the Gospel of John*, 2 vols., Hermeneia [Philadelphia: Fortress, 1984]) contain numerous references to support the point.

encounter with the Samaritan woman. Jesus' action in the temple is interpreted by his own disciples as a foreshadowing of his own death and resurrection — even though they understood this only after Jesus' death. The risen Jesus was subsequently interpreted as the focal point of God's presence. In the second account in this section, Nicodemus, the representative inquirer, hears from Jesus not a rationale for his activity but a challenge to be "born from above," by the life-giving power of the Spirit ("unless you are born by water and the spirit"). Both these narratives point the reader away from the human being as self-sufficient actor to the human being as recipient of the activity and Spirit of God. It would then seem odd if in conversation with the Samaritan woman Jesus were to urge her to "look within," as it were, for the strength and capacity to offer true worship. Quite the contrary, one is brought into the eschatological hour by God's saving activity in Jesus and by the divinely sent Spirit of God. Worship "in spirit" is the work of the Spirit.

Hence chapters 3 and 4 form a sustained argument emphasizing the necessary and renewing work of the Spirit for proper relationship to God, whether that relationship be construed in terms of "entering the kingdom" or "worshiping the Father." While the Spirit, because it is God's spirit, clearly belongs to the realm "above," nevertheless the tension exists not only between the realms "above" and "below," but also between the coming and present hour. For the coming hour, the hour of Jesus' death and resurrection, releases a new work of the Spirit. It is by participating in the realities effected by Jesus' death that one receives the Spirit, enters the kingdom of God, and offers "worship in spirit and in truth." Because God is Spirit, and Jesus brings the Spirit, he also "supplies the necessary medium and vehicle of worship."[56]

Thus the emphasis on the coming hour and the gift of the Holy Spirit indicates the appropriate eschatological framework for "true worship"; the statement "God is spirit" seems not to need such a framework but rather to point to an "essential" definition of God as "spirit." Few commentators take the statement "God is spirit" in this manner, construing it rather as comparable to affirmations in the epistles that "God is light" and "God is love," which emphasize God's activity towards human beings. In the present context, then, the statement that "God is spirit" would again underscore the point that true worship of the Father results from the action of

56. Barrett, *John*, p. 228.

God's spirit, the wind which "blows where it wills."[57] Just as in the conversation with Nicodemus, Jesus emphasizes that entry into the kingdom of God requires a fresh work of God's spirit, so here Jesus insists that a similar work of the Spirit calls forth "true worship."[58] The Spirit who enables rebirth to new life empowers worship of the true God.

The dialogue with the Samaritan woman does not furnish us with a criticism of Jewish worship, its rites, or its institutions in and of themselves. There is no criticism of sacrifice, of the priesthood, or even of the temple or conceptions about the temple. The Gospel focuses on the arrival of the hour that brings the fulfillment of the hope for the new temple. Thus the rebuke that could be offered of Jewish worship is that it is behind the times, failing to keep in step with God's spirit and the messianic fulfillment brought by Jesus. Jesus announces to the woman: "*The hour is coming* when neither on this mountain nor in Jerusalem will you worship the Father" (4:21). This statement is followed almost immediately with the pronouncement that this hour had come: "But the hour is coming, and *is now here,* when the true worshipers will worship the Father in spirit and truth" (4:23). In other words, Jesus' criticism of worship offered in any realm other than "in spirit and in truth" because of the arrival of "the hour" indicates that the primary critique of these other modes of worship is lodged in their failure to keep step with the times.

Indeed, Jesus has already enacted his death and resurrection in the context of the temple itself, in which he prophetically demonstrated that the locale for true worship would be his own person. After his resurrection and glorification to the Father, he also becomes the focal point of this worship, the "sanctuary" in and through which God's presence is manifested. That Jesus speaks of an alternative worship does not demonstrate that Christian worship of God renders irrelevant protected sacred spaces and holy places; precisely the opposite. The alternative "holy place" is Jesus himself.[59] As the

---

57. E. C. Hoskyns, *The Fourth Gospel* (London: Faber & Faber, 1947), p. 238.

58. Hoskyns (*The Fourth Gospel*, p. 238) comments that true worship of the Father "is spiritual because it makes room for the reverse and corresponding action of God from above. This reverse operation and power of God is defined as Spirit, just as elsewhere it is defined as love and light." I would modify this statement so that it is clear that such worship begins with the action of God from above.

59. For the argument that the Fourth Gospel understands worship of God as completely severed from sanctuaries and the very notion of sacred space made useless by Jesus himself, see Dunn, *Partings of the Ways,* pp. 93-95.

locus of God's presence, Jesus serves as the "place" of epiphany, and so reidentifies the "place" of worship.[60] The holy ground of revelation becomes the sanctified "space" of worship. Here it is that "you will see heaven opened and the angels ascending and descending upon the Son of Man" (1:51). Worship "in" this holy place, then, is worship "in spirit and in truth."

The Johannine polemic with respect to the temple does not so much contrast two rites, or two religions, or two forms of piety, but rather two eras and their respective manifestations of the presence of God. True worship is not a matter of first discovering a new object of worship but is rather a reorientation of one's worship through and in the presence of God in the living temple, Jesus, and in the realm of the Spirit. What David Aune says generally about early Christian worship applies also to John:

> The widespread views that Jesus was a radical critic of traditional Jewish worship, that early Christianity did not have a cult in the proper sense of the term, and that Christianity eliminated the usual distinction between the sacred and the profane, are exaggerated claims based on modern theological biases with tenuous historical support in early Christian literature.[61]

Indeed, a close examination of the Gospel leads to a somewhat more nuanced understanding of the arguments regarding worship in the Fourth Gospel: The Gospel is not a "radical critic of traditional Jewish worship" so much as it is a critic of the failure to recognize the eschatological hour and the way in which worship is appropriately offered in that hour. Insofar as it understood Jesus to be the manifestation of God's glory and presence, early Christianity validates "sacred space," while nevertheless "relocating" it and rendering it metaphorically. The symbols of Judaism that are used to explicate his identity are therefore taken up into the person of Jesus, the Messiah of Israel.

Jesus, Passover, and the Worship of God

Aune's contention that early Christianity *did* have a cult leads us to cast a quick glance at John's treatment of the Passover, one of the major festivals

60. See Haenchen, *John*, 1:222.
61. David E. Aune, "Early Christian Worship," in *ABD* 6:974.

of first-century Judaism and of symbolic importance to the Gospel of John, particularly as it lies behind the account of the feeding miracle in John 6. Just as the Gospel of John "relocates" sacred space in Jesus, so too it envisions a Passover that is God's saving work through the person of Jesus.

The Johannine treatment of the festivals has provided some of the most important data for Christologically focused readings of the Gospel that emphasize the sharp discontinuity with and criticism of Judaism. We may recall some of the statements quoted earlier: "All previous religious institutions, customs and feasts lose meaning in [Jesus'] presence."[62] Or: "Jesus supersedes the great pilgrim festivals; he fulfills the symbolism of the feast of tabernacles. . . . Jesus fulfills and thus supersedes the purity regulations of Judaism. . . . in Jesus the Messiah the old Temple and cult has been rendered redundant."[63] Or: "Jesus even replaced the Sabbath, Passover, Feast of Booths, and Feast of Dedication."[64] Before proceeding further, we should note the awkwardness of such statements, which, for example, in contrasting Jesus with the Passover, contrast a *person* with a *festival,* something that people *do* in order to commemorate something that has happened or that has been done by someone else. One can imagine a comparison between two figures, such as Moses and Jesus, or between two festivals, such as the Passover celebration and the Lord's Supper, but to argue that Jesus replaces Passover would be analogous to arguing that the Lord's Supper replaces Moses. Stated so baldly, it will be immediately evident that the argument is highly compressed and not particularly helpful in illuminating the Gospel.

Similarly jarring is the statement that "Jesus supersedes the great pilgrim festivals." What, exactly, does it mean to speak of a person replacing a festival? Presumably such arguments intend to speak of *the religious significance* of Passover somehow being superseded by what Jesus has done or by Jesus himself. This, however, does not help us very much until we know exactly what it is that Jesus is understood to "replace" or "supersede." If the feast of Passover commemorates God's deliverance of Israel from Egypt and God's leading of the people through the wilderness, then it makes little sense to speak of Jesus as "superseding" or "replacing" either God's activity or Israel's remembrance of it. More precisely, the contrast lies between

62. Brown, *John,* 1:104.
63. Dunn, *Partings of the Ways,* pp. 93, 94, 95.
64. Koester, *The Dwelling of God,* p. 108.

God's saving action in the deliverance from Egypt, the provision in the wilderness, and the giving of the law at Sinai, and God's saving action in the deliverance, provision, and teaching now offered through Jesus Christ, who is the bread of life. The festival of Passover celebrates God's acts of deliverance, provision, and guidance, while the Johannine interpretation of Passover strikes the note of finality and fulfillment. Thus, rather than saying that "Jesus supersedes the great pilgrim festivals," it would be more precise to argue that even as the great pilgrim festivals celebrate God's work, so too Christians commemorated God's acts of salvation — here, the act of eschatological salvation in Christ.

When the issue is framed in this way, it also becomes apparent that Jesus does not "supersede" or replace the action of God through Passover; rather, Passover clarifies and illumines the nature of Jesus' own work. Just as God delivered Israel and provided for it, so now, too, through Jesus, the true manna from heaven, God again promises deliverance and provision. Passover is not "replaced"; rather, the great pilgrim festivals anticipate God's work in Jesus. Yet Jesus himself neither replaces nor displaces that earlier act of God. John's presentation of Passover assumes that God did indeed act to deliver, sustain, and guide Israel in the wilderness. Through Jesus, God is now providing food that leads to life rather than death in the wilderness (6:27, 33, 35, 47-51, 51-58). In this hour, God renews the covenant (6:44-46) and gives the gift of faith (6:29, 36, 40), so that those on the journey may not grumble as did the faithless wilderness generation. Just as God sustained the life of the people of Israel in the wilderness, so now God provides through the "true bread from heaven," the "bread of life."

The juxtaposition of these two life-giving acts of God is not merely a heuristic device, as though the first Passover provided a template that could simply be discarded once it had been grasped that salvation was now accomplished in Jesus. To be sure, the stakes in John 6 are high. Specifically, what is at stake in the argument there is the recognition and acknowledgment of God's activity in Jesus, construed in terms of God's working (6:29), provision of bread and life (6:32-33, 50-51, 57), and teaching (6:44-45). Through the ministry and person of Jesus, the salvation of God comes to its fullness. Eschatological fulfillment inevitably assumes some discontinuity between past and present, or present and future. However, the discontinuity does not eradicate all continuity because the eschatological activity is always ultimately lodged in the one life-giving God. Just as Israel's God is one God, so the life-giving work of God is one story.

219

In John 6, then, the emphasis falls *first* on the continuity of the narrative of God's redeeming work from Moses to Jesus, and *then* on the discontinuity brought about by the striking of the eschatological hour. Consequently, to assert that in Jesus' presence all Jewish festivals lose their meaning is to misinterpret the character of Johannine polemic. Jesus does not replace the Jewish festivals; and neither does God's deliverance "replace" the deliverance of the Exodus from Egypt. Rather, the festivals of Israel, which present and represent that narrative of God's saving work, are taken up into those festivals that celebrate the continuation of that narrative. More sharply than in the Synoptics, the interpretation of the Lord's Supper in John, as it is found in 6:51-58, finds its meaning in Israel's Passover.

Jesus, Worship, and the Synagogue

"They will put you out of the synagogues. Indeed, an hour is coming when those who kill you will think that by doing so they are offering worship to God" (16:2). This verse — or, more correctly, the one word *aposynagōgos* (ἀποσυνάγωγος; "out of the synagogue") — has played an important role in recent reconstructions of the history of the Johannine community. It predicts the conflict between "Church" and "synagogue" that would lead to the eventual expulsion of the Johannine Christians from the synagogue. If we return the verse to its immediate context, however, we will see that further light is shed upon the question of worship we are considering here.

> "The hour is coming and now is, when those who worship the Father must worship him in Spirit and in truth, for such the Father seeks to worship him." (John 4:23)

> "They will put you out of the synagogues. Indeed, an hour is coming when those who kill you will think that by doing so they are offering worship to God." (John 16:2)

In putting these two verses side by side, we note that both refer to a coming hour and to worship that will be carried out in that hour. John 4:23 refers to worship apart from either the Samaritan or the Jewish temple; John 16:2 envisions worship outside the synagogues. John 4:23 makes explicit the link between worship and the Spirit; in context, John 16:2 comes after the promise of the coming of the Spirit of Truth. These striking parallels are worth exploring a bit further.

The words for worship in 4:23 (προϲκυνεῖν) and 16:2 (λατρεία) do differ. The Greek word in 16:2 (λατρεία) occurs only here in John, seldom in the NT (Rom. 9:4; 12:1; Heb. 9:1, 6), and then never in combination with "offer" (προσφερεῖν). In the LXX λατρεύειν and its cognates consistently render the Hebrew עבד and its cognates when the reference is to religious service. More precisely, λατρεία and its cognates refer to cultic service or worship. Here, in John 16:2, joined as it is with the word "offer" (προσφερεῖν), it virtually means "sacrifice."[65] That word can, of course, take on metaphorical significance, as it does in Paul's use of it to speak of "spiritual worship" (Rom. 12:1). The time is coming when those who seek to kill Jesus' followers — as they did Jesus himself — will view such a deed as a sacrifice to God. There are parallels to this thought in Jewish writings. For example, *Numbers Rabbah* 21:3 (on Num. 25:6-13) reads as follows:

> "And it shall be unto [Phinehas], and to his seed after him . . . because he . . . made atonement." But did he offer a sacrifice, to justify the expression "atonement" in this connection? No, but it serves to teach you that if a man sheds the blood of the wicked it is as though he had offered a sacrifice.

It may well be that the language in John of "offering sacrifice" to God reflects underlying disagreement about the shape of proper worship of God. We can trace this argument in the Farewell Discourses. In 15:18, Jesus introduces the theme of the world's hatred for the disciples, leading up to the scriptural proof "They hated me without a cause" (15:25; see Ps. 35:19; 69:4).[66] In order to keep the disciples from falling away under these pressures, Jesus promises the Spirit of Truth, who will bear witness to him (15:26–16:1). Then Jesus makes the threat more precise: not only will "they" expel the Johannine Christians from the synagogue, but "they" will even seek to kill these Christians, vainly thinking that by so doing they are offering a sacrifice to God (16:2). Finally, Jesus offers the rationale for such behavior: "They will do this because they have not known the Father, nor

---

65. H. Strathmann, "λατρεύω," in *TDNT* 4:59-65.

66. For extensive analysis and argumentation that 15:18–16:4a constitutes a unified and coherent whole, see Fernando F. Segovia, *The Farewell of the Word: The Johannine Call to Abide* (Minneapolis: Fortress, 1991), pp. 170-208.

me" (16:3). In short, those who think that they are worshipping God by "sacrificing" Jesus' disciples will show that they do not know God. John affirms the risen Jesus as the locus of God's presence and hence of true worship of God, but there are others who think that it is actually the death of Jesus' followers that merits the designation "true worship of God." The time would come when Jesus' followers would be viewed as idolaters, or apostates, those who had "fallen away" from the worship of the one God. To slay them would be an instance of proper zeal for God.[67]

This leads us to consider whether the Gospel affirms or testifies to the currency of the practice of worship of the risen Lord. There are verses that suggest an affirmative answer. For example, the statement in 5:23 urges that all should "honor the Son, even as they honor the Father. He who does not honor the Son does not honor the Father who sent him." The language of paying honors may well point to worship. Thomas's confession of Jesus as "My Lord and my God!" (20:28) may be taken not simply as a statement about the identity of the risen Lord but rather as an acknowledgment and confession of him in keeping with religious or cultic practice. As already noted above, J. L. Martyn suggested that the charge against Johannine Christians was that they worshipped Jesus as a second God. The Johannine Christians were really di-theists, and their developing high Christology provided the basis for their expulsion from the synagogue. So also J. D. G. Dunn, in discussing the "partings of the ways" between Judaism and Christianity, writes, "The Jesus of the Fourth Gospel would have put a severe strain on Jewish monotheism and probably could not have been retained within Judaism."[68] In short, the charge is that the Johannine trajectory led to precisely the sorts of views attacked by rabbinic polemic against "two powers in heaven" as an infringement upon the most fundamental of Jewish beliefs, "Hear, O Israel, the Lord our God is one."[69] Hence, it will be useful to ask whether the Gospel testifies to the practice of worshipping Jesus and, if so, how then the identity of God is to be understood.

---

67. Segovia calls attention to the irony in this contrast in *Farewell of the Word*, pp. 204, 212.

68. Dunn, *Partings of the Ways*, p. 176. For another view, see Richard Bauckham, *God Crucified: Monotheism and Christology in the New Testament* (Grand Rapids: Eerdmans, 1998).

69. This whole matter is discussed fully by Hurtado, *One God, One Lord*; and Alan Segal, *Two Powers in Heaven: Early Rabbinic Reports about Christianity and Gnosticism*, Studies in Judaism in Late Antiquity 25, ed. Jacob Neusner (Leiden: Brill, 1977).

Worship of Jesus in the Fourth Gospel?

Several passages in the Gospel suggest worship of the risen Jesus. Three passages in the Gospel either refer to or imply expulsion from the synagogue, and these passages have to do with believing in Jesus as Lord and Son of Man, and possibly also worshipping him as such (9:38), "confessing" Jesus (12:42), and "offering service to God" (16:2).[70] These verses speak of belief in and confession, and perhaps worship, of Jesus, practices that lead to expulsion from the synagogue. Hence these passages also lend credence to the interpretations of Martyn and Dunn that the Johannine Christology and, particularly, worship of Jesus led to a "parting of the ways" between the Church and the synagogue. Elsewhere Jesus notes that those who do not honor the Son (ὁ μὴ τιμῶν τὸν υἱὸν) do not honor the Father (5:23), a noteworthy passage since the Greek word *timaō* (τιμάω) frequently designates cultic honors.[71] While this passage distinguishes the Father and the Son, it joins them in speaking of both as proper recipients of honor, stating that failure to honor the Son is a failure to honor the Father.

Finally, there is the climactic resurrection appearance of Jesus, which results in Thomas's acclamation, "My Lord and my God!" (20:26-29). This acclamation of Jesus as "God" comes only after the resurrection and is found in the personal form, "my Lord and my God." While it forms an inclusio with the prologue's acknowledgment of the Word as "God" (1:1), this is the only place in the Gospel where an individual directly addresses Jesus in this way. Although Thomas is not said to confess or worship Jesus, the acknowledgment of Jesus as "my Lord and my God" can hardly be construed in any other way. The personal pronouns indicate that this is a confession addressed to Jesus and, hence, properly judged an acclamation not only of his identity but an act of worship. In light of the climactic position of Thomas's confession, it is perhaps surprising that it is followed immediately by a statement of the Gospel's purpose couched in terms of leading people to believe in Jesus as the "Messiah and Son of God." That the evangelist sees no contradiction between confession of Jesus as "my God" and as "Son of God" reveals the basic contours of his Christology and sheds

---

70. In 12:42 and 16:2, the word ἀποσυνάγωγος ("out of the synagogue") is used. In 9:34-35 the blind man, now healed, has been "cast out," but it is not explicitly stated that he is "cast out" of the synagogue.

71. See here Moxnes, *Theology in Conflict*, p. 71.

some light on the question of what it might mean to worship the risen Jesus. Specifically, it cannot mean to worship a figure alongside of God, or in addition to God, but to acknowledge the propriety of speaking of the one who is the Son of God, the incarnation of the Word of God, as "my God." For John, the incarnation is nothing other than God's self-manifestation. The incarnate Son is neither an exalted agent figure nor a second deity but the very embodiment of the Word of God and, therefore, merits address as "my God."

In keeping with the specific question of the relationship of Jesus to the feasts and institutions of Judaism, we may put this differently. At the outset of this chapter, we noted the regularity with which scholars assert that John intends to show how Jesus "replaces" or "supersedes" Jewish festivals and rites by focusing on the Christological significance of Jesus' actions in relationship to various acts and practices of Jewish worship and ritual. In all cases, it is important to consider the ways in which Jesus *mediates* worship of God. According to the Fourth Gospel, Jesus manifests the glory of God (1:14) and the presence of God (1:51) in such a way that he can even be identified with the temple, the symbolic dwelling place of God (2:21-22). Hence, worship in that holy place is necessary, not optional.

As we saw earlier in this chapter, one of the most frequent biblical and Jewish polemics against those who do not worship idols rather than the living God is that they worship that which is created rather than the Creator. Similarly, one of the most frequent characterizations of God is that God is the living God, the Creator of all that is, and hence the unique and sovereign Lord.[72] Therefore, it is highly significant that John repeatedly speaks of the reality mediated through Jesus as the reality of life. Through Jesus, God gives life. Not only so, but the one who is the "living Father" has even granted it to the Son "to have life in himself." At this point the subtle movement from worship *through* Jesus to worship *of* Jesus begins, shadowing the movement from "God gives life through Jesus" to "Jesus himself gives life." If the Creator, the Giver of life, is to be worshipped, and Jesus is both the means through whom God gives such life and, indeed, the very possessor of divine life, it is not a far step to offering worship to the one through whom life comes, inasmuch as life-giving is a unique divine power.

All these passages offer an interesting comparison between directing honor or worship *to* Jesus and offering it *through* him. Honors are offered

72. See chapter 2, "The Living Father," esp. pp. 73-77.

to Jesus as the Son of Man (9:38), as "my Lord" and "my God," and through him as Son (of God) to the Father. Each of these ways of thinking of and confessing Jesus underscores that he is the embodied presence of God, the one through whom one knows and acknowledges the "living Father" (6:57), "the only true God" (17:3). As the Son of Man, Jesus becomes the place of revelation (1:51) and the one to whom the Father has given the right and power of judgment (5:27). As the risen and living one, he is the living "house of God" or manifestation of God's presence (2:21-22), the one who is ever with the Father (1:18; 8:58). Because he is the one who embodies the very Word and glory of God, and who now lives with the Father, the Son may be honored and confessed as "my Lord" and "my God." He does not "take the place of God" but comprehensively and fully manifests the Word, presence, glory, and life of God. As the Son of the Father, Jesus has and brings the very life of God and fully reveals the Father.

John thus presents Jesus as the one *through* whom worship is directed to God. In so doing, John also speaks of the Son not just in terms that assign to him a prominent, distinct, or exalted role of agency but that predicate an inseparable unity with God. As noted in an earlier chapter, terms such as Wisdom, Word, and glory are the best explications of the sort of relationship and unity that already exist between the Father and Son by virtue of that Father-Son relationship. To confess the risen Jesus as "my Lord" and "my God" always takes into account the character of this relationship and the way in which the one who is acknowledged as the incarnate Word and Son comes from God. To honor the Son as one honors the Father pays equal honor to both but also recognizes that the Son is who he is precisely because he is the Son of the Father. Hence, honor of the risen Jesus is never honor of a second god but honor of the One who manifests the glory, Word, and life of God.

Not by accident does Thomas's acknowledgment of Jesus as "My Lord and my God!" follow the resurrection, for Jesus' appearances attest to the disciples that he is indeed alive. Whatever else one may predicate of the divine, it is clear that in Jewish writings "divinity" is always defined by the prerogative and power to give life. God is eternally alive. Philo, in the *Embassy to Gaius*, argues that worship is due to the one who is Benefactor, Creator, and Father of all the world, not to that which is mortal and corruptible (118). In hailing Jesus as "my God" Thomas confesses him to be, like God the living Father, eternally alive. Again, the prologue of the Gospel speaks of the Word as "God" when it points to his eternal existence: "In the beginning was the Word, and the Word was with God, and the Word was God." He was before Abraham (8:58); he lays down his life to take it again; he returns to the glory he had with God before creation; and he is ever at the Father's side. Life belongs to God, and because Jesus has life as God does, and so has it eternally, the disciples are led to the confession, "My Lord and my God!"

The God of the Gospel of John

In this book I have taken up the implicit challenge issued over two decades ago by Nils Dahl in his assertion that God is the neglected factor in NT theology by offering, as he also suggested, a "monograph that concentrates upon one topic in such a way that it contributes to a better understanding of an aspect of the whole."[1] Yet even the "one topic" pursued here — namely, the characterization and identity of God in the Gospel of John — is obviously vast and could be approached in a number of different ways. I have endeavored to focus attention on some specific aspects of the topic, particularly as they emerge from the Gospel itself. I have further suggested that the oft-repeated and widely shared characterization of the Gospel as "Christocentric" has contributed to the neglect of God in the delineation of Johannine theology. Instead, I have proposed that the Gospel would better be termed "theocentric," in that it directs our attention to God, and that this designation is particularly apt in light of the fact that Johannine Christology itself regularly, comprehensively, and insistently seeks to relate Jesus to God. This is evident from titles applied to Jesus such as Son (of God), Lamb of God, Word, and Messiah; from the description of God as "my Father" or as "the Father who sent me"; and from Jesus' repeated affir-

1. Nils A. Dahl, "The Neglected Factor in New Testament Theology," in *Jesus the Christ: The Historical Origins of Christological Doctrine,* ed. Donald H. Juel (Minneapolis: Fortress, 1991), p. 157.

227

mations that he comes from God and that he brings life and revelation from God. Indeed, "every statement about Christ implicates God."[2] It is time, then, to draw some of the threads of our analysis together and to offer some summary comments.

The Use of "God" in the Gospel of John

In almost every case, the word "God" applies in the Gospel of John to the God of Israel. While that phrase is in and of itself never used in John, it is clear that the one designated as "God" is also the one to whom "the Jews" refer as their God (8:41, 54). Echoing the words of the *Shema*, the Gospel speaks of God as "the one who alone is God" (5:44) and as "the only true God" (17:3). This God is the one who created the world (1:1-3); gave the law through Moses (1:17; cf. 9:16, 29); teaches his people, even as the Scriptures promised (John 6:45; Isa. 54:13); has never been seen by any human being (1:18; 5:37; 5:46); and over whose proper worship the Samaritans and Jews quarrel (4:19-22). Certain institutions and feasts are particularly linked to God. Jesus refers to the Jerusalem temple as "my Father's house," alluding to the description in the Psalms of the temple as God's house (Ps. 69:9). The Scriptures are God's inviolable word (5:37-47; 10:34-36). Observance of the Sabbath law, precisely because it is God's law, looms large in the conflict between Jesus and his adversaries (e.g., 5:16-18; 9:16, 24). The God of the Gospel of John is the God of Israel, who is made known through the feasts and institutions of Israel — such as the Sabbath, the temple, and the law.

However, the most telling and frequent characterization of God is to be found on Jesus' lips, for he calls God "my Father" and refers to him regularly as "the Father" or "the Father who sent me." Indeed, as indicated earlier, the most common designation of God in John is Father, a term that appears about 120 times. More importantly, however, the actions of God as Father are distinctly and peculiarly concentrated on and through Jesus as the Son.[3] Of all the functions and activities of God, the one that defines God as Father is that of giving life. God is the one who, as Father, gives life

---

2. Leander Keck, "Toward the Renewal of New Testament Christology," *NTS* 32 (1986): 363.

3. See chapter 2, "The Living Father," pp. 77-80.

to and through the Son. Or, put differently, the designation of God as Father indicates that God is the source and origin of the life of the one who is designated as Son (e.g., 5:25-26). Because God is "Father" in relationship to the Son, that relationship constitutes God's very identity as Father in the Gospel of John. God is known as the Father through the Son, and God is known as the Father of the Son.

The Father-Son relationship underscores the fundamental portrayal of God in the Gospel of John as the living God and creator of all life (1:1-3; 6:57). That God is the living and life-giving God so regularly characterizes biblical assertions and assumptions about God that it scarcely needs to be repeated in later Jewish sources — and yet it is. This understanding of God is assumed rather than argued for in John, and it provides the linchpin of the argument that Jesus' work is the work of God. These are one work because Jesus' work brings life, and the prerogative and power to give life belong to God alone. Even as the opening words of the prologue echo the opening words of Genesis and its account of God's creation of the world, so the Gospel echoes the repeated affirmations of the Scriptures, particularly the prophets, that there is one Creator of all that is. As Creator, God merits honor, obedience, and worship. In short, then, God is the living God and source of life and is known through the life-giving work of the Son, who himself has life from the Father (5:25-26).

The characterization of God as the God of life colors the portrayal of the Spirit as well, for the Spirit is virtually by definition the life-giving force or power of God. Through the Spirit one is born from above to become a child of God (1:12-13; 3:3-5), for it is the Spirit that gives life (6:63) and that becomes a source of life within the believer (4:14; 7:38). The Spirit of Truth empowers true worship of God (4:23-24) and guides believers into all truth. Because "truth" belongs solely and necessarily to "the one true God" (17:3), the Spirit confers life insofar as and because through the Spirit believers are led from the realm of darkness and death to truth and life.

To put it differently, God is the Father who is the source of life. Jesus, the Son of the Father, confers God's life but, even more, is God's life-giving Word embodied in the flesh for the life of the world. The Spirit of God is the power of life and the agency through which life is received. To a large extent, then, John sketches the identity of God through what God does and, even more specifically, primarily through the various ways in which God gives life through the Son and the Spirit. Hence, God is made known through the life and work of the Son, and through the life and work of the Spirit. The God of the Gospel of John is the God of life. We may make these observations somewhat more precise and concrete.

Divine Prerogatives and Functions

In the first chapter of this study, we observed several instances in which "God" was used of figures other than Israel's God. Yet while the bare "god" can be applied to figures human and heavenly, various descriptive or qualifying phrases often make clear the limitation of such usage. For example, phrases such as "the Most High," or "the Almighty" are not similarly used of figures such as Moses or Melchizedek. Most often even the simple "god" refers to the God of Israel, as is evidenced by the regular substitution in the LXX of *theos* (θεός) for the Tetragrammaton. When we find "god" used of other figures, such usage is typically based on a biblical text and linked with that figure's exercise of a divine prerogative, such as judgment or sovereignty. For just as some adjectival phrases are reserved for God, so are some activities or prerogatives. In the Gospel of John, Jesus exercises a number of these divine prerogatives, including the power to give life (5:25-26; 10:28-29), the authority to work on the Sabbath (5:16-18), sovereignty over or knowledge of "all things" (3:35; 4:25; 13:3; 16:30), the power and authority of judgment and salvation (5:27, 30; 8:16), and the capacity to bestow the divine spirit of creation and salvation (6:63; 20:22).

Jesus exercises these divine prerogatives through the signs that embody God's life-giving work, and he speaks words that confer life. Among them are the various "I am" sayings, for they point to the life that is to be found in Jesus and given through his work. His saving work is characterized in these sayings as sustaining and nurturing (6:35; 15:1), illuminating and revealing (8:12; 9:5; 14:6), protecting and guiding (10:9, 11), and, simply, bestowing life (11:25). These functions can, however, be made more specific. For example, Jesus nurtures with the "bread from heaven" because he is the bread of God (6:33) that comes down from heaven (6:32, 33, 50, 51) and gives life to the world (6:51). This sustaining and life-giving bread comes from God; those who receive it show that they have been taught by God, drawn by God into fellowship, and heard the words of God (6:44-46). Jesus' life-giving work is not an additional work alongside that of God's but a work in and through which God carries out his own. Similarly, the context of the statement "I am the way, the truth, and the life" (14:6) indicates that Jesus is the way that leads to the truth and by which one enters into the life of God. Just as Jesus is the door that opens to life, and the shepherd who guides the sheep to the abundant and nurturing pastures, and the bread that sustains life, so he is the means or way that leads one to the truth and life of God.

In other words, although John makes a point of showing that Jesus exercises God's own prerogatives, he does not exercise them independently of God. Rather, Jesus' exercise of these prerogatives indicates his expression of God's work in the world, and his embodiment of that work leads in turn to knowing the truth and having eternal life (14:6; 17:3). Another way to summarize the point is to say that Jesus is not presented as a second divine being, not a god alongside the one true God, but as the Son who is authorized and even commanded to speak God's words and to do God's work. The identification of Jesus as the Son, and the language of authorization and command, make it clear that the Son is not the Father, but that the Son always carries out the work of the Father — and that he does so by the Father's explicit command and authorization (e.g., 5:19-20, 25-26; 10:18, 32, 37-38). Hence John's Christology is, as we argued above, both *functional* and *relational*.[4] John's Christology may be called *relational* in that it seeks to delineate the dependence of Jesus on God. John articulates that dependence in a number of ways and with a variety of metaphors and assertions, including the fundamental description of Jesus as "Son," explicit statements that Jesus does the will of the Father, the description of God as "giving" certain powers to the Son and of issuing him certain commands, and the assertion of the unity of their work. John's Christology is also *functional* in that it lays particular stress on Jesus' exercise of divine prerogatives. As one writer has put it, the Early Church did not develop its Christology by beginning with "divine agent" figures. Rather, "Jesus' relation to God was formulated in terms of the major divine activity which constituted the faith of Israel: creation, redemption, reconciliation, law, kingship, and judgment."[5] In John, these activities include creation, salvation, revelation, kingship, sovereignty, and judgment, and precisely here it

4. See the discussion in chapter 1, "The Meaning of God," pp. 46-48.
5. Brevard S. Childs, *Biblical Theology of the Old and New Testaments: Theological Reflection on the Christian Bible* (Minneapolis: Fortress, 1992), p. 367.

becomes clear that "every statement about Christ implicates God" and that "christology functions within theology."[6]

The Unity of God

John's argument for the dependence of the Son on the Father constitutes an argument for their unity. Father and Son are not two independent deities and not "two powers in heaven." Rather, there is — to quote the Gospel itself — one "true God," the living Father, whose life is given to and whose divine power is exercised in and through Jesus, the Son, and through the agency of the life-giving Spirit. Yet the very description of Jesus as the Son does not in the first instance point to the exercise of divine prerogatives or functions but rather to the character of the relationship and unity between the Father and Son. In other words, Jesus is not the Son because he exercises these divine functions; rather, he exercises them because he is the Son. Out of and by virtue of his relationship to the Father, the Son gives life to the world, makes the Father known, carries out the Father's will in the world, and so on. The activity and character of the Father are embodied in and through the Son. Hence, the determinative elements of the Christology of the Fourth Gospel are those that present Jesus as the one who carries out the functions of God and embodies the activity of God because he is identified with God in the way that a Son is identified with a Father, and that glory, Wisdom, and Word, as the manifestation and expression of God, are identified with God.

Within the monotheistic framework of Judaism and early Christianity, a framework clearly shared by the Gospel of John, there is no "thing" or attribute called "deity" or "divinity" that God may share with another.[7] The attributes and activities of God, such as eternal existence, the power to create, omniscience, and sovereignty over all things, do not characterize "divinities" or even "divinity" but belong solely to God. Hence, if "divinity" is to be predicated of a figure, that predication will necessarily imply a relationship to the "only true God." John articulates this relationship primarily through the Father-Son dyad, through the emphasis on Jesus' car-

6. For these quotations from Leander Keck and James D. G. Dunn, see the introduction to this volume, pp. 1, 7, 10-11.

7. See above, chapter 1, "The Meaning of God," pp. 46-47.

rying out divine functions and activities, and through categories that posit the closest possible unity between them.

The Gospel of John, which testifies most vigorously to the unity of Father and Son, nevertheless also unequivocally differentiates between them. In every possible formulation, Jesus is portrayed as one whose identity and actions originate with God, and whose ministry points and leads to God. Jesus is a prophet, the Son of Man to whom judgment has been entrusted, the Messiah, the Son of God, the one who does the work of God and who speaks the words of God, and the one who has seen God and so makes him known. He comes from God, the Father who sent him. As the one who has seen God, Jesus reveals God; as the one who hears from God, Jesus speaks words of life. Jesus embodies God's glory in the flesh. This emphasis on the unity of Jesus with God, and particularly on the way that Jesus manifests God's presence and work through his signs and in his words, accounts to a large extent for the Gospel's accent on *seeing* the Father in the Son. Seeing requires the presence of the one who is seen, and to the extent that knowledge arises from or is even equated with seeing, knowledge of God depends upon the presence of the one who is to be known. Because the Father is present in and through the Son, knowledge of God is not knowledge that is separate from the person of Jesus, as though it could be summed up in some theses statements or reduced to a list of propositions. Rather, knowledge of God is mediated through the work and person of Jesus.

This leads us directly to a consideration of the designation of "God" for the Word (1:1) and for the risen Jesus (20:28).[8] We note, first, the very limited attribution of "God" to Jesus in the Gospel. Specifically, "God" is used of the Word in 1:1, and it is this Word that becomes flesh (1:14). Then "God" is not used again of the incarnate Word until after the resurrection. In other words, "God" is used with reference to the Word (of God) and with reference to the risen One who has returned to the glory he had with the Father before the creation of the world (17:5). Properly speaking, then, the term is not used of Jesus of Nazareth during his life and ministry in first-century Judea, Galilee, and Samaria. Here we may speak of the enfleshment of God's Word and the manifestation of God's glory. Yet not even in John does any person ever confess Jesus, prior to the resurrection,

---

8. The textual evidence may suggest that θεός was used of the Son in 1:18, but this usage would not change the conclusions reached here.

as "God." That this is so surely reflects the Johannine emphasis on the living Father as God and creator of all that is.

In the Gospel the charge is twice raised against Jesus that "he makes himself equal to God" (5:18; 10:33). It is a charge that Jesus does not flatly deny, but rather interprets in two ways. In the first instance, the charge that Jesus makes himself "equal to God" is countered by showing that the Son does all that he does through his dependence on the Father (5:19). Hence, the Son is not independent of, but rather dependent upon, the Father in all things. The Father has authorized the Son precisely to exercise divine activities and prerogatives, including the giving of life, passing judgment, and working on the Sabbath. In the second instance, Jesus refutes the charge that though he is a human being he "makes himself God" (10:33) through an appeal to Psalm 82. This Psalm speaks of *elohim* (אֱלֹהִים; gods), and in John Jesus applies the designation to "those to whom the word of God came." He subsequently reasserts his identity as the Son of God. This tacit claim to dependence upon God is borne out in an appeal to the unity of the work of the Father and Son that testifies to their mutual indwelling (10:37-38).

John is working within the same constraints that bind Jewish authors such as Philo and the translators of the Targums: namely, the biblical affirmation that there is one God and the scriptural warrant for referring to individuals as "god" or "gods." As we saw in the first chapter, Jewish authors interpret the attribution of "god" to individuals because they either have attained a particularly intimate status with God or have been assigned a particular function or status by God. Philo acknowledges the existence of one God, "the God who is," the Most High God, and understands Moses' designation as "god" in Exodus 7:1 as a title bestowed upon him because of his virtue and nobility, and as a token of his partnership with God. The Targums similarly take seriously the application of "god" to Moses in Exodus 7:1, but they refer it to the exercise of sovereignty or rule as commissioned by God.

Again, like Philo, John uses "god" to refer both to the "only true God" — for Philo, the "one who is" — and to the manifestation of that God as the Logos. While John understands the Logos somewhat differently and posits an incarnation in human flesh that Philo does not, nevertheless, that Logos is both identified with and differentiated from God in ways that allow a dual usage of the term "God." Ultimately, the Logos may be called "God" because the Logos derives from God and is an expression of God.

John's problem may, if anything, be deemed more acute than Philo's since John must account not only for the unity of God and the Logos but also for the identity of Jesus, a human being of flesh and blood, with the God who is Spirit.

The risen Jesus is addressed by Thomas as "My Lord and my God!" According to the Roman historian Suetonius, the emperor Domitian affected the title "Our lord and god" *(dominus et deus noster)*.[9] It is possible that Thomas's language reflects the imperial title, but one of the most common adjectives or descriptive phrases attached to "God" in the OT and Jewish sources is the personal possessive pronoun, either in the singular, "my God," or the plural, "our God." The "god" in question is thus identified with a specific group or people who honor and worship that deity as God. In light of the rest of the Gospel of John, Thomas's confession cannot mean that the risen Jesus is the only God. That epithet has already been used by Jesus himself in a context that clearly distinguishes the Father and the Son (17:3). Moreover, in a resurrection appearance to Mary Magdalene, Jesus had commanded her to go tell his disciples that he was "ascending to my Father and to your Father, to my God and to your God" (20:17). It is highly unlikely that John intends the reader to understand that at some point the Father and Son are simply "collapsed" into one, or that the one identified by Jesus as "my God" somehow has become the risen Lord himself. Rather, the Gospel has made it clear that the identity of Jesus cannot be fully comprehended unless grasped as the manifestation and revelation of God. Hence, when Thomas confesses Jesus as "My Lord and my God!" he acknowledges the exclusive and comprehensive revelation of God through the person of Jesus, and the identity of Jesus with God.[10]

The Genre of John

Any summary analysis of a document's content or "ideas" runs the risk of transforming the document under study into something that it is not. In the case of the Gospel of John, this danger is acute, since this Gospel lends

9. Suetonius, *Dom.* 13. Suetonius's characterization of Domitian has been challenged in recent scholarship as satirical slander.

10. At this point there are striking overlaps with Philo's view that the Most High God is known in the world through the visible manifestation of the Logos.

itself, perhaps more easily than the other Gospels, to theological reflection and synthesis in ways that too quickly leave behind the actual narrative as we have it. In his reflections on the content of the Fourth Gospel, John Ashton poses the question, "What is the Gospel attempting to reflect or describe, a man, a god, an event, or an idea?"[11] It is clear from Ashton's posing of the question that the answer is not at all simple. While it is easy enough to assert that the genre of the Fourth Gospel is that of a Gospel, such assertions beg the prior questions of what a Gospel is and to what extent the author of the Fourth Gospel intended his work to belong to a specific category.

Still, as D. Moody Smith points out, the Gospel of John is a first-order account of the life of Jesus, and not second-order Christological reflection.[12] Smith comments on the Gospel's distinctive presentation of Jesus:

> The presentation of Jesus in the Fourth Gospel is multidimensional. He is still the Jewish man of Galilee. But he is also the spiritual presence with, and head of, the community of disciples which we may safely call his church. He has been with the church in its past struggles and will continue with it into the foreseeable future. His nature is, however, never understood until his origin and destiny with God is truly comprehended. . . . What is uniquely Johannine is the way these aspects of, or perspectives on, Jesus are made to coalesce into a single narrative so that each is always present in almost every part of the narrative.[13]

John narrates what happened when the Word of God "became flesh and dwelt among us" (1:14). While John's Gospel is often labeled the most theological or the most interpretative — characterizations often understood as equivalent — of the four Gospels, John's creativity operates within definite limits, and his theological reflections remain tethered to historical realities.[14] Clearly, for the evangelist, this Gospel presents the ul-

---

11. John Ashton, *Understanding the Fourth Gospel* (Oxford: Clarendon, 1991), p. 4.

12. D. Moody Smith, "The Presentation of Jesus in the Fourth Gospel," in his *Johannine Christianity: Essays on Its Setting, Sources, and Theology* (Columbia, S.C.: University of South Carolina Press, 1984), p. 175. Ashton comments, "John is not a dogmatist but an evangelist; what he writes is not doctrine but gospel" (*Understanding the Fourth Gospel*, p. 517).

13. Smith, "Presentation of Jesus," p. 187.

14. I have discussed some of these issues in "The Historical Jesus and the Johannine Christ," in *Exploring the Gospel of John: In Honor of D. Moody Smith*, ed. R. Alan Culpepper and C. Clifton Black (Louisville: Westminster/John Knox, 1996), pp. 21-42.

timate identity of Jesus of Nazareth when it refers to his origins and destiny in God. However, because John does so by speaking of the enfleshment of the Word, this Gospel also presents the *historical* significance of Jesus. This account intends to render for the reader, in a genuine sense, *"wie es eigentlich gewesen ist"* — as it really was. The Gospel makes the earthly life of Jesus (who he was) transparent to his ultimate significance (who he is). Because, for John, Jesus' significance is to be expressed in terms that speak of him as the embodiment of God's glory, Word, Wisdom, and life, then the explication of the historical significance of Jesus becomes, for John, an account of the character and purposes of God.

Paul Meyer comments on the way that understanding of God is mediated through the narrative of the Gospel:

> God is known and God's presence felt only because the Son alone "presents" God to the world, is wholly transparent to God, and is the only reliable vehicle for God's presence and action in the world; *"apart from the revelation God is not here and is never here."* The only "presentation of God" in the Fourth Gospel is the self-presentation of Christ in its narratives and discourses. . . . The "presentation" of God takes place for the reader in attending to the Gospel narrative, which fuses historical recollection of the figure of Jesus with theological interpretation. This is far truer to the nature of the Gospel's genre and more satisfying theologically than a notion of revelation that remains empty. But it still means that one may not abstract from the Gospel some detached doctrine of God.[15]

The actions attributed to God in the Gospel are made known to the reader by the words of Jesus and are embodied in the deeds of Jesus. Although God's activity is rather fully described, nowhere are God's actions dramatized. As a result, the character of God in the narrative remains only indirectly accessible to the reader, and accessible only through the words of Jesus or editorial comment by the narrator. While Jesus frequently asserts that he speaks the words of God, he virtually never recounts a message delivered to him by God. On this point, John Ashton comments, "What the divine agent 'heard' from God is disclosed not in his words but in his life;

---

15. Paul W. Meyer, "'The Father': The Presentation of God in the Fourth Gospel," in *Exploring the Gospel of John: In Honor of D. Moody Smith*, ed. R. Alan Culpepper and C. Clifton Black (Louisville: Westminster/John Knox, 1996), pp. 255, 256.

the 'what' is displayed in the 'how.' The matter of the Gospel, its true content, is indistinguishable from its form: the medium is the message."[16]

John thus provides the starkest instance of what a Gospel is: a Gospel is the narrative account of God's encounter with humankind through the life, death, and resurrection of Jesus of Nazareth. The framing of that narrative is therefore inescapably a form of theological argument that invites response. John's Gospel shows us what a Gospel *is* by showing us what a Gospel *does:* it presents an interpreted account of God's encounter with humankind through Jesus and narrates how that embodied encounter engenders both belief and unbelief. John puts it this way: "The world was made through him, but the world did not know him. . . . But to as many as received him, who believed in his name, he gave power to become children of God." John's Gospel recounts a series of incidents showing how Jesus' work and word drew forth both unbelief and belief. The narrative presents Jesus' work as firmly anchored in the historical circumstances of the first-century world and as leading ultimately to reflections on and about the character of God's work.

These observations with respect to the genre of John confirm what has been argued on other grounds, namely, that the Christology of the Gospel of John focuses on the agency of Jesus as mediating the presence or carrying out the will of God. Various designations for Jesus, including prophet (4:19, 44; 6:14; 7:40, 52), king (1:49; 6:15; 12:13, 15; 18:33, 37, 39; 19:3, 12, 14, 15, 19, 21), Son of Man (1:51; 3:13, 14; 5:27; 6:27, 53, 62; 8:28; 9:35; 12:23, 34; 13:31); Messiah (1:20, 25, 41; 3:28; 4:25, 29; 7:26-27, 31, 41; 9:22; 10:24; 11:27; 12:34; 20:31), and Word (1:1, 14) all fall within the broad category of "agent of God." Other categories, such as personified Wisdom and Word, are also pressed into service to speak not only of Jesus as God's agent but of the unity of Jesus with God. Because John takes seriously the incarnation of the Word of God as an historical event, the Gospel consequently narrates the life of the one who was the embodiment of God's word. In that sense, the Gospel elucidates the historical significance of the ministry of Jesus, but never apart from acknowledgment of those factors of Jesus' identity — his ultimate origin and destiny with God — that finally answer the question who he is and what he offers to humankind. Because the Gospel of John is an articulation of the significance of Jesus' ministry as the embodiment of the glory, Wisdom, and Word of God, it is also, finally, theocentric in focus and content.

16. Ashton, *Understanding the Fourth Gospel,* p. 553.

The Theocentric Character of John

John's fundamental assumption about God is that there is one God, and that this God is the "only true God," the living Father, the one who alone is God and has "life in himself." As the living God, God is also the source of all life, the creator of all that is. John is not interested in the unmoved mover but the living life-giver. Jesus is the Son who has been granted by the Father to have life in himself, and so who confers, in word and deed, through the Spirit, God's gift of life. Just as the Son comes from God and returns to God, so he embodies in this world God's Word and glory so as to grant to those who hear and see a true understanding of God. However, precisely because Jesus embodies the Father in flesh, word, and deed, the revelation of God always remains hidden; and knowledge of God, mediated through the work and words of Jesus, is always indirect. Because in this world the Son makes the Father known, one may truly "see" God, but always and only indirectly. It is the role of the Paraclete to enable such continued "seeing" after the departure of Jesus from his disciples, by recalling to them the words and deeds of Jesus in such a way as to re-present Jesus among them.

The figures of the Father and the Son are not simply fused, but neither are they to be so completely distinguished and held apart as though they could simply be known and comprehended separately and apart from each other. For John, to know the Father is to know the Son; to know the Son is to know the Father. It is not that their identities are merged but that the identity of the Father lodges in his relationship to the Son, and the identity of the Son in his relationship to the Father. It is this feature of John particularly that justifies the interpretation offered by C. K. Barrett: "There could hardly be a more Christocentric writer than John, yet his very Christocentricity is theocentric."[17] It is not as though we are to imagine an ellipse with two foci; or as though we had two "centers" in John that simply exist side by side. Rather, the image is that of concentric circles, in which the Christological circle lies within and shares its center with the larger theological circle. Through focusing attention on the figure of Jesus as the Revealer and Son of God, the one who brings life from God, the Gospel always directs its reader's attention to God.

17. C. K. Barrett, "'The Father is Greater than I' (John 14.28): Subordinationist Christology in the New Testament," in his *Essays on John* (Philadelphia: Westminster, 1982), p. 246.

239

While it is possible that these assumptions are implicit in the regular description of John as "Christocentric," they are less seldom made explicit. It is the failure to make the theological correlates of Christology explicit that has led to neglect of the figure of God in NT theology. Furthermore, it is the conception of "Christology" as a task or enterprise separable from "theology" or as standing alongside of it that has contributed to this neglect. The NT and early Christian literature bear witness to the necessity to interpret, explain, and defend the identity of Jesus, and, hence, to engage in Christological reflection. It is surely no less true that when they engaged in Christological reflection, they also understood themselves to be engaging in explicit theological reflection. Paul makes this clear when, in Romans, he sets the death of Jesus within the context of the revelation of the righteousness of God. John makes this clear when he writes a Gospel about Jesus who reveals the unseen God. The Christological task at root implies the articulation of its theological framework and correlates.

To make explicit the theological correlates of John's presentation of Jesus means to take as the polestar of the interpretation of the Gospel the statements in its prologue that the Word who "was with God" and who "was God" became flesh and "dwelt among us." In the incarnation God has taken on human form and entered into the world of death and darkness, has taken on an embodied presence that reveals that God's ultimate purposes for the world are life-giving, and that God persistently and faithfully works to that end. Salvation is construed primarily as knowing God, as participation in God's life, and as having fellowship with God through the one in whom God's presence became embodied in this world, for the salvation and life of this world.

Bibliography

Allison, Dale C. *The End of the Ages Has Come: An Early Interpretation of the Passion and Resurrection of Jesus.* Philadelphia: Fortress, 1985.

Appold, Mark. *The Oneness Motif in the Fourth Gospel: Motif Analysis and Exegetical Probe into the Theology of John.* Wissenschaftliche Untersuchungen zum Neuen Testament 2/1. Tübingen: Mohr, 1976.

Argyle, A. W. *God in the New Testament.* Philadelphia: J. B. Lippincott, 1966.

Ashton, John. *Studying John: Approaches to the Fourth Gospel.* Oxford: Clarendon, 1994.

———. *Understanding the Fourth Gospel.* Oxford: Clarendon, 1991.

Aune, David E. *The Cultic Setting of Realized Eschatology in Early Christianity.* Leiden: Brill, 1972.

———. "Orthodoxy in First Century Judaism? A Response to N. J. McEleney." *Journal for the Study of Judaism in the Persian, Hellenistic, and Roman Periods* 7 (1976): 1-10.

———. "Worship, Early Christian," *ABD* 6:973-89.

Ball, David Mark. *"I Am" in John's Gospel: Literary Function, Background, and Theological Implications.* Journal for the Study of the New Testament: Supplement Series 124. Sheffield: Sheffield Academic Press, 1996.

Barker, Margaret. *The Great Angel: A Study of Israel's Second God.* Louisville: Westminster/John Knox, 1992.

Barr, James. *Biblical Faith and Natural Theology: The Gifford Lectures for 1991.* Oxford: Clarendon, 1993.

Barrett, C. K. "Christocentric or Theocentric? Observations on the Theological Method of the Fourth Gospel." Pages 361-76 in *La Notion biblique de Dieu.*

241

Bibliotheca ephemeridum theologicarum lovaniensium 41. Leuven: Leuven University Press, 1976.

———. "'The Father is Greater than I' (John 14.28): Subordinationist Christology in the New Testament." Pages 19-36 in *Essays on John*. Philadelphia: Westminster, 1982.

———. *The Gospel According to St. John*. 2d ed. Philadelphia: Westminster, 1978.

———. "The Old Testament in the Fourth Gospel." *Journal of Theological Studies* 48 (1947): 155-69.

Bassler, Jouette M. *Divine Impartiality: Paul and a Theological Axiom*. Society of Biblical Literature Dissertation Series 59. Chico, Calif.: Scholars Press, 1982.

Bauckham, Richard J. "For Whom Were the Gospels Written?" Pages 9-48 in *The Gospels for All Christians: Rethinking the Gospel Audiences*. Edited by Richard J. Bauckham. Grand Rapids: Eerdmans, 1998.

———. *God Crucified: Monotheism and Christology in the New Testament*. Grand Rapids: Eerdmans, 1998.

Beasley-Murray, George R. *John*. 2d ed. Word Biblical Commentary. Nashville: Nelson, 1999.

Becker, Jürgen. *Das Evangelium des Johannes*. 2 vols. Ökumenischer Taschenbuchkommentar zum Neuen Testament 4/1. Gütersloh: G. Mohn, 1979, 1981.

Behm, Johannes. "παράκλητος," *TDNT* 3:800-814.

Beker, J. Christiaan. *Paul the Apostle: The Triumph of God in Life and Thought*. Rev. ed. Philadelphia: Fortress, 1989 [1980].

Bernard, J. H. *The Gospel According to St. John*. 2 vols. International Critical Commentary. Edinburgh: T. & T. Clark, 1928.

Betz, Otto. *Der Paraklet: Fürsprecher im häretischen Spätjudentum, im Johannes-Evangelium und im neugefundenen gnostischen Schriften*. Leiden: Brill, 1963.

Bickerman, Elias. *The God of the Maccabees: Studies on the Meaning and Origin of the Maccabean Revolt*. Translated by Horst R. Moehring. Studies in Judaism in Late Antiquity 32. Leiden: Brill, 1979.

Blank, Josef. *Krisis: Untersuchungen zur johanneischen Christologie und Eschatologie*. Breisgau: Lambertus-Verlag, 1964.

Borgen, Peder. *Bread form Heaven: An Exegetical Study in the Concept of Manna in the Gospel of John and the Writings of Philo*. Supplements to Novum Testamentum 10. Leiden: Brill, 1965.

———. "God's Agent in the Fourth Gospel." Pages 83-95 in *The Interpretation of John*. Edited by John Ashton. Philadelphia: Fortress; London: SPCK, 1986. Repr. from pages 137-48 in *Religions in Antiquity: Essays in Memory of E. R. Goodenough*. Edited by Jacob Neusner. Leiden: Brill, 1968.

———. "The Gospel of John and Hellenism: Some Observations." Pages 98-123 in *Exploring the Gospel of John: In Honor of D. Moody Smith*. Edited by R. Alan Culpepper and C. Clifton Black. Louisville: Westminster/John Knox, 1996.

Boring, M. E. "The Influence of Christian Prophecy in the Johannine Portrayal of the Paraclete and Jesus." *New Testament Studies* 25 (1978): 113-23.

Bornkamm, Günther. "Der Paraklet im Johannes-Evangelium." Pages 68-89 in *Geschichte und Glaube. Gesammelte Aufsätze*. Erster Teil. Band III. Munich: Kaiser, 1968.

Brown, Raymond E. *The Gospel According to John*. 2 vols. Anchor Bible. Garden City, N.Y.: Doubleday, 1966, 1970.

Bühner, J.-A. *Der Gesandte und sein Weg im 4. Evangelium*. Wissenschaftliche Untersuchungen zum Neuen Testament 2/2. Tübingen: Mohr-Siebeck, 1977.

Bultmann, Rudolf. *The Gospel of John*. Philadelphia: Westminster, 1971.

———. *Theology of the New Testament*. 2 vols. New York: Scribner's, 1951, 1955.

———. "ζάω." *TDNT* 2:861-72.

Burge, Gary. *The Anointed Community: The Holy Spirit in the Johannine Tradition*. Grand Rapids: Eerdmans, 1987.

Burridge, Richard. *What Are the Gospels? A Comparison with Graeco-Roman Biography*. Cambridge: Cambridge University Press, 1992.

Caird, G. B. "The Glory of God in the Fourth Gospel: An Exercise in Biblical Semantics." *New Testament Studies* 15 (1969): 265-77.

———. *New Testament Theology*. Completed and edited by L. D. Hurst. Oxford: Clarendon, 1994.

Carson, D. A. *The Gospel According to John* Grand Rapids: Eerdmans; Leicester: InterVarsity, 1991.

Casey, Maurice. *From Jewish Prophet to Gentile God: The Origins and Development of New Testament Christology*. Louisville: Westminster/John Knox, 1991.

Casurella, Anthony J. *The Johannine Paraclete in the Church Fathers: A Study in the History of Exegesis*. Tübingen: J. C. B. Mohr (Paul Siebeck), 1983.

Charlesworth, James H. ed. *Old Testament Pseudepigrapha*. 2 vols. Anchor Bible Reference Library. Garden City, N.Y.: Doubleday, 1983, 1985.

Chester, Andrew. *Divine Revelation and Divine Titles in the Pentateuchal Targumim*. Texte und Studien zum Antiken Judentum 14. Tübingen: J. C. B. Mohr (Paul Siebeck), 1986.

Childs, Brevard S. *Biblical Theology of the Old and New Testaments: Theological Reflection on the Christian Bible*. Minneapolis: Fortress, 1992.

———. *The New Testament as Canon: An Introduction*. Philadelphia: Fortress, 1984.

Chilton, Bruce. "God as 'Father' in the Targumim, in Non-Canonical Literatures of Early Judaism and Primitive Christianity, and in Matthew." Pages 39-73 in *Judaic Approaches to the Gospels*. International Studies in Formative Christianity and Judaism 2. Atlanta: Scholars Press, 1994.

Cohen, Shaye J. D. *From the Maccabees to the Mishnah*. Library of Early Christianity 7. Edited by Wayne A. Meeks. Philadelphia: Westminster, 1987.

Collins, John J. *The Scepter and the Star: The Messiahs of the Dead Sea Scrolls and*

Other Ancient Literature. Anchor Bible Reference Library. New York: Doubleday, 1995.

Corell, Alf. *Consummatum Est: Eschatology and Church in the Gospel of St. John.*
London: SPCK, 1958.

Culpepper, R. Alan. *Anatomy of the Fourth Gospel: A Study in Literary Design.* Philadelphia: Fortress, 1983.

Dahl, Nils A. "The Neglected Factor in New Testament Theology." Pages 153-63 in
Jesus the Christ: The Historical Origins of Christological Doctrine. Edited by
Donald H. Juel. Minneapolis: Fortress, 1991.

————. "The One God of Jews and Gentiles (Romans 3:29-30)." Pages 178-91 in
Studies in Paul: Theology for the Early Christian Mission. Minneapolis:
Augsburg, 1977.

————. "Sources of Christological Language." Pages 113-36 in *Jesus the Christ:
The Historical Origins of Christological Doctrine.* Edited by Donald H. Juel.
Minneapolis: Fortress, 1991.

Dahl, Nils A., and Alan F. Segal. "Philo and the Rabbis on the Names of God." *Journal for the Study of Judaism in the Persian, Hellenistic, and Roman Periods* 9
(1978): 1-28.

D'Angelo, Mary Rose. "*Abba* and 'Father': Imperial Theology and the Jesus Traditions." *Journal of Biblical Literature* 111 (1992): 611-30.

de Jonge, Marinus. *Jesus, Stranger from Heaven and Son of God: Jesus Christ and the
Christians in Johannine Perspective.* Society of Biblical Literature Monograph
Series 11. Missoula, Mont.: Scholars Press, 1977.

Dodd, C. H. *The Bible and the Greeks.* London: Hodder & Stoughton, 1954.

————. *The Interpretation of the Fourth Gospel.* Cambridge: Cambridge University
Press, 1953.

Dunn, James D. G. "Christology as an Aspect of Theology." Pages 202-12 in *The
Future of Christology: Essays in Honor of Leander E. Keck.* Edited by Abraham J.
Malherbe and Wayne A. Meeks. Minneapolis: Fortress, 1993.

————. *Christology in the Making: A New Testament Inquiry into the Origins of the
Doctrine of the Incarnation.* 2d ed. London: SCM, 1989 [1980].

————. "Let John Be John: A Gospel for Its Time." Pages 309-39 in *Das Evangelium und die Evangelien: Vorträge vom Tübinger Symposium 1982.* Edited by
Peter Stuhlmacher. Wissenschaftliche Untersuchungen zum Neuen Testament 28. Tübingen: Mohr, 1983.

————. *The Partings of the Ways between Christianity and Judaism and Their Significance for the Character of Christianity.* London: SCM; Philadelphia: Trinity,
1991.

Epp, Eldon Jay. "Wisdom, Torah, Word: The Johannine Prologue and the Purpose
of the Fourth Gospel." Pages 128-46 in *Current Issues in Biblical and Patristic
Interpretation.* Edited by G. F. Hawthorne. Grand Rapids: Eerdmans, 1975.

Evans, Craig A. "Obduracy and the Lord's Servant: Some Observations on the Use of the Old Testament in the Fourth Gospel." Pages 221-36 in *Early Jewish and Christian Exegesis: Studies in Memory of William Hugh Brownlee*. Edited by Craig A. Evans and William F. Stinespring. Atlanta: Scholars Press, 1987.

———. *Word and Glory: On the Exegetical and Theological Background of John's Prologue*. Journal for the Study of the New Testament: Supplement Series 89. Sheffield: JSOT Press, 1993.

Fennema, David A. "Jesus and God According to John: An Analysis of the Fourth Gospel's Father/Son Christology." Ph.D diss., Duke University, 1979.

Fitzmyer, Joseph A. *Paul and His Theology: A Brief Sketch*. Englewood, N.J.: Prentice-Hall, 1989.

———. "The Semitic Background of the New Testament *Kyrios*-Title." Pages 115-42 in *A Wandering Aramean: Collected Aramaic Essays*. Society of Biblical Literature Monograph Series 25. Missoula, Mont.: Scholars Press, 1979.

Forbes, Christopher. *Prophecy and Inspired Speech in Early Christianity and Its Hellenistic Environment*. Wissenschaftliche Untersuchungen zum Neuen Testament 2/75. Tübingen: J. C. B. Mohr (Paul Siebeck), 1995.

Fossum, Jarl. *The Name of God and the Angel of the Lord: Samaritan and Jewish Concepts of Intermediation and the Origin of Gnosticism*. Wissenschaftliche Untersuchungen zum Neuen Testament 36. Tübingen: J. C. B. Mohr (Paul Siebeck), 1985.

Freedman, David Noel, ed. *The Anchor Bible Dictionary*. 6 vols. New York: Doubleday, 1992.

Grant, Robert M. *Gods and the One God*. Philadelphia: Westminster, 1986.

Grayston, Kenneth. *The Gospel of John*. Narrative Commentaries. Philadelphia: Trinity, 1990.

Gruenwald, Ithamar. *Apocalyptic and Merkavah Mysticism*. Leiden: Brill, 1980.

Haenchen, Ernst. *A Commentary on the Gospel of John*. 2 vols. Hermeneia. Philadelphia: Fortress, 1984.

Hagner, Donald A. "The Vision of God in Philo and John: A Comparative Study." *Journal of the Evangelical Theological Society* 14 (1971): 81-93.

Hahn, Ferdinand. "The Confession of the One God in the New Testament." *Horizons in Biblical Theology* 2 (1980): 69-84.

Harner, Philip B. *The "I Am" of the Fourth Gospel: A Study in Johannine Usage and Thought*. Facet Books 26. Philadelphia: Fortress, 1970.

Harris, J. Rendel. *The Origin of the Prologue to St. John's Gospel*. Cambridge: Cambridge University Press, 1917.

Harris, Murray J. *Jesus as God: The New Testament Use of Theos in Reference to Jesus*. Grand Rapids: Baker, 1992.

Harvey, A. E. "Christ as Agent." Pages 239-50 in *The Glory of Christ in the New Testament: Studies in Christology in Memory of George Bradford Caird*. Edited by L. D. Hurst and N. T. Wright. Oxford: Clarendon, 1987.

———. *Jesus and the Constraints of History*. Philadelphia: Westminster, 1982.

Hayman, Peter. "Monotheism — A Misused Word in Jewish Studies?" *Journal of Jewish Studies* 42 (1991): 1-15.

Hengel, Martin. *Judaism and Hellenism: Studies in Their Encounter in Palestine during the Early Hellenistic Period.* Translated by John Bowden. 2 vols. Philadelphia: Fortress 1974.

————. *Studies in Early Christology.* Edinburgh: T. & T. Clark, 1995.

Holladay, Carl. *Theios Aner in Hellenistic Judaism: A Critique of the Use of This Category in New Testament Christology.* Society of Biblical Literature Dissertation Series 40. Missoula, Mont.: Scholars Press, 1977.

Hoskyns, E. C. *The Fourth Gospel.* London: Faber & Faber, 1947.

Howard, George, "The Tetragram and the New Testament." *Journal of Biblical Literature* 96 (1977): 63-83.

Hurtado, Larry W. *One God, One Lord: Early Christian Devotion and Ancient Jewish Monotheism.* Philadelphia: Fortress, 1988.

————. "What Do We Mean by 'First-Century Jewish Monotheism?'" Pages 348-68 in the *SBL Seminar Papers, 1993.* Society of Biblical Literature Seminar Papers 32. Atlanta: Scholars Press, 1993.

Isaacs, M. E. *The Concept of Spirit: A Study of Pneuma in Hellenistic Judaism and Its Bearing on the New Testament.* Heythrop Monographs 1. London: Heythrop, 1976.

Jeremias, Joachim. *The Prayers of Jesus.* Philadelphia: Fortress, 1967.

Johansson, N. *Parakletoi. Vorstellung von Fürsprechern für die Menschen vor Gott in der alttestamentlichen Religion, im Spätjudentum, und Urchristentum.* Lund: Gleerup, 1940.

Johnson, Luke T. "The New Testament's Anti-Jewish Slander and the Conventions of Ancient Polemic." *Journal of Biblical Literature* 108 (1989): 419-41.

Johnston, George. *The Spirit-Paraclete in the Gospel of John.* Society for New Testament Studies Monograph Series 12. Cambridge: Cambridge University Press, 1970.

Juel, Donald H. *Messiah and Temple: The Trial of Jesus in the Gospel of Mark.* Society of Biblical Literature Dissertation Series 31. Missoula, Mont.: Scholars Press, 1977.

Kanagaraj, Jey J. *"Mysticism" in the Gospel of John: An Inquiry into Its Background.* Journal for the Study of the New Testament: Supplement Series 158. Sheffield: Sheffield Academic Press, 1998.

Käsemann, Ernst. *The Testament of Jesus: A Study of the Gospel of John in the Light of Chapter 17.* Translated by Gerhard Krodel. Philadelphia: Fortress, 1968.

Keck, Leander E. "Toward the Renewal of New Testament Christology." *New Testament Studies* 32 (1986): 362-77.

Keener, Craig. *The Spirit in the Gospels and Acts: Divine Purity and Power.* Peabody, Mass.: Hendrickson, 1997.

Kittel, G., and G. Friedrich, eds. *Theological Dictionary of the New Testament.* Translated by G. W. Bromiley. 10 vols. Grand Rapids: Eerdmans, 1964-1976.

Kleinknecht, Hermann, Ethelbert Stauffer, and Gottfried Quell. "θεός." *TDNT* 3:65-119.

Koester, Craig R. *The Dwelling of God: The Tabernacle in the Old Testament, Intertestamental Jewish Literature, and the New Testament.* Catholic Biblical Quarterly Monograph Series 22. Washington, D.C.: Catholic Biblical Association, 1989.

―――. "Hearing, Seeing, and Believing in the Gospel of John." *Biblica* 70 (1989): 327-48.

―――. *Symbolism in the Fourth Gospel: Meaning, Mystery, Community.* Minneapolis: Fortress, 1995.

Kraus, Hans-Joachim. "Der lebendige Gott. Ein Kapitel biblischer Theologie." *Evangelische Theologie* 27 (1967): 169-99.

Kreitzer, L. Joseph. *Jesus and God in Paul's Eschatology.* Journal for the Study of the New Testament: Supplement Series 19. Sheffield: JSOT Press, 1987.

Kümmel, W. G. *The Theology of the New Testament.* Nashville: Abingdon, 1973.

Kysar, Robert. "The Fourth Gospel: A Report on Recent Research." *ANRW* 25.3:2389-2480. Part 2. *Principat,* 25.3. Edited by H. Temporini and W. Haase. New York: de Gruyter, 1985.

La Notion biblique de Dieu. Bibliotheca ephemeridum theologicarum lovaniensium 41. Leuven: Leuven University Press, 1976.

Lane, Dermot A. *The Reality of Jesus: An Essay in Christology.* Dublin: Veritas, 1975.

Levenson, Jon. *The Death and Resurrection of the Beloved Son: The Transformation of Child Sacrifice in Judaism and Christianity.* New Haven: Yale University Press, 1993.

Levison, John R. *The Spirit in First Century Judaism.* Leiden: Brill, 1997.

Lincoln, Andrew. "Trials, Plots, and the Narrative of the Fourth Gospel." *Journal for the Study of the New Testament* 56 (1994): 3-30.

Lindars, Barnabas. *The Gospel of John.* New Century Bible Commentary. Grand Rapids: Eerdmans, 1972.

Loader, William. *The Christology of the Fourth Gospel: Structure and Issues.* Beiträge zur biblischen Exegese und Theologie 23. Frankfurt am Main: Peter Lang, 1989.

McEleney, Neil J. "Orthodoxy and Heterodoxy in the New Testament." *Proceedings of the Catholic Theological Society of America* 25 (1971): 54-77.

―――. "Orthodoxy in Judaism of the First Century Christian Church." *Journal for the Study of Judaism in the Persian, Hellenistic, and Roman Periods* 4 (1973): 19-42.

Malina, Bruce J. *The Palestinian Manna Tradition: The Manna Tradition in the Palestinian Targums and Its Relationship to the New Testament Writings.* Leiden: Brill, 1968.

Marcus, Ralph. "Divine Names and Attributes in Hellenistic Jewish Literature." *Proceedings of the American Academy for Jewish Research* 3 (1931-1932): 43-120.

Marmorstein, A. "Philo and the Names of God." *Jewish Quarterly Review* 22 (1931-1932): 295-306.

———. "The Unity of God in Rabbinic Literature." *Hebrew Union College Annual* 1 (1924): 467-99.

Martin, Francis. *The Feminist Question: Feminist Theology in the Light of Christian Tradition.* Grand Rapids: Eerdmans, 1994.

Martyn, J. Louis. "Glimpses into the History of the Johannine Community." Pages 149-75 in *L'Évangile de Jean: sources, redaction, théologie.* Edited by M. de Jonge. Gembloux: Duculot, 1977.

———. *History and Theology in the Fourth Gospel.* 2d ed. Nashville: Abingdon, 1979.

Mason, Rex. *Old Testament Pictures of God.* Regent's Study Guides. Oxford: Regent's Park College; Macon: Smyth and Helwys, 1993.

Meeks, Wayne A. "The Divine Agent and His Counterfeit in Philo and the Fourth Gospel." Pages 43-67 in *Aspects of Religious Propaganda in Judaism and Early Christianity.* Edited by Elisabeth Schüssler Fiorenza. Notre Dame: University of Notre Dame Press, 1976.

———. "The Ethics of the Fourth Evangelist." Pages 317-26 in *Exploring the Gospel of John: In Honor of D. Moody Smith.* Edited by R. Alan Culpepper and C. Clifton Black. Louisville: Westminster/John Knox, 1996.

Meier, John P. *A Marginal Jew: Rethinking the Historical Jesus.* Vol. 2: *Mentor, Message, and Miracles.* Anchor Bible Reference Library. New York: Doubleday, 1994.

Meyer, Paul W. "'The Father': The Presentation of God in the Fourth Gospel." Pages 255-73 in *Exploring the Gospel of John: In Honor of D. Moody Smith.* Edited by R. Alan Culpepper and C. Clifton Black. Louisville: Westminster/John Knox, 1996.

Meyers, Carol. "Temple, Jerusalem," *ABD* 6:350-69.

Michaels, J. Ramsey. *John.* New International Biblical Commentary. Peabody, Mass.: Hendrickson, 1989.

Mitchell, Margaret M. "New Testament Envoys in the Context of Greco-Roman Diplomatic and Epistolary Conventions: The Example of Timothy and Titus." *Journal of Biblical Literature* 111 (1992): 641-62.

Moore, George Foot. *Judaism in the First Centuries of the Christian Era: The Age of the Tannaim.* 3 vols. Cambridge, Mass.: Harvard University Press, 1927-1930.

Moule, C. F. D. "The Meaning of 'Life' in the Gospels and Epistles of St. John: A Study in the Story of Lazarus, John 11:1-44." *Theology* 78 (1975): 114-25.

Mowinckel, Sigmund. "Die Vorstellung des Spätjudentums vom heiligen Geist als

Fürsprecher und der johanneische Paraklet." *Zeitschrift für die neutestament-liche Wissenschaft und die Kunde der älteren Kirche* 32 (1933): 97-130.

Moxnes, Halvor. *Theology in Conflict: Studies in Paul's Understanding of God in Romans.* Supplements to Novum Testamentum 53. Leiden: Brill, 1980.

Newbigin, Lesslie. *The Light Has Come: An Exposition of the Fourth Gospel.* Grand Rapids: Eerdmans, 1982.

Newman, Carey C. *Paul's Glory-Christology. Tradition and Rhetoric.* Supplements to Novum Testamentum 69. Leiden: Brill, 1992.

Newsom, Carol. *Songs of the Sabbath Sacrifice: A Critical Edition.* Atlanta: Scholars Press, 1985.

Neyrey, Jerome. *An Ideology of Revolt: John's Christology in Social-Science Perspective.* Philadelphia: Fortress, 1988.

———. "'My Lord and My God': The Divinity of Jesus in John's Gospel." Pages 152-71 in the *SBL Seminar Papers, 1986.* Society of Biblical Literature Seminar Papers 25. Atlanta: Scholars Press, 1986.

Nickelsburg, George W. E. *Jewish Literature between the Bible and the Mishnah: A Historical and Literary Introduction.* Philadelphia: Fortress, 1981.

———. "Resurrection (Early Judaism and Christianity)," *ABD* 5:684-91.

Nock, Arthur Darby. "Deification and Julian." Pages 833-46 in *Essays on Religion and the Ancient World.* Edited by Zeph Stewart. 2 vols. Cambridge, Mass.: Harvard University Press, 1972.

Olsson, Birger. "*Deus Semper Maior? On God in the Johannine Writings.*" Pages 143-71 in *New Readings in John: Literary and Theological Perspectives.* Edited by Johannes Nissen and Sigfred Pedersen. Journal for the Study of the New Testament: Supplement Series 182. Sheffield: Sheffield Academic Press, 1999.

Painter, John. "Theology, Eschatology and the Prologue of John." *Scottish Journal of Theology* 46 (1993): 27-42.

Pancaro, Severino. *The Law in the Fourth Gospel: The Torah and the Gospel, Moses and Jesus Judaism and Christianity According to John.* Supplements to Novum Testamentum 42. Leiden: Brill, 1975.

Peterson, Erik. *HEIS THEOS: Epigraphische, formgeschichtliche und religions-geschichtliche Untersuchungen.* Göttingen: Vandenhoeck & Ruprecht, 1926.

Placher, William. *The Domestication of Transcendence: How Modern Thinking about God Went Wrong.* Louisville: Westminster/John Knox, 1996.

Porsch, Felix. *Pneuma und Wort. Ein exegetischer Beitrag zur Pneumatologie des Johannesevangeliums.* Frankfurt am Main: Josef Knecht, 1974.

Prestige, G. L. *God in Patristic Thought.* London: Heinemann, 1936.

Price, S. F. R. "Gods and Emperors: The Greek Language of the Roman Imperial Cult." *Journal of Hellenic Studies* 104 (1984): 79-95.

Rainbow, Paul A. "Monotheism and Christology in 1 Corinthians 8:4-6." D.Phil. diss., Oxford University, 1987.

Reinhartz, Adele. *The Word in the World: The Cosmological Tale in the Fourth Gos-*

pel. Society of Biblical Literature Monograph Series 45. Atlanta: Scholars Press, 1992.

Rensberger, David. *Johannine Faith and Liberating Community*. Philadelphia: Westminster, 1988.

Ricca, Paolo. *Die Eschatologie des vierten Evangeliums*. Zürich und Frankfurt a. M.: Gotthelf-Verlag, 1966.

Richardson, Alan. *An Introduction to the Theology of the New Testament*. London: SCM, 1958.

Richardson, Neil. *Paul's Language about God*. Journal for the Study of the New Testament: Supplement Series 99. Sheffield: Sheffield Academic Press, 1994.

Riches, John K. *Jesus and the Transformation of Judaism*. New York: Seabury, 1980.

Ridderbos, Herman. *The Gospel of John: A Theological Commentary*. Grand Rapids: Eerdmans, 1997.

Rowland, Christopher. *The Open Heaven: A Study of Apocalyptic in Judaism and Early Christianity*. New York: Crossroad, 1982.

————. "The Visions of God in Apocalyptic Literature." *Journal for the Study of Judaism in the Persian, Hellenistic, and Roman Periods* 10 (1979): 137-54.

Runia, David T. "God of the Philosophers, God of the Patriarchs: Exegetical Backgrounds in Philo of Alexandria." Pages 206-18 in *Philo and the Church Fathers: A Collection of Papers*. Supplements to Vigiliae Christianae 32. Leiden: Brill, 1995.

Safrai, S., and M. Stern, eds. *The Jewish People in the First Century: Historical Geography, Political History, Social, Cultural and Religious Life and Institutions*. 2 vols. Assen: Van Gorcum; Philadelphia: Fortress, 1974, 1976.

Sanders, E. P. *The Historical Figure of Jesus*. London: Penguin Books, 1993.

————. *Judaism: Practice and Belief, 63 BCE–66 CE*. London: SCM; Philadelphia: Trinity, 1993.

————. *Paul and Palestinian Judaism: A Comparison of Patterns of Religion*. Philadelphia: Fortress, 1977.

Schlatter, Adolf von. *Wie Sprach Josephus von Gott?* Beiträge zur Förderung christlicher Theologie 1/14. Gütersloh: Bertelsmann, 1910.

Schnackenburg, Rudolf. *The Gospel According to St. John*. 3 vols. Vol. 1: New York: Seabury, 1968. Vol. 2: New York: Seabury, 1980. Vol. 3: New York: Crossroad, 1982.

————. *Jesus in the Gospels: A Biblical Christology*. Translated by O. C. Dean. Louisville: Westminster/John Knox, 1995.

Schürer, Emil. *The History of the Jewish People in the Age of Jesus Christ*. Revised and edited by Geza Vermes and Fergus Millar. 3 vols. Edinburgh: T. & T. Clark, 1973.

Schweizer, Eduard. "πνεῦμα," *TDNT* 6:437-44.

Scott, Martin A. *Sophia and the Johannine Jesus*. Journal for the Study of the New Testament: Supplement Series 71. Sheffield: JSOT Press, 1992.

Segal, Alan F. *Paul the Convert: The Apostolate and Apostasy of Saul the Pharisee.* New Haven: Yale University Press, 1990.

—. *Two Powers in Heaven: Early Rabbinic Reports about Christianity and Gnosticism.* Studies in Judaism in Late Antiquity 25. Edited by Jacob Neusner. Leiden: Brill, 1977.

Segovia, Fernando F. *The Farewell of the Word: The Johannine Call to Abide.* Minneapolis: Fortress, 1991.

Shutt, R. J. H. "The Concept of God in the Works of Flavius Josephus." *Journal of Jewish Studies* 31 (1980): 171-89.

Smalley, Stephen. "Pneumatology in the Johannine Gospel and Apocalypse." Pages 289-300 in *Exploring the Gospel of John: In Honor of D. Moody Smith.* Edited by R. Alan Culpepper and C. Clifton Black. Louisville: Westminster/John Knox, 1996.

Smith, D. Moody. "The Presentation of Jesus in the Fourth Gospel." Pages 175-89 in *Johannine Christianity: Essays on Its Setting, Sources, and Theology.* Columbia, S.C.: University of South Carolina Press, 1984.

—. *The Theology of John.* Cambridge: Cambridge University Press, 1995.

Strathmann, Hermann. "λατρεύω," *TDNT* 4:59-65.

Talbert, Charles H. *Reading John: A Literary and Theological Commentary on the Fourth Gospel and the Johannine Epistles.* New York: Crossroad, 1992.

Temporini, Hildegard, and Wolfgang Haase, eds. *Aufstieg und Niedergang der römischen Welt: Geschichte und Kultur Roms im Spiegel der neueren Forschung.* Part 2, *Principat,* 25.3. New York: de Gruyter, 1985.

Theissen, Gerd. *The Miracle Stories of the Early Christian Tradition.* Edited by John Riches. Translated by Francis McDonagh. Edinburgh: T. & T. Clark, 1983.

Thompson, Marianne Meye. "The Historical Jesus and the Johannine Christ." Pages 21-42 in *Exploring the Gospel of John: In Honor of D. Moody Smith.* Edited by R. Alan Culpepper and C. Clifton Black. Louisville: Westminster/John Knox, 1996.

—. *The Promise of the Father: Jesus and God in the New Testament.* Louisville: Westminster/John Knox, 2000.

Torrance, Thomas F. "The Christian Apprehension of God." Pages 120-43 in *Speaking the Christian God: The Holy Trinity and the Challenge of Feminism.* Edited by Alvin F. Kimel, Jr. Grand Rapids: Eerdmans; Leominster: Gracewing, 1992.

Turner, Max. *The Holy Spirit and Spiritual Gifts: In the New Testament Church and Today.* Rev. ed. Peabody, Mass.: Hendrickson, 1998.

—. *Power from on High: The Spirit in Israel's Restoration and Witness in Luke-Acts.* Sheffield: Sheffield Academic Press, 1996.

Unnik, W. C. van. "A Greek Characteristic of Prophecy in the Fourth Gospel." Pages 211-29 in *Text and Interpretation: Studies in the New Testament Pre-*

sented to Matthew Black. Edited by Ernest Best and R. McL. Wilson. Cambridge: Cambridge University Press, 1979.

Urbach, Ephraim. *The Sages: Their Concepts and Beliefs.* Translated by Israel Abrahams. Cambridge, Mass.: Harvard University Press, 1987.

Volz, Paul. *Der Geist Gottes und die verwandten Erscheinungen im Alten Testament und im anschließenden Judentum.* Tübingen: J. C. B. Mohr (Paul Siebeck), 1910.

Weder, Hans. "The Hermeneutics of Christology in the Johannine Writings." Pages 327-45 in *Exploring the Gospel of John: In Honor of D. Moody Smith.* Edited by R. Alan Culpepper and C. Clifton Black. Louisville: Westminster/John Knox, 1996.

Wicks, Henry J. *The Doctrine of God in the Jewish Apocryphal and Apocalyptic Literature.* New York: KTAV, 1971.

Wijngaards, John. *The Spirit in John.* Zacchaeus Studies. Wilmington, Del.: Michael Glazier, 1988.

Windisch, Hans. *The Spirit-Paraclete in the Fourth Gospel.* Philadelphia: Fortress, 1968.

Wire, Antoinette C. "Pauline Theology as an Understanding of God: The Explicit and the Implicit." Ph.D. diss., Claremont Graduate University, 1974.

Witherington, Ben, III. *Jesus the Sage: The Pilgrimage of Wisdom.* Minneapolis: Fortress, 1994.

Wolterstorff, Nicholas. *Divine Discourse: Philosophical Reflections on the Claim That God Speaks.* Cambridge: Cambridge University Press, 1995.

Wright, N. T. *Jesus and the Victory of God.* Vol. 2 of *Christian Origins and the Question of God.* Minneapolis: Fortress, 1996.

—————. *The New Testament and the People of God.* Vol. 1 of *Christian Origins and the Question of God.* Minneapolis: Fortress, 1992.

Zeller, Dieter. "God as Father in the Proclamation and in the Prayer of Jesus." Pages 117-29 in *Standing Before God: Studies on Prayer in Scriptures and in Tradition with Essays in Honor of John M. Oesterreicher.* Edited by Asher Finkel and Lawrence Frizzell. New York: KTAV, 1981.

Index of Modern Authors

Index of Ancient Sources

Letter of Aristeas		3:631	200	17:23	26		

Letter of Aristeas
15-16   197

Lives of the Prophets
21:8   90

Prayer of Manasseh
1   25, 26

Psalms of Solomon
17:26-32   66

Sibylline Oracles
2:214-20   75
2:284   75
2:318   75
2:330   75
3:11   200
3:11-12   200
3:13   200
3:15   200
3:24   200
3:29-39   200
3:35   200
3:48   200
3:56   200
3:81   200
3:101   200
3:174   200
3:276-78   200
3:283   200
3:286   200
3:295   67
3:296   200
3:301   200
3:542   200
3:550   67, 200
3:583   200
3:593   200
3:601   200
3:604   67, 200
3:617   200
3:628   200
3:629   200

3:631   200
3:672   200
3:693   200
3:698   200
3:708   200
3:711   200
3:717   200
3:718   200
3:719   200
3:721-723   200
3:726   200
3:742   200
3:757   200
3:760   200
3:763   200
5:33-35   39
5:137-54   39
5:214-21   39

Testament of Job
33:3   66
33:9   66
40:2-3   66
47:11   66
50:3   66

Testament of Judah
19:1   203
20   150
23:1-5   203

Testament of Naphtali
3:4   139

Testament of Simeon
2:8   25

DEAD SEA SCROLLS

1QH
9:7   136
9:14   136
9:19   136

17:23   26
17:35   64
17:35-36   66
20:3   210

1QpHab
2:6-7   204
8:10   204
10:7   23
10:14   23
12:8-10   204
12:10–13:4   204

1QM
10:8   26
13:1   26
13:2   26
13:7   25
13:13   26
18:7   28

1QS
2:11-12   205
2:16-17   205
3:15-16   138-39
3:24   26
3:25   139
4:5   205
4:20-22   167-68
5:5   204
5:5-7   210
6:27–7:2   24
8:4-10   210
8:5-14   204
8:6   210
8:10   210
8:14   23
9:3-6   204, 210
9:26   204, 210
10:6   204, 210
10:11-13   139
10:12   29
10:14   204, 210
11:15   26, 29

INDEX OF ANCIENT SOURCES

Berakot
5:5 — 126

Soṭah
9:15 — 68

Babylonian Talmud
Baba Meṣiʿa
96a — 126

Ḥagigah
10b — 126
14a — 45
15a — 45

Menaḥot
93b — 126

Nazir
12b — 126

Qidduŝin
42b — 126
43a — 126

Sanhedrin
38b — 45

Tosefta
Šabbat
13:5 — 205

Mekilta on Exodus
12:3 — 126
12:6 — 126
13:17 — 132
14:19 — 68

Midrash Rabbah
Genesis Rabbah
1:1 (on Gen. 1:1) — 136
70:5 (on Gen. 28:20) — 132

Exodus Rabbah
8:1 (on Exod. 7:1) — 33, 39
25:7 (on Exod. 16:4) — 132
46:4-5 (on Exod. 34:1) — 68

Numbers Rabbah
17 (on Num. 15:2) — 68
21:3 (on Num. 25:6-13) — 221

Song of Songs Rabbah
2:16 §1 — 68

TARGUMIM

Targum Neofiti
Genesis
32:31 — 112

Exodus
3:14 — 90
4:16 — 32, 42
7:1 — 32, 42, 234
15:3 — 43
24:10 — 112
33:23 — 112

Numbers
14:14 — 112

Targum Onqelos
Genesis
32:31 — 112

Exodus
3:14 — 90
4:16 — 32, 42
7:1 — 32, 42, 234
15:3 — 43

24:10 — 112
33:14 — 112
33:15 — 112
33:20 — 112

Numbers
14:14 — 112

Deuteronomy
32:6 — 68

Targum Pseudo-Jonathan
Genesis
32:31 — 112

Exodus
1:19 — 68
3:14 — 90
4:16 — 32, 42
7:1 — 32, 42, 234
15:3 — 43
24:10 — 112

Leviticus
22:28 — 68

Numbers
14:14 — 112

Deuteronomy
32:6 — 68

Targum 1 Samuel
10 — 174
10:11-12 — 174
19 — 174

Targum Isaiah
6:1 — 113, 124
6:5 — 124
63:16 — 62
64:8 — 62